CAPTIVE VOICES

The Report of the Commission of Inquiry into
High School Journalism

Convened by the Robert F. Kennedy Memorial

Prepared by Jack Nelson

Distributed by
Schocken Books • New York

Commission of Inquiry into High School Journalism

Dr. Franklin Patterson, Chairman
Chairman of the Board of Trustees of Hampshire College; Frank L. Boyden Professor of the University of Massachusetts; former Staff Director of the Carnegie Commission on Educational Television.

Msgr. Geno Baroni
President of the National Center for Urban Ethnic Affairs, Washington, D.C.; active in civil rights and community development needs of poor and working class people.

Karen Blank
Former high school editor of yearbook and newspaper editorial staff member in Wichita, Kansas; currently a freshman at University of Kansas majoring in journalism.

Miguel Berry
Former staff member of Texas Institute for Educational Development, San Antonio, Texas, developing communications for Chicano community programs. Currently staff member and adult education teacher at Centro de Servicos Sociales Aztlan.

Mae Churchill
Director, Urban Policy Research Institute, Beverly Hills, California, an institute focused on the criminal and juvenile justice systems as well as on the rights of young people.

Dr. Jean Grambs
Professor of Secondary Education at the University of

Maryland. Author of *Schools, Scholars and Society*, co-author of *Black Self-Concept*.

Sr. Ann Christine Heintz

Teacher and administrator at the St. Mary's Center for Learning in Chicago. Author of three journalism textbooks: *Persuasion, Mass Media,* and *Independent Learning.*

Dr. Joseph Kuklenski

Superintendent of Schools, Springfield, Missouri, a district that has five high school and eight junior high school newspapers.

Charlayne Hunter-Gault

Reporter for *The New York Times,* former reporter for WRC-TV in Washington, D.C., contributing reporter for *The New Yorker.* Staff member at Columbia University Summer Program for Minority Journalists.

Alan Levine

Director of New York Civil Liberties Union, Student Rights Project, N.Y.C.L.U. staff attorney, principal author of *The Rights of Students.*

Ida Lewis

Editor and publisher of *Encore* magazine, former BBC reporter African Desk; contributor to *Jeune Afrique, L' Exprés* and *Life,* former editor-in-chief of major fashion magazine.

Dr. Carl Marburger

Former teacher, principal, and assistant superintendent of schools; former (until 1973) Commissioner of Education for the State of New Jersey; currently Senior Associate, National Committee for Support of the Public Schools.

Suzanne Martinez

Staff attorney at the Youth Law Center in San Francisco, specializing in education and youth rights litigation; member of the Commission of Inquiry on School Governance.

Dorothy McPhillips

Teacher and publications adviser at R.A. Lang High School, Longview, Washington; former Journalism Education Association second vice-president; active in several local and national scholastic journalism associations.

Maurine Neuberger

Former United States Senator from Oregon; former secondary school teacher; active member of Women in Communications.

Trilla Ramage

Former newspaper editor of South Brunswick High School and graduate of Blair Summer School for Journalism. Staff member of New Jersey Student Union; currently a freshman at Livingston College.

John Seigenthaler

Publisher of *The Tennessean,* Nashville, Tennessee; former administrative assistant to the United States Attorney General and Nieman Fellow at Harvard University.

Rev. Douglas Still

Former director of Ministries for Educational Justice for the National Council of Churches and United Ministries in Public Education.

Sander Vanocur

Former broadcast journalist at WNBC and N-PACT. Currently a consultant to the Center for the Study of Democratic Institutions.

Tillie Walker

Executive Director of the United Scholarship Services, Inc., Denver, Colorado; active in the development of counseling and service programs for Native American students.

Rufus Washington

Former member of the North Carolina Student Task Force and chairman of the Charlotte Student Coordinating Council. Currently a freshman at North Carolina Central University.

Jules Witcover

Reporter for the *Washington Post;* contributor to the *Columbia Journalism Review;* 1973 Chairman of the

Robert F. Kennedy Journalism Awards Program; member of the Board of Advisers, Washington Scholastic Press Association.

Commission Staff
Richard Brodsky, director
Libby Keefer, co-director
Lenny Conway
Frank Smith

Research Assistants
Sharon Bouldin
Wendy Cook-Henry
Maureen Finnigan
Maria Maldonado

Consultants
Fraser Barron
Frank O'Leary

Acknowledgments

The Commission of Inquiry into High School Journalism would like to express appreciation to young people, teachers, administrators, university staffs, community groups, and professional and citizens' organizations who made this study possible and provided the Commission with information and advice.

The Commission wishes to give special thanks to the staff of the Robert F. Kennedy Memorial for its invaluable assistance in the development and completion of this Report.

In addition to the substantial support received from the Robert F. Kennedy Memorial, the work of the Commission would not have been possible without grants from the following:

Board of Missions of the United Methodist Church
Center for Community Change
Cummins Engine Foundation
Field Foundation
The Laras Fund
New York Foundation
Norman Foundation
Stern Fund
Third World Fund
John Hay Whitney Foundation
Young Generation Ministries, Executive Council of the
    Episcopal Church

Appreciation is expressed to those who donated their time and expertise to the development of the surveys and content analysis. The Commission wishes to thank

Dr. Henry Walbesser, Assistant Dean, School of Education, University of Maryland, and Ms. Margaret Perry, formerly of the Department of the Navy and the University of Massachusetts Computer Center for their work on the surveys; and thanks to Dr. Barbara Finkelstein, School of Education, Dr. R. Hiebert, Dean, School of Journalism, University of Maryland and the University of Maryland Computer Science Center for their assistance in developing and completing the content analysis.

Table of Contents

Introduction xi

Part I Censorship

1. Jann Wesolek 3–7
2. Demetrius Hopkins and David Rabin   7–11
3. Janice Fuhrman 11–16
4. Armando Castro 16–19
5. Don Patrick Nicholson 19–24
6. Censorship from the Top 24–28
7. Advisers as Censors 29–37
8. Self-Inflicted Censorship 37–40
9. Kind of Material Censored 40–47
Specific Commission Findings: Censorship . 47–49

Part II Minority Participation

10. "Three-fourths of One Percent—
    .0075" 53–57
11. Alternative Papers 58–61
12. Journalism and the Integrated
    School 61–66
13. Institutional Discrimination 66–77
Specific Commission Findings:
Minority Participation 77–78

Part III Journalism and Journalism Education

14. The Role of Journalism in the
    School 81–89
15. Journalism Teachers and Advisers .. 89–97
16. Electronic Media 97–103
17. Alternative Journalism Education ... 103–105

18. Journalism as Career Education 105–107
19. Scholastic Journalism Organizations .. 108–111
Specific Commission Findings:
Journalism and Journalism Education 111–113

Part IV Established Media

20. The Isolation of the High School
    Media 117–123
21. Substantive Contacts Do Help 123–126
22. Programs and Organizations 126–136
Specific Commission Findings:
Established Media 137–138

Part V Toward Action

Recommendations of the Commission.... 141–149

Appendix A

1. A Legal Guide for High School
   Journalism 153–163
2. Model Guidelines for Student
   Publications 164–166

Appendix B

1. List of Hearing Sites and
   Consultation Meetings 169–170
2. Student Survey Analysis 170–188
3. Faculty Adviser Survey Analysis 189–201
4. Journalism Teacher Survey Analysis . 201–207
5. Managing Editor Survey Analysis ... 207–215
6. Content Analysis 215–227
7. Selected Readings 227–236
8. Organizations 236–242

Appendix C

1. *The Lion* 245–248
2. *Ram-Page* 248–249
3. *The Sword and Shield* 250–251
4. *Editor and Publisher* 251–255

Index 257–264

Introduction

When the Robert F. Kennedy Memorial asked me to serve as chairman of the Commission of Inquiry into High School Journalism, three factors impelled me to accept the responsibility. I believe that other Commission members were moved by similar considerations.

One factor was a long-term personal concern for the improvement of youth's effective participation in the civic and political life of our country. The Memorial reflects Robert Kennedy's own dedication to strengthening youth's role and presented an opportunity through the Commission for this concern to be expressed in a practical way.

A second factor was the Commission's proposed focus on the high school. Out of long experience, I have learned to respect what high schools, even under enormous economic and social constraints, have managed to accomplish in the way of providing general and special educational opportunity for our children. The Commission's inquiry proceeded with respect for such achievement and with the knowledge that high schools represent a significant contribution as well as an unfulfilled potential in American life.

But in addition to the good things creative teachers do and enlightened principals encourage, we were aware of a less happy side, in whose shadow far too much of the high school world stands. More than it should, the American high school in the twentieth century has become an institution for the custodial care of adolescents. It serves as a systematic instrument of social control, to deal with some millions of young

Americans who would otherwise have no place in an advanced industrial society.

In addition to their educational contribution, American high schools are characterized by three interrelated, dominant functions assigned to them by the larger social order, and one of these indeed is *control.* A second function is *classification,* i.e., the sorting-out of youth in terms of their "appropriate" futures, a process that operates through counseling, curricula, scores, grades, and other overt mechanisms, and tends to reinforce inequality. A third function is *certification,* the culmination of one's having been classified, stamped as essentially unsuitable for further training, or suitable for limited kinds, or fitted for higher education.

American high schools have for the most part been tightly and hierarchically organized to perform these three functions, notwithstanding that one can find some notable creative exceptions. High school teachers, principals, and superintendents have lived and worked at the center of community and societal pressure that puts these things first. Personnel who take a different view, or who put other priorities first, often endanger their support by the community and risk their employment.

There is at present, however, the potential for a much better reality. New conditions in our society—in the reach for racial justice, for the conquest of poverty, for equality of the sexes, for responsible roles by youth —are opening up again the possibility of important, positive change in the high schools. Lawrence Cremin, in *The Transformation of the School,* presented a history of the earlier progressive movement in American education, whose vision was far different from the reality we have now in conventional high schools. At the end of his book, Cremin commented that a reformulation and resuscitation of the progressive vision might "ultimately derive from a larger resurgence of reform in American life and thought."

My sense is that we are approaching the threshold of such a resurgence, out of the long, confused struggles of the sixties, and the sordid aftermath of Vietnam and Watergate. If that is true, the high school again will be exciting for its creative possibilities, as the progressive movement once proved it could be and as its best teachers know it can.

A third factor persuading my fellow commissioners and me to undertake this truly arduous task was the stated intention of examining the nature, problems, and possibilities of journalism in the high school context. Here was an opportunity to examine the high school and its relationship to youth in a very tangible way and from a fresh perspective. Journalism is the central organized means for information and communication in our general society, and its freedom and quality are inextricable from the public interest. Given this, it would be instructive to investigate what high schools are doing and failing to do in providing students with the experience of journalism as part of their education. American high schools are the only secondary schools anywhere that provide experience in journalism as part of their curriculum.

A basic strength of the Commission lay in the nature of its membership. Individuals asked to serve as members of the Commission did so without remuneration. They included high school students, high school teachers, professional journalists, teachers of teachers, lawyers, educational administrators, and community organizers. All were alike in their dedication to the proposition that the work of the Commission was of major importance. Each brought a special background, experience, or point of view, adding up to an unusual range of capabilities relevant to our task.

The Robert F. Kennedy Memorial, particularly through its Director, Richard W. Boone, gave the Commission the fullest encouragement throughout the fifteen months of its life, combined with an independence to go ahead as we saw best. The Memorial formed the Commission and sponsored its study and present report because of the Memorial's commitment to youth in American society and its concern with individual freedom, educational opportunity, and active participation in community life. The Memorial, founded in 1968, carries forward Robert F. Kennedy's active work for the young and the poor by assisting programs that address poverty, discrimination, and civil liberties and by involving youth in learning about, reporting, and acting on such issues.

Part of the Memorial's initial concern about the state of high school journalism stemmed from the results of two surveys. One of these, by the National Education Association, indicated that most high school faculty advisers to newspapers in one way or another favored censorship. The other, by the American Society of Newspaper Editors, indicated that less than 1 percent of all professional journalists in the United States were nonwhite. The question arose within the Board of the Memorial whether conditions within the schools accounted for or were related to these findings.

The Memorial and the Commission it brought into being to answer this question sought funding to support a study never before undertaken. The Commission's work has been financed by $65,000 in grants from twelve churches and foundations, including the Memorial itself. With these funds the Commission was enabled to have the assistance of a small but excellent staff and conduct its investigations.

The Commission's work effectively began at the beginning of 1973. Our first step as individual members and with the assistance of staff, was to undertake a preliminary reconnaissance of our field of inquiry. This reconnaissance was summarized in our first Commission meeting in Washington, D.C., in February, 1973. At that time we agreed to specify four principal areas of inquiry for ourselves:

1. *Censorship* Our preliminary inquiries convinced us that we should examine the degree to which direct and indirect censorship of high school journalism operated to deny student journalists the protection of the First Amendment of the United States Constitution. We felt further that our inquiry should clarify the legal and constitutional framework within which high school journalism should be able to operate, and that we should, after inquiry, arrive at concrete recommendations that would be useful to high school

students, teachers, administrators, and school boards.

2. *Minority Participation* Our preliminary reconnaissance made it clear that the Commission should investigate the degree to which minority youth found access to the experience of high school journalism unavailable to them. Further, we agreed to try to determine causes for limited access and practical suggestions for enlarging this kind of educational opportunity for minority youth.

3. *Journalism and Journalism Education* At the outset, the Commission agreed that one of its principal responsibilities should be to examine the educational and journalistic quality of secondary school journalism. We agreed that we should investigate the degree to which journalism experience in the high school contributes to general education, and whether high school journalism education helps to prepare students for later careers in the field of professional journalism.

4. *Established Media* Our preliminary investigation convinced us that we should attempt to determine the degree to which editors and others in the established media were aware of the problems and possibilities of high school journalism. Members of the Commission believed that high school journalism deserved consideration as part of the larger media context of our society.

These four areas of inquiry thereafter became the main agenda of the Commission. This is reflected in the Report itself, where each of these considerations has a section ending with specific Commission findings. In addition, the final section of the Report, "Toward Action," presents the Commission's recommendations with regard to these four areas.

At our February, 1973, meeting, members of the Commission agreed that we should be a *working* body, committing a substantial amount of our own time and energy to inquiry in the four areas I have outlined.

Commission members thereafter participated in regional planning meetings, field preparation and briefings for the public hearings themselves, consultation meetings, development and analysis of surveys, and long working sessions.

Five basic data gathering techniques were selected by the Commission in order to obtain a wide spectrum of information and ensure access to a variety of opinions and attitudes.

1. *Public Hearings* During the spring of 1973, the Commission conducted a series of six formal hearings in separate locations across the country: San Francisco; South Bend; San Antonio; Washington, D.C.; Charlotte, N.C.; and New York City. The preparation for public hearings was made with considerable care by staff of the Commission. Prior visits by staff to each hearing location resulted in identification of key persons whom it would be helpful for the Commission to hear.

   Individual witnesses—teachers, student editors, administrators, journalists, and others—were asked to respond to questions by Commission members, in order to illumine the several areas of concern to the inquiry. Witnesses appeared in one of two ways. In addition to scheduled witnesses, the Commission instituted a policy of inviting testimony from any person attending the hearing. Both kinds of witnesses provided Commission members with substantial opportunity to explore questions and concerns related to the four areas of the inquiry. By transcribing the testimony of witnesses, a verbatim record was preserved that has helped the Commission to reach the findings and recommendations contained in this Report. Through the public hearings, the Commission heard over 130 witnesses (seventy-seven students, twenty-four teachers, ten administrators, nine professional journalists, two attorneys, one college professor, one college journalist, five community organizers, three representatives of scholastic journalism organizations), gained 1,725 pages of testimony, and acquired a series of background papers submitted to the Commission at each hearing.

2. *Consultation Meetings* Twelve informal consultation meetings were held in various regions of the country to enable Commission members to benefit from the advice of experts and from the experience of persons involved in uncommon aspects of high school journalism. These sessions included meetings with Native American high school journalists at the Navajo reservation in Ramah, New Mexico, at the Oglala Sioux reservation in Pine Ridge, South Dakota, and at the Little Big Horn School for urban Native Americans in Chicago, to discuss their cultural magazines, radio programming, and newspapers. A consultation was held with the director of the Blair Summer School for Journalism to review supplementary and summer journalism education programs, with specific reference to recruitment and financing to support the participation of minority youth. Other consultations included meeting with professional journalists; with Eliot Wiggington, teacher-organizer of the student-researched publication *Foxfire;* a meeting with students and educators concerning the potential of radio, videotape, film and open access cable in Chicago; attendance at the Missouri Scholastic Press Association Workshop in Columbia, Missouri; and other sessions. Information gathered at the informal consultations substantially added to the data gained by the Commission through its formal hearings.

3. *Surveys* The Commission also gathered useful data through four surveys directed at specific populations having a relationship to the subject matter of the inquiry. It should be emphasized that the resources available to the Commission did not enable the conduct of surveys that would be fully satisfactory in terms of social science research design and methodology. But the Commission considers that data gained through the surveys that were conducted provided useful

supportative information and additional background for its deliberations.

In a student survey, 1,789 questionnaires were returned from forty-eight secondary schools that were selected as being reasonably representative of national distributions in terms of factors such as size, racial composition, location, and urban, suburban, or rural character. These responses, while not providing the validity and reliability one would expect from a stratified random sample of the kind used by professional polling organizations, gave the Commission what it felt was credible evidence of student opinion.

In two other surveys, random samples of journalism teachers and faculty advisers who are members of the National Council of Teachers of English or the Journalism Education Association were selected and surveyed by direct mail. Out of the 800 questionnaires mailed, 363 were returned. These responses permitted comparison of perceptions and attitudes of surveyed teachers and advisers with impressions gathered by the Commission during public hearings, regional meetings, and consultations.

A fourth survey was addressed to a random sample of one-third of all of the managing editors of daily newspapers listed in the *Editor and Publisher Yearbook*. Information regarding involvement with and opinions about high school journalism was solicited from 465 editors of established newspapers. The questionnaire was returned by 38.6 percent of the editors surveyed.

4. *Content Analysis* An additional information-gathering technique consisted of content analysis of 293 high school newspapers. Based on a non-random effort to obtain a representative cross section of high school publications, the analysis included 183 entries in the Columbia Scholastic Press Association Journalism Contest, publications submitted to the Commission as part of testimony at public hearings, and papers mailed to the Commission either by students or by ad-

visers. The analysis sought to gather data as to the possible relationship among variables such as geographic region, size of town and school, and the existence of advertisements and the content of the papers.

5. *Research* The Commission and its staff also looked into relevant research undertaken by others. This process included a review of masters' and doctoral theses, papers written under the auspices of the Quill and Scroll Society, and many other published papers. An intensive study of judicial decisions and opinions, and of relevant law, was undertaken and summarized.

In its various efforts to gather data, I believe it is accurate to say that the Commission undertook the single largest national inquiry into American high school journalism so far conducted. We do not pretend that a more thorough and informative inquiry could not be accomplished given greater resources of time and money. But these meetings, hearings, and consultations, together with surveys and research reviews, represent the most comprehensive investigation we were able to accomplish in a period of a year and a half. The results constitute the basic evidence in the Commission's possession, and from this evidence patterns have emerged that we feel apply to high school journalism throughout the country. The Commission's findings and recommendations are based upon careful review of these patterns.

Before the reader considers the Commission's findings and recommendations there are two aspects of our work that we hope will be emphasized and borne in mind.

One of these is that the Commission was sensitive to the fact that school teachers and administrators work in a situation that is subject to many kinds of pressure from many different directions. We understand that often the easiest course seems to be to play it safe. But we are also convinced that school people can deal with such pressures effectively, with wisdom and courage, when they see that really important things are at stake.

If we were not so convinced, it would be pointless for us to offer the findings and recommendations that are contained in this Report.

We know that school people can—and in some cases do—find remedies for the kinds of needs and problems our inquiry discovered. In our public hearings and other investigations, we encountered exciting examples of positive programs being conducted in junior and senior high schools in all parts of the country. We heard from teachers and administrators and students whose very work itself demonstrated that negative conditions of censorship, minority access, and educational quality in journalism are not inevitable. Their stories gave us confidence that the kind of recommendations we have presented can indeed become the general reality if school people want it so.

A second point to emphasize is that the reader may find it useful to precede a reading of the section on censorship by reviewing the appendix material dealing with constitutional and legal aspects of the First Amendment and official school publications. This material provides a very current context of law within which the kinds of issues we deal with under the subject of censorship should be considered.

The Commission trusts that in all four areas with which this Report deals a lasting and beneficial dialogue will have been begun. We know that many school people and other citizens share in the conclusions to which we have come, and we are hopeful that serious discussion of these conclusions by students, teachers, and administrators will lead to more freedom, more participation, and more quality in what should be one of the most important and rewarding parts of high school education for thousands of youths.

In a real sense, this Report shows how far we have to go in inducting youth into the true meaning of democratic citizenship. We hope that educators at all levels will read this Report and know, as we do, that the repressive conditions we found ought to be the exception rather than the rule. We hope that they will conclude with us that *any* censorship of journalism is a dangerous thing, that *any* limitation of student participation in journalism because of minority status is undesirable, that the quality of educational experience in journalism should be higher than it is, and that the established media have a major responsibility to work cooperatively with schools and students in journalism. We believe that high school journalism for too long has existed in a gray, shadowy area of public concern. We believe it is time to bring it forth as one of the most potential, most educational, most exciting means available for young people to meet and come to understand their world and ours.

FRANKLIN PATTERSON
Chairman

PART I

Censorship

Chapter 1

Jann Wesolek

Jann Wesolek, editor-in-chief of *Liberty Link,* a school newspaper in North Liberty, Indiana, was intrigued by the discussions of school censorship she heard at a Youth Coalition newspaper clinic in South Bend in January, 1973.

Wesolek was one of the few high school editors in the country who was well versed in the rights of a student editor. She was a member of the Youth Coalition, which had as its principal speakers at the newspaper clinic two attorneys with expertise in the field of student rights: the Coalition's own counsel and a staff member of the Commission of Inquiry.

They both assured the young journalists in the audience that although traditionally there had been questions about how broadly the Bill of Rights applied to students, recent court decisions had tended toward a broad interpretation of student rights. In 1969, for example, the Supreme Court, upholding the right of a student in Des Moines, Iowa, to wear an arm band as a sign of protest, held that "students in school as well as out of school are persons under the Constitution" and do not "shed their constitutional rights to freedom of speech or expression at the schoolhouse gate."[1]

Despite such assurances, Wesolek knew that many school authorities censored any material they considered objectionable. A case in point involved a student editor who told the young journalists at the clinic

---

[1] *Tinker v. Des Moines Independent School District.*

that she had been unable to get approval for publication of a story on planned parenthood.

Planned parenthood! It was just the kind of subject to arouse some interest among the readers of her own school paper, Wesolek thought. It was a thought that when transformed into action would raise the hackles of the faculty adviser of her newspaper and ultimately would result in a censorship controversy and a federal court ruling affirming the free press rights of high school journalists.

On April 7, 1973, several months prior to the court ruling in her case, Wesolek testified about her experiences at a Commission of Inquiry hearing at South Bend. She told of writing the brief article on planned parenthood and of routinely giving it to the adviser for review.

Later, she said, she walked into the hall and "the adviser was standing in front of the principal's office and was making all kinds of wild gestures. I walked back in the room. Pretty soon she came back, tossed the paper at me, and said, 'This isn't going in the paper.' I said, 'Yes,' and she said, 'No.' She said, 'No, it is my paper, and it is not going in.' "

Wesolek then consulted the principal, who read the article and decided it was too controversial for the community—a decision principals are prone to make frequently, according to evidence compiled by the Commission. The principal, Wesolek told the Commission, "said he didn't want to take a hassle from the community—there would be a lot of backlash—it is a small community."

A school secretary, Wesolek said, talked about how "it would be discussed in every pulpit if the article got in the paper."

The young journalist finally appealed to the school counselor, but "the counselor stated that he might be biased. He has seven children, is a devoted Catholic, and was not exactly happy about the fact I wanted to print an article on planned parenthood. He proceeded to give me a forty-five-minute lecture on morals."

Still seeking official sanction for the article, Wesolek attempted to tone it down to meet the objections of the adviser and the principal. The article quoted a pamphlet sponsored by Planned Parenthood and she thought that the wording might be the problem, that the principal might find it objectionable. She consulted an English teacher who advised her to make a slight change.

Explaining the matter to the Commission, she said, "In one of the paragraphs there was a little problem because it said you go to Planned Parenthood for birth control. We put 'birth control counseling.' I thought that was the problem."

However, the adviser and principal were adamant in their disapproval and Wesolek, determined to exercise her First Amendment rights as editor of the paper, notified the adviser she was going to consult an attorney, Tom DiGrazia. "Go ahead," the adviser told her, "it won't do you any good."

When word circulated around school that she was consulting an attorney, Wesolek said, "Teachers would come in and talk to the adviser about it, and she would start crying. She was all upset. . . . She told me it was like a slap in the face because I was going against her . . . something about I had agreed to let her censor all articles—which I don't recall—when she selected me to be the editor at the end of last year."

Why did it mean so much to Wesolek to have the article printed? She told the Commission, "Not only was it informative, it was with the times. It is important to the students. I think it is important for the students to see this. Students have a right to publish something they are really concerned with. It is not a vulgar article. It was not dirty. I wouldn't print something like that. It was merely informative, and students know now I have taken a stand and I want to see the article in the paper. They are behind me. I feel I can't let the students down, now, plus it is a personal conviction."

In the article that the principal banned Wesolek noted that the article's first two paragraphs were reprinted with permission from Planned Parenthood. There were also this notation: "This article does not reflect the views of the school administration, paper staff, or any member affiliated with either group."

The article was written beneath this heading: "Babies

Aren't Found Under a Cabbage Leaf (And You Know It!)." It read as follows:

> And so do over one-quarter of a million girls under 18 that will bear children this year. . . . And one-half of the teenagers that are married this year will know it. And over one million women in the United States that have pregnancies aborted this year will know it.
>
> When a couple . . . whether married or unmarried . . . makes an unwanted baby, the results are often fear, disbelief, anger and disappointment . . . anything but the love that should be there. And the effects last much longer than just nine months. Becoming parents when you aren't emotionally or financially prepared can leave you self-defeated and personally devastated.
>
> So, for your sake, your parents and the sake of the unborn child . . . be honest with yourself. You either don't have sex at all, or you have responsible sex that requires the use of effective and reliable contraception.
>
> You can get birth control counselling at Planned Parenthood, 201 South Chapin Street, South Bend. Or check with your doctor or go to your neighborhood hospital or clinic. You can call Planned Parenthood, 289-7027, to find out where to get help and counselling about anything else you want to know.

After being informed by her adviser that "the only way the article would get in the paper was if I went to court," Wesolek authorized DiGrazia to file suit in U.S. District Court in South Bend against the Board of Trustees of the South Bend Community School Corp.[2]

On October 2, 1973, a final order in the case by Judge George Beamer applied First Amendment rights protecting journalists on official, in-school newspapers from prior restraint by school officials. Although courts generally had applied such rights to journalists for unofficial school newspapers, Judge Beamer's decision was only one of several in recent years to embrace the same rights for staff members of official school papers.

Judge Beamer pointedly ruled: "The School Cor-

---

[2] See Appendix A for discussion of case and legal arguments.

poration shall not prohibit publication of articles in official school newspapers on the basis of the subject matter or terminology used unless the article or terminology used is obscene, libelous or disrupts school activities."

Through her perseverance and with the aid of a concerned attorney, Wesolek had secured a court ruling that emphasized the constitutional basis for free expression within the schools.

Chapter 2

Demetrius Hopkins and David Rabin

When seniors Demetrius Hopkins and David Rabin sought to secure a greater voice in school affairs for students at Chicago's Lane Technical High School, they ran into an obstacle familiar to students seeking such goals—a wall of resistance from the school administration.

Hopkins was president of the Student Council and ranked in the upper one-fourth of a class of 1,000. Rabin was president of the school's Key Club and ranked 20th in the class.

A principal issue between the students and the administration was the fact that the administration insisted on appointing the faculty sponsor to the Student Council instead of permitting the Council to make the appointment.

The student leaders favored other changes that also irritated school authorities, including formation of a Student Union, establishment of drug treatment centers in high schools, and an open enrollment plan that would abolish school districts and allow students to attend any school in the city.

But there was little opportunity for circulating their ideas and proposals among other students. They told the Commission of Inquiry that their regular school newspaper eschewed controversy and rarely mentioned the school administration.

Rabin said, "The adviser is our journalism teacher and claims he has no censorship power over the paper. He says he does not see it before it goes to press. I'm not going to go on record as calling him a liar, but I would question the veracity of that statement. Perhaps, once in a while, he will publish something about the Student Council, but will not print anything that hints of controversy."

To air their ideas and grievances, Hopkins and Rabin followed a course used by many students before them in scattered communities around the country. They established an alternate school paper, *The Oppressed.* Rabin told the Commission, "We try not to make it libelous. We don't use any improper language. In six issues, there has been only one profane word, and that was used in a quote. We prefer not to call our paper an underground paper, because when somebody says 'underground paper' it conjures up communism, free love, or something. We call it an independent student publication."

In outlining their well-documented case to the Commission, Hopkins and Rabin gave some of the most articulate and compelling testimony presented at the Commission hearings—a story of censorship, harassment, suspension, legal action, and recalcitrant school officials.

Hopkins told the Commission:

We believe that Student Councils, and in fact, all students, should be allowed to freely express their opinions about and make suggestions concerning the operation of their schools.

The Administration of my school—in the persons of the acting principal and the Student Council sponsor whom he appointed—opposed and retarded all efforts to obtain such freedom of expression for students. Their tactics were harassment of student leaders. This harassment included suspensions, threat of suspensions, constant removal of students from important classes for conferences, and innuendos of adverse college recommendations.

Our response . . . was the historic response of groups whose rights are retarded. We put our grievances into print and distributed our publication, *The Oppressed,* to the students at our school. The immediate response of the administration was to attempt to suspend us for an infraction of a rule, Section 6-19 of the rules of the Chicago Board of Education, which states the following: 'No person shall be permitted . . . to distribute on the school premises any books, tracts, or other publications . . . unless the same shall have been approved by the General Superintendent of Schools.'

There was a similar infraction of this rule last year by two Lane students and another student from a Chicago public high school. The three students were suspended for breaking the rule and subsequently filed suit in U.S. District Court. The case became known as Fujishima v. the Board of Education.[3]

Hopkins went on to explain that the judge in the Fujishima case ordered that the school expunge any notice of disciplinary action from the records of the student plaintiffs, but also dismissed the class suit and left the question of the constitutionality of Section 6-19 unanswered.

The student plaintiffs appealed the decision, Hopkins pointed out, and the Seventh U.S. Circuit Court of Appeals ultimately ruled that Section 6-19 was unconstitutional because it provided for prior restraint in violation of the First Amendment. The court's opinion also sustained the claim of class action, thus extending the effect of the ruling to all Chicago high schools, and provided that students should be notified by the defendant school authorities that they would not have to submit material for review before publication.

Despite the court order, Hopkins testified, officials at

---

[3] See Appendix A for discussion of case and legal arguments.

Lane failed to notify students of the rule change. "The principal and assistant principal completely ignored the decision of the court and acted as though 6-19 was still in effect," Hopkins said. "These were the same two people who were involved in the Fujishima case."

Moreover, Hopkins and Rabin were notified that they were being suspended from school. The day before the suspension was to become effective, however, they secured a restraining order from a U.S. District Court after they filed suit against the principal, assistant principal, and the Board of Education, alleging First Amendment violations.

Since litigation is both costly and time consuming, Hopkins and Rabin considered themselves fortunate with the board and school authorities agreed to an out-of-court settlement that included a court order guaranteeing them most of their demands.

It was an order that (1) permitted the two students to continue publishing *The Oppressed;* (2) provided that neither they nor other persons associated with the newspaper would be disciplined for anything related to the paper; and (3) provided that all adverse matter in their school records deriving from publication of the paper be expunged.

Despite the court order, the student editors continued to be harassed. Rabin told the Commission they were continually called out of classes for conferences by school authorities. "They don't call us out of classes like gym, studies, or division—that's home room—they call us out of classes like math, English, or science, which are majors," he said. "After a while, when you are called out of three classes in five days, the teacher gets a little angry with you and the administration. You miss class time. I have been called out on a test before. I have been called out of important classes and missed work. Usually, the nature of these conferences is they call you out to tell you they are very distressed with your actions and wish you wouldn't do it again. . . ."

Rabin said, "We have been threatened with suspensions, and I was given ten periods of discipline for attending a Student Council meeting—which I had every right to be at. The administration tried to turn people against us, so to speak, by speaking against us publicly and privately. If we attempted to do anything like this, they say we are speaking behind their backs."

Such harassment "definitely" continued after the court order had been issued, Rabin said, adding, "I guess a court order is the ultimate kind of protection you can have, but it has not done any good."

Chapter 3

Janice Fuhrman

Stanley Onderdonk, the principal of Novato (California) High School, was understandably upset. The *Hornets Buzz,* the school's newspaper, had just devoted more attention to him than anyone else in an editorial column that awarded "right on's" for worthy deeds and "left off's" for unworthy deeds. And Mr. Onderdonk was among the "left off's."

He had banned from the high school campus a county-wide publication called *Free Youth.* The paper had been widely distributed in high schools throughout Marin County and previous issues had been distributed on the Novato campus without incident. But Onderdonk found the fifth issue offensive.

Janice Fuhrman, editor of the *Hornets Buzz,* careful to use the style of many professional newspapers in using dashes to truncate the spelling of words considered obscene, wrote:

Left Off to Mr. Stanley Onderdonk who banned the fifth issue of *Free Youth* from being distributed on the Novato High Campus. Mr. Onderdonk objected to the use of the words chicken ———— and bull ————

(words he called obscene), and an article about the
Viet Nam war which suggested a violent act (burning
a school building down), and the fact that the author
of the article was not named. Principals of San Rafael,
Drake, Terra Linda, Redwood and Tamalpais high
schools did not see it necessary to forbid distribution
and because of the objections by Novato . . . the Free
Youth committee decided to censor out the objectionable article. Novato seems to be some kind of puritan-
ical community and I guess Mr. Onderdonk wants to
keep it that way.

Fuhrman, a junior at the time, was summoned to Mr.
Onderdonk's office while completing a final examina-
tion. As she later recalled in testimony before the Commission of Inquiry, the principal told her that the
column was libelous and that she had made him look
like a "bad guy." She said he ordered her off the school
grounds.

For Fuhrman it was the culmination of a frustrating
year as a high school journalist. She had been a member of the *Free Youth* news staff as well as editor of
her school newspaper. *Free Youth* was supported by
the County Board of Supervisors and it seemed, Fuhrman said, that "every time we came out with something the least bit controversial they would threaten to
cut off our funds, and we had to answer to them, because they were paying for it. . . ."

Like most high schools, Novato had no tradition of a
free student press and like many schools it had no journalism courses and a high school newspaper adviser
with no journalism experience. So when Fuhrman
sought to print articles of substance that might involve
controversy, she had few allies at the school.

She competed for space in the newspaper with
another editor who thought the newspaper should be
more concerned with social activities and other matters
safely removed from controversy. That policy also
seemed to be to the liking of the faculty adviser.

Fuhrman speculated that if the adviser had read the
article criticizing Onderdonk before it was published he

would have censored it. "But he didn't even look at it," she told the Commission. "He didn't even bother. He never did."

Although Fuhrman told of her experiences as a high school journalist during a Commission hearing in San Francisco, Onderdonk declined an invitation to present his side of the dispute. He explained that his schedule was too tight to permit an appearance and that it would be inappropriate to open old wounds. Besides, he said, the issue was "a tempest in a teapot."

Of her suspension from school by Onderdonk, Fuhrman told the Commission:

> I only had one final examination, which I was taking when he called me in his office, and my teacher said, "Well, finish it and then go in there."
>
> So I went in there, and when he told me to get off the school grounds, he said, "You are not going to be able to finish your examinations." And I said that I only had one and that I just took it.
>
> He got really upset and he started out into the hall where all the student schedules are kept and he took mine out and he said, "What about this class, what about this class?"
>
> And I said I had a paper or we were on a field trip.
>
> He said, "I don't understand this. You are not supposed to be doing this. I am going to talk to your teachers and find out why you don't have examinations."
>
> He was real upset. He was yelling and everything, and he said, "Well, I am going to talk to your teachers."

At Novato High, a school of some 1,300 mostly white, middle-class students, Fuhrman had learned little about students' rights. She also found relatively little interest in the subject among the school's students.

Fuhrman told the Commission, "This may sound zany, but I don't think the majority of kids in our school care that much about individuals expressing themselves. I think a lot of the problem is that they are very poorly educated on constitutional rights. . . ."

But Fuhrman was aware of her rights, having studied

them at student rights' workshops conducted off the
school grounds by civil liberties groups. And she did
not take her suspension from school lightly. She went
immediately to a lawyer who was a family friend and
told of her encounter with the principal. The lawyer,
she said, advised her, "This is an infringement of your
constitutional rights, the First Amendent."

Instead of resorting to legal action, however, her
attorney prescribed an antidote long recognized for its
effectiveness in cases of First Amendment violations—
exposure by the press. Although the established media
often overlooks First Amendment violations in the high
schools, in this case the lawyer supplied details of the
case to the *San Francisco Chronicle* and the newspaper
published a story about it.

The reaction was almost immediate. "What was supposed to happen," Fuhrman told the Commission, "was
two days later my parents were supposed to have a
conference with Mr. Onderdonk and myself. The next
morning, while I was suspended, the article came out in
the *Chronicle,* and five minutes later Mr. Onderdonk
called my father and said, 'It is all a big misunder-
standing. I didn't mean to suspend her. We want her
back in school.' "

But if Fuhrman secured a personal measure of
justice, neither her high school paper nor high school
journalism gained from her experience. For although
she was reinstated in school, the administration continued its censorship policies.

She told the Commission that when she returned to
school the principal "talked to me and said that I was
not the owner of the school paper, that the school
district was, and they had a right to determine editorial
policy, and that as long as the district was giving us the
money to write the paper, we weren't going to criticize
the district."

As a senior the following year (1972–73), Fuhrman
passed up the chance to work on the paper again because of her previous frustrations and because she felt
that the majority of the students, although they expressed support for what she had done, would not be

willing to undertake such risks themselves and would not want to see her or any other student do it again. Members of the paper's staff, she said, "are avoiding things like that now" and the adviser appointed as editor a student he could count on to steer the paper clear of articles critical of school policy.

Now, Fuhrman said, "The paper does revolve around school activities. Mostly drama, actually, because the adviser is drama teacher at our school."

Throughout its hearings the Commission heard testimony similar to Fuhrman's about the use of staff selection procedures by advisers to ensure a "safe" student staff. Since advisers usually have the ultimate authority of selection, they often wring a promise from prospective editors that they will submit all articles for review and approval before publication.

After her problems at North Liberty, Indiana, Jann Wesolek told the Commission, her adviser "told me next year she will find an editor who will listen to her, and sign a paper saying she can censor everything before it goes in the paper."

The Fuhrmans and Wesoleks of high school journalism sometimes voice concern, too, that their insistence on a free student press may cause them problems when they seek admission to colleges. Fuhrman said she was worried that she might receive poor recommendations from her high school "because for some of my colleges there were really long things that had to be filled out by the principal, and personal, subjective opinion."

Although students such as Fuhrman and Wesolek and others who challenge censorship policies demonstrate a high degree of maturity, they are the very ones labeled as "immature" by advisers who seek a staff they can control. The mature students, these advisers insist, are the ones that know the rules and stay in line. As one adviser told the Commission, "I consider my students mature and they know my thinking and they know what their responsibility is. They never come up with anything I would really veto, as such."

These advisers avoid the Fuhrmans and Wesoleks if

at all possible. Said Fuhrman, "The adviser was really careful about not getting someone like me in there because he didn't want the trouble that happened last year. I don't think he knew me."

Chapter 4

Armando Castro

To Armando Castro, who had grown up among a Chicano majority dominated by a white minority, the fact that Anglos controlled the staff of *The Wheel,* the student newspaper at McAllen (Texas) High School, precluded a fair hearing for chicano students. And he found this intolerable, especially since Chicanos comprised about 75 percent of the school's 2,200-member student body.

So Castro and some fellow students, all members of the local Mexican American Youth Organization, began an alternate newspaper, *El Chicano,* which published articles in Spanish as well as English. Unlike *The Wheel, El Chicano* related directly to the problems of the chicano community, and it became an immediate success, so much so that it propelled Castro on a meteoric, if ill-fated, high school political career.

Castro had carefully sought sanction of the newspaper by school authorities at the outset, even though he personally felt that distribution of the paper at the school was within his rights. He later told the Commission of Inquiry that he and his colleagues went before Homer M. Morris, the principal, "and we asked him if we could distribute the paper and he said fine, as long as we did not disrupt any classes or make a big scene of it, which we didn't. We used to pass out the paper during lunchtime and during breaks."

The newspaper and Castro himself became so popular that within four months he decided to run for Student Council president, a post never held by a Chicano. His decision to run was too late to get his name on the ballot so he ran as a write-in candidate against three other candidates whose names were on the ballot. Despite that handicap and the fact he was only a sophomore, he won the election.

When Castro returned to school in September, 1970, after the summer vacation and began his administration as Student Council president, however, Homer Morris was no longer principal. His successor was Charles E. Haynes, a former football coach who had resigned as principal at Carroll High School after twenty years with the Corpus Christi school district to take the same position at McAllen.

The *Corpus Christi Caller* reported that in explaining his decision to leave Carroll High, Haynes cited a desegregation suit that he said would not "help the education process at all." Although Haynes would be administering a predominantly chicano school at McAllen, he would be working with a Board of Education whose members included five Anglos and only two Chicanos.

During the summer recess, the Board had enunciated a clear policy of prior approval by school authorities before any unofficial school papers could be distributed on school grounds. And Castro told the Commission he followed "the procedure and channels" and advised Haynes he would like to again circulate the paper because "it did so good last year and it is very good for the student body and it is reaching where the students and the people are." He gave the principal a copy of an earlier issue of the paper for review.

Haynes told him he would "think about it." Castro said, "He thought about it a week and I called him and he said that he hadn't seen the paper yet, that he was too busy and I said, 'Okay.' So I waited and then I approached him again. I approached him about two or three times in a period of three weeks."

Although Haynes never gave specific orders for

banning the paper, Castro said, the principal did comment at one time, "No, I don't think this paper is going to be too good for the campus here."

After three weeks of inaction by Haynes, Castro and his colleagues decided that press freedom delayed was press freedom denied "and the only way we were going to get through was to reach the school board . . . we then devised a petition to be circulated among students to present it to the school board."

The circulation of the petition infuriated Haynes, according to Castro, who said the principal summoned him to his office and demanded to know if he was one of the instigators. "I said yes, that I was trying to do my duty as president of the student body in trying to reinstate freedom of speech in our school," Castro told the Commission. "After that, Mr. Haynes said, 'Well, you have done a very wrong thing.' And he . . . said, 'You are no longer to state yourself as president of the student body. You are to leave these premises as soon as you walk out of this door.' "

Castro said, "I was removed from my office and suspended as a result of that. And he said, 'Don't come back and leave the premises as soon as you can. If you don't I will call the police.' "

Castro left, but, like Janice Fuhrman of Novato High, he was aware of his First Amendment rights and immediately contacted a lawyer. Through his lawyer's efforts, the school board finally reinstated him as a student.

But Castro never served again as Student Council president. He decided against taking legal action to recover the office because "my lawyer advised me it would have taken about eight or nine months to get the case to court. By that time I would have already been out of school and there was no way I could have been reinstated as the president."

El Chicano folded in the wake of the principal's order banning it from the school campus. Castro then turned to *The Wheel,* the school paper, submitting for publication an article about a medical study that showed widespread malnutrition among Chicanos.

The article was written, Castro said, after "we had

found out that a staff of medical doctors from Washington had come to the valley and had made some findings that . . . fifty percent of the population in Hidalgo was suffering from malnutrition, another term for starvation, and saying that they needed Vitamin C, which we have in abundance there in the valley."

Another article he submitted, he said, reported that "the medical staff had found out that in the past five years there have been three or four cases of polio and all of them have been in Hidalgo County."

The articles were never published. "When I turned them into the sponsor," Castro said, "I believe the sponsor later reviewed them with Mr. Haynes, who was still there, and I guess he rejected these articles because at a later date I picked them up and they weren't published."

The only explanation he was ever given, Castro said, was that the newspaper had "no space" for the articles.

Despite such adversities, Castro emerged from his struggles for a free high school press with a determination to continue trying to help solve the problems of Chicanos through a free press. He lost academic credits for a semester because of his suspension and his graduation was delayed from January, 1972, until May, 1972.

He told the Commission his experience "instilled in me this courage to continue on with my education and . . . right now I am studying to go into social work." He said he hoped that after completing college he could start a chicano community newspaper.

Chapter 5

Don Patrick Nicholson

The Torrance (California) school district had no guidelines concerning the contents of its high school newspapers, but left the matter in the hands of school principals.

At Torrance High School, the principal, Carl Ahee, had a simple set of rules—the "Four-Way Test" of Rotary International, a service organization of business and professional men. As a Rotarian, Ahee frequently cited the test as a daily guide to live by and he saw no reason why the high school press should not live by it, too.

The first time Don Patrick Nicholson, the school's journalism teacher and newspaper adviser, asked Ahee about any guidelines, the principal pointed to a small Rotary plaque on his desk. If Nicholson followed the "Four-Way Test" lettered on the plaque, Ahee said, he "couldn't go wrong."

The test consisted of four questions:

1. Is it the truth?
2. Is it fair to all concerned?
3. Will it build goodwill and better friendships?
4. Will it be beneficial to all concerned?

The trouble with such a test, Nicholson recognized immediately, was that even if an article was the truth and fair to all concerned, it still might do nothing for goodwill and friendships and might not be beneficial to all concerned.

Nicholson had perhaps one of the broadest backgrounds in journalism and public affairs of any high school newspaper adviser in the country. Before moving to Torrance, he had been in professional journalism for eight years, working first on a Seattle newspaper, then as a wire service writer and as a news broadcaster. He had won a national award for a public affairs radio documentary. He had a B.A. degree and a law degree and had been a student journalist in college and high school. Also, he had served six years as a Washington state legislator.

After his conference with Ahee, Nicholson went back to his classroom and discussed the Rotary test with the editors of the paper—the *Torrance News Torch*. They decided that the *News Torch* would be dim indeed if it lived by the test. Later, in recounting his experiences at Torrance in an affidavit, Nicholson said:

The student editors and I had absolutely no quarrel with the first two points of the Rotary code—truth and fairness—if "accuracy" were substituted for the word truth to eliminate the latter word's far-ranging moral connotations. The stubborn problem was that the second two parts of the code (goodwill and friendships, beneficial to all concerned) were restrictive and unworkable if applied to newspaper production. For many reasons.

Their absolutism becomes especially censorial when read together with all four parts: a story can be accurate, fair and otherwise legitimized by the nature of its subject matter *without* creating better friendships.

Newspaper production is a highly creative and demanding activity. A good reporter has to have the curiosity to follow the facts wherever they lead, to dig them out, so that he writes from a position of strength and authority. He cannot do this if every news lead which comes to his attention, every fact, has to be screened through a mind prism which rejects anything that may not create goodwill or better friendships.

One of the most basic skills my job required me to teach was the ability to distinguish a perception from an inference. It is a difficult, specialized skill essential to objective newswriting, acquired by study and practice. It means sharpening the senses and mental discipline to the point of being able to see a fact without adding something to it.

For a reporter, it's the difference between objective and subjective writing, between newswriting and editorializing. To measure all reportage by "goodwill" and "better friendships" is to color over this process, to cloud the perception of reality with the inference that only a "pleasant" reality is acceptable.[4]

Despite Ahee's insistence on the Rotary code as the newspaper's guideline, Nicholson and the *News Torch* editors composed an alternate Four-Way Test:

---

[4] Affidavit filed in *Nicholson v. Board of Education, Torrance Unified School District, et al.*

1. Is it accurate?
2. Is it fair?
3. Is it in good taste?
4. Does it avoid libel and obscenity?

Nicholson continued to work with Ahee, too, hoping to persuade the principal that the Rotary test was too oppressive and should be abandoned. Student editors also argued that it was unfair. One of them, Joseph Schwartz, later recalled "tense meetings" in the principal's office between Ahee and the editors.

Schwartz, in an affidavit, said:

> Many things would be discussed during these meetings, but ultimately the discussion would end up on the subject of negativism. At that point, Dr. Ahee would point to his Rotary Four-Way Test plaque and make sure we all re-read it. It was in his office, behind closed doors, that I first saw the impractical applications of this test. He would discuss each point of the test, and then compare it to the story we discussed, and tell us that, more or less, we were not being good Rotarians. I do not recall a story that we discussed in these group sessions that ever passed.[5]

Nicholson finally decided that Ahee's censorship was so violative of the student journalists' First Amendment rights that he began passing some articles without sending them to the principal for prior review. These included a controversial series of articles on the problems of Chicanos living in Torrance's Pueblo, as well as the results of a survey of police-student relationships. Ahee had ordered that the student journalists not be permitted to conduct the survey. Reviews of the musical *Hair* and of the movie *Midnight Cowboy,* both written in low-key style, also were published without Ahee's approval.

By Ahee's standards, the news articles flunked the Rotary test. And he ruled the reviews were on subjects

---

[5] Affidavit filed in *Nicholson v. Board of Education, Torrance Unified District, et al.*

"unsuitable" for high school readership. The most serious offense in the principal's view, of course, was that the press copy had not been submitted for prior review.

Despite his differences with Ahee, Nicholson had managed to remain as adviser from 1968 until early 1970, when they clashed over the articles and reviews that were passed without going through the censorship process.

In March, 1970, Ahee accused Nicholson of insubordination and fired him from the faculty. Although some 500 students and parents urged the Torrance Board of Education to reinstate the teacher, the Board upheld the firing.

Almost four years later Nicholson was still battling Ahee and the Board over the censorship issue. A suit he filed against both in 1973 in the U.S. District Court in Los Angeles alleging violation of his constitutional rights was expected to be brought to trial in 1974. The suit seeks reinstatement of $118,500 in damages.[6]

The DuShane Fund of the National Education Association retained Roy Lucas, a Washington attorney, to represent Nicholson. Lucas, a Rotarian and former Rotary Foundation Fellow, called the Four-Way Test an excellent personal guide for business relationships. But he said, "If the Four-Way Rotary Test had been applied to the Watergate, news of the first story of the burglary would never have been published because it would have been unfair to the burglars."

Supporting Nicholson's cause, the Journalism Education Association, the nation's largest organization of high school newspaper advisers, issued a statement criticizing the Rotary test as applied to the high school press:

> Truth sometimes is not pleasant. It may hurt a person's reputation. It may make us sick at heart. But it must be found and reported to the public, and this

---

[6] *Nicholson v. Board of Education, Torrance Unified School District, et al.*

certainly includes students. For some persons, it may be more comfortable to live in a fantasy world in which nothing is bad and no one suffers. But ignoring a problem does nothing to solve it. It is up to the press, including the scholastic press, to make these problems known so that they may be solved. The professional journalism educator is trained in good journalistic practices as well as how best to pass this understanding of journalism, reporting and the democratic process along to his students. He is aware that a simple test, such as the Four-Way Rotary test, does not help the press fulfill its democratic mission and that it would greatly mislead the students in their search for the truth.

Chapter 6

Censorship from the Top

The cases cited here and other cases documented by the Commission of Inquiry reflect the most destructive form of censorship of school journalists—that administered by school authorities.

Not only does direct administrative censorship stifle the free expression of ideas in specific cases, but also it creates an atmosphere in which faculty and students alike know that to deal with controversial issues is to court official disapproval and perhaps disciplinary action. It breeds faculty censorship and self-censorship by students who otherwise would be more inclined toward participating in a free press.

The result usually is an unquestioning attitude among students, an unhealthy acquiescence in pronouncements of school authorities no matter how unfair or oppressive they may be. In such authoritarian schools, student rights are routinely denied, with little or no protest by students. The cost of such controls is not only the absence of a free student press, but also bland, apathetic students who are unaware or uninterested in their rights.

In schools generally the strongest force for censorship comes from the top—principals with support of superintendents and boards of education. And teachers or advisers with courage and commitment enough to defend the students' rights of free expression may run the risk of loss of their jobs, as in the case of Don Patrick Nicholson. Or they may face reassignment, as in the case of Dorothy McPhillips, a member of the Commission of Inquiry who lost her assignment as adviser to the *Crusader,* the school paper at Los Alamitos (California) High School, because she opposed the principal's policies of prior review and censorship of articles he considered offensive or unworthy of publication.

The Commission found that some boards of education put their censorship policies in writing, although they eschew the word "censorship." One of these was the Board of Trustees of Anaheim Union High School District, which adopted a new policy in the wake of McPhillips' clash with the principal.

The Anaheim Board decreed that advisers should serve as "consultants," but noted that they could reject articles. "If student articles must be edited, redirected or refused," the Board ruled, "counseling with the student as to the effects of his proposed activities shall be an integral part of the teaching process."

In its policy statement the Board also pointedly noted that the Board and the principal held the purse strings to school publications:

As a learning tool, school-sponsored student publications are in the main supported by public funds. In the normal chain of authority, the principal is responsible for school publications. . . . Therefore, he has final authority, including budgetary support. . . . As a matter of necessity, the principal delegates his authority to one or more faculty members, usually as a part of regular teaching assignments. The teacher may delegate to student editors the task of publication, though the responsibilities and authority of the sponsor and administrator remain undiminished.

The policy statement also forbade the use of quotes from faculty members without first verifying the quotes with the faculty members. Concerning reviews of school events, the Board decreed: "Since criticism of school-sponsored productions and athletic events can have disruptive effects on concerned groups within the school, reviews of these productions and contests shall be constructive in character."

A policy statement of somewhat different character had been advocated by Dorothy McPhillips, who had had eleven years experience as a teacher and adviser at the time she resisted the principal's censorship policies in 1971.

In arguing her case before the Board, she suggested that the adoption of a policy guaranteeing a free press should have priority over her own reinstatement as adviser to the school paper. "Perhaps even more important," she told the Board, "is the need for you to establish a policy before next September, one which guarantees freedom of expression to all high school students in the . . . district, and one which will not allow a trained and experienced journalism teacher and publications adviser to be put out to pasture because some coaches, some Boosters' Club members, or even one board member does not like or agree with what students have to say."

The Board not only upheld the reassignment of McPhillips, but, as previously noted, it put its censorship policies in writing.

In New York, Ron Vandor, student editor and president of the New York City High School Press Council, described interference by the Board of Education as "the biggest problem we've had." He told the Commission:

In the last year they succeeded in hampering the Press Council to the point where they have set us back a full year, and now we're in the process of re-organizing ourselves, but by next year we will hopefully be able to function again normally. Thus, the Press Council has been censored in a way by the Board of Education, and that censorship by the Board comes in line with censorship of school newspapers by administrators and teachers and ... there is a serious question here of the First Amendment.

The Board then proceeded to postpone meetings, Council meetings. In essence, they impeded the process of the Press Council, that process being electing officers, setting up steering committees, and they hampered all that, and when this wasn't done last year, it kept us from organizing ourselves this year. There hasn't been a Press Council—the Press Council just wasn't in existence from May of last year till about January of this year. There was no president, no officers, no steering committee. Finally, a group of students working with Board of Education people were able to set up a Press Council again, after repeated visits to the New York Civil Liberties Union, and various ombudsmen at the Board of Education.

Although some school administrators are reluctant to talk publicly about restrictions they impose on the high school press, others feel so deeply that such policies are justified and necessary that they unhesitatingly discuss them.

Despite other pressing obligations, Joseph Endry, principal of Reynoldsburg (Ohio) High School, traveled more than 200 miles to a Commission of Inquiry hearing in South Bend to defend his policies. He had confiscated a copy of *Doubloon,* the school newspaper, in 1971. Because of that and other alleged acts of censorship, at the time of the hearing he was a defendant in a federal court suit brought by student journalists.[7]

Endry told the Commission he thought the op-

---

[7] *Hannahs v. Endry.* On Dec. 13, 1973, a U.S. District Court in the Southern District of Ohio upheld Endry, ruling that he had the responsibility to maintain order and that restraint of distribution of the material in question was not unconstitutional. The Ohio ACLU has appealed the ruling.

portunity to present his side of the case was so important that he missed his first senior play in twenty-two years to attend the hearing. He suggested that other principals would have given the Commission opinions similar to his if they had been involved in censorship cases and had been able to spare the time to attend Commission hearings. He said:

> Let's remember the silent majority, those who do not have a cause to promote and, therefore, do not respond to your request to testify. Not only did I miss the senior play to get here, but I had to leave the office to catch my plane in the middle of a conference with a student high on drugs; a distraught parent; and a policeman who wanted to bust a kid. I had to wrestle with my conscience to say my flight here was more important before I called the assistant principal in to take over. You may have to go to those people, rather than have them come to you. I think many high school principals—and I don't want to sound like a martyr—but they are long, hard jobs that take a lot of their time and they really are not free to leave them. I don't think their conscience permits them to be away from their work that much.

Endry voiced concern about community pressures and about the possibility that articles and editorials in the school paper would be interpreted in the community as representing the attitude of the administration. The mere fact that material is published in the school paper, he said, convinces many persons "we are sympathetic with views expressed therein."

In his opinion, some stories are not "proper" for school newspapers. "An article on planned parenthood, telling students where to obtain information to prevent pregnancy," he said, "implies we accept premarital sex and advise those who engage in it how to keep from getting pregnant." Such articles belong in health classes and government classes, Endry said, and possibly in English classes, "provided it is preceded with discussion of problems premarital sex can cause. . . ."

Chapter 7

Advisers as Censors

While a written policy is a clear warning to the faculty, neither a stated nor an implied policy of censorship is necessary in some cases for advisers to censor the papers. They do it because they believe in it and see it as a duty to the school, as reflected by a National Education Association survey that found that 62 percent of American secondary school teachers favored censorship of school papers.

In their eyes, the paper belongs to the administration, not to the students. For example, Susan Kemp, an adviser from San Antonio, Texas, told the Commission:

Administrators look on the paper as an educational tool, depending on the administrator and how well he communicates with sponsors. Most items he desires are those that show the best side of the school, listing winners and spreading joy and sunshine. Administrators look on the paper as a house organ and rightfully so. Paper staff should do its darndest to uphold the administrators and present them in the best possible light. However, the staff also has the right to investigate administrative mistakes or injustices because the staff is a part of the administration. This right is just as long as the staff conducts its investigation in a mature reportive fashion. We are not censored. Period. I am the censor.

The extent to which many advisers feel they must go to satisfy the school administration was indicated in an article in the October–November, 1970, *Quill and Scroll* by Sandra Grasinger, publications adviser at Rolling Hills (California) High School. Suggesting ways for advisers to avoid censorship problems, Grasinger emphasized the public relations aspect of the school paper and urged advisers to:

(1) Consider the paper's publisher to be the school administration and work within that framework;
(2) Learn the personal philosophy of the principal and pay him allegiance in print;
(3) Have respect for all "sacred cows"; and
(4) Limit the newspapers to news and features that "concern the school and students."

It is not uncommon for teachers to inject their own moral code or to consider community pressures in deciding what they feel is fit to print in high school papers. For example, Jann Wesolek's North Liberty High School counselor lectured her when she discussed the possibility of publishing her story on planned parenthood.

And Marilyn Fodor, an adviser from South Bend, told the Commission: "I was asked about an article on abortion, or planned parenthood. . . . I think I have personal Christian convictions I would have to put into this, I'm sure, because I would have to consider the community we publish our paper in. I do not think I would personally put this in if it was given to me. If somebody else wanted to put it in, I don't know what I would do. . . . I have personal convictions, because I am the parent of four children."

Trudy Martin, student editor from Millbrae, California, quoted the adviser to her newspaper, the *Thunderbolt,* as saying that there were "things that would never be able to go into any paper, simply because of the reaction of the community. She fears retaliatory action if she would presume to put anything of a questionable nature in the paper."

The control some advisers exercise over newspapers is so tight that the title "editor" is meaningless for students. Take the case of Linnell Hickson, a student editor from Washington, D.C., whose adviser, he told the Commission, rules with an "iron hand" and "seems to favor more praising the school."

Hickson said, "It's almost like it's his paper, it's not the students'. . . . He puts sort of a ban on really provocative issues and he makes sure that certain materials never appear in the paper. It's censorship in all forms of the word because he'll look at a certain article or a certain topic and won't even take it or he'll use some other excuses and he won't let you develop certain subjects."

Advisers insensitive to the youth culture have engaged in some of the most blatant and restrictive acts of censorship, backed up by harsh disciplinary measures for those who rebel at the restrictions. Kathleen Sullivan, a student editor from San Francisco, told the Commission:

Well, the most problem I have with [the adviser]—and she's in charge of the whole journalism, everything—is she doesn't want you to write anything—which I can understand—which could offend anybody else, or that is obscene. But she goes to extremes. . . .

Another thing is, she kicks people out of her class left and right. If you don't put up with her . . . you will be out in a week. I have been threatened to be put out of the class three times. The only reason I haven't is because I am a senior and I will, of course, be nice —"Oh, please, don't get rid of me." I don't want to be put out in the last couple of weeks.

This, you know, happens to everybody. I mean, since I have been in her class, since the tenth grade, she has kicked out about five people. Each semester somebody mysteriously is gone the next day. . . .

Everybody finds out about these things, so nobody wants to take that class. Last semester we only had, I think, eight people, nine people in the whole class. There has never been more than fifteen in the whole class.

Not all advisers are insensitive, of course. Some of them agonize over the problems involved in trying to assure that the school paper is as responsible as it is free. One of these is John Wheeler, adviser to the *Lion,* the paper of Lyons Township High School in La Grange, Illinois.

The *Lion,* one of the best high school publications examined by the Commission, generally has operated free of any censorship policies. However, in one instance Wheeler, after repeated conferences with the editors, suppressed an editorial endorsing candidates for student government.

Testifying before the Commission he acknowledged that he may have made the wrong decision:

> I tried to suggest to them they could be irresponsible and the candidates could not have legitimate opportunity to respond if they weren't endorsed, since they would not have another issue before the election. It could provide an unfair advantage, including the fact I thought the job of the paper was to represent the candidates' position, not to tell voters how they should vote.
>
> I searched, personally, for alternatives. I tried to raise questions with editors about it. I searched for help.
>
> I checked books; I asked another adviser-teacher what he felt about it; I tried to talk to the adviser at school who had carried an endorsement policy; I talked at some length to the Student Activities adviser about what could happen. The only thing I found, that gave me any guide at all in terms of legal aspects, was a statement in a copy of *Communication: Journalism Education Today* (a J.E.A. publication) that said the I.R.S. might be concerned if a school newspaper endorsed political candidates because the institution might lose its tax-exempt status. No more definition than that.
>
> I don't think it is a legal question. I think it is an ethical question. Most of the arguments I put to the editors against the endorsement were ethical arguments.
>
> I let the thing simmer down for a long time. Finally, on Monday, I decided that I had to make a decision. It was not a popular one—it was one that involved prior restraints. I told them I could not support their view and, as adviser to the paper, I could not allow them to do it. It was very painful. After I had made

the decision, I checked with the superintendent to make sure he would support me on it and could assure me I would not illegally interfere with their rights—I was very concerned about this.

It was hoped this would stimulate discussion and get some feedback, because I thought it was very important. They knew—and the Commission might as well know—I could have done nothing.

Perhaps the healthiest thing would have been if I could have removed myself from the situation and said, "I don't agree with what you are doing. I will put a disclaimer in the paper. Go ahead, it is your baby." Maybe that is what I should have done, but that is not what happened.[8]

Most advisers readily acknowledge that they or the school administration, rather than the students, have the final word on publication of articles. The Commission, in a survey of advisers and journalism teachers, asked, "Who in school have final right of approval of articles to be published in the paper?"[9]

The replies showed that students are unlikely to have the final word regardless of the racial makeup of the school. The adviser was listed as having the final word by 64 percent of the advisers polled in predominantly white schools; by 87 percent of advisers surveyed in racially balanced schools; and by 74 percent of advisers in schools where minorities were predominant.

Some teachers and school administrators do not stop at trying to control what students write in campus publications. Not only do they ban or discourage distribution of alternate school newspapers, they seek to curb stories of a controversial nature that are written about school activities by students for the established media.

Nancy Sulok, editor of the High School Page of the *South Bend Tribune* (one of relatively few newspapers that encourage student journalists to submit articles directly rather than through school channels), has ex-

---

8 Article from the *Lion* appears in Appendix C.
9 Summary of survey appears in Appendix B.

perienced pressure from school administrators more than once. She told the Commission:

> A student from Riley, writing for the High School Page, wrote a story about the confiscation of a student survey and included in it a copy of the survey. The day after the story appeared in the paper, the managing editor of the *Tribune* had a telephone call. . . . The assistant principal wanted to know why we printed a story like this—do we really think it is necessary to say things like that in the paper? The editor said, "Yes. It is newsworthy and it was a good story," and more or less told the assistant principal that he was not going to get anywhere.
>
> Another incident came up after one of the staff writers for *Student Supplement* (an alternate school paper) turned in a story for the High School Page explaining that the *Student Supplement* had been founded at Mishawaka High School. It was a very well-written story. It was not emotional at all. It was just plain news. After that appeared in the paper, the managing editor again got a telephone call. Mr. Smith, from Mishawaka High School, was unhappy about the fact the story was printed. He didn't think it was the type of news that the community should be aware of.

Not only school administrators, but also some teachers disapproved of the *Tribune's* use of student-written stories that were considered controversial. Nancy Sulok told the Commission of a meeting with journalism students, advisers, and teachers in South Bend where she explained to the students they were responsible to her as their editor but assured them the *Tribune* would print any responsible, newsworthy article, even if it was controversial and might be turned down for publication in the school newspaper.

She said, "I think some of the teachers were upset. I saw them frowning in the audience when I made that statement. The students seemed to appreciate it."

No matter how blatant the act of censorship or how harsh the treatment of students who rebel at the act, administrators generally find wide faculty support for their policies. For many teachers as well as administrators find a free high school press a threat to their own concept of institutionalized control of students.

David Plylar, a San Antonio teacher, told the Commission of a censorship case involving MacArthur High School of San Antonio that resulted in a court decision vindicating the students and criticizing the school board for harsh reprisals against the students.

Even while the case was in litigation, Plylar said, "there were a lot of teachers who believed that the school board was entirely in the right in doing what it did; that candor of the type expressed in the MacArthur newspaper, poses a threat to people, to many people in the education profession." Most censorship of high school newspapers goes virtually unnoticed outside the school unless litigation develops. And for a variety of reasons, such as expense, the amount of time involved, and lack of knowledge of student rights, students seldom resort to legal action.

In a written report to the Commission, John Roemer III, executive director of the American Civil Liberties Union of Maryland, explained that in his own state "students are afraid to complain, articles and editorials get watered down, administrators give 'good' reasons to editors for toning down essays, and so on." He cited several Maryland cases, however, that had come to the ACLU's attention in the early 1970s:

- Refusal of permission to distribute a pamphlet attacking prior censorship in Montgomery County schools.
- Seizure of antiwar pamphlets in a Baltimore County high school.
- Disciplinary action for distributing flyers about a Black Panther benefit in a Baltimore city school.
- Ban on a Baltimore city junior high school newspaper for an article asking students to write to their Congressmen to protest the war.
- Student initially refused staff position on Garrett County school paper on grounds she was "too radical."

- Harford County student editor in many battles over articles in school paper critical of school— paper finally dropped by school for "lack of money."

School administrators and teachers are not solely to blame for repression of student journalists. For parents generally take little interest in the rights of students and, in fact, many support rigid school controls.

Parent Teacher Associations have been known to assist school administrations in censorship efforts. In Baltimore County, Maryland, the PTA of the Milford High School went so far in 1970 as to write advertisers and discourage them from continuing to advertise in an underground paper. A letter from the PTA noted that the school's executive board was "greatly concerned about a newspaper called 'Harry,'" and added, "We consider the paper not to be in the best interest of young people."

In a Louis Harris survey in 1969, nearly two-thirds of parents polled said they believed "maintaining discipline is more important than student self-inquiry" in high schools. The comparable figure among teachers was only 27 percent.

As Charles Silberman wrote in *Crisis in the Classroom,* "The most important characteristic schools share in common is a preoccupation with order and control."[10]

It is a preoccupation that chokes a free press, stifles other freedoms of inquiry and expression, and produces the gloomy picture of public schools Silberman painted in the same book:

It is not possible to spend any prolonged period visiting public school classrooms without being appalled by the mutilation visible everywhere—mutilation of spontaneity, of joy in learning, of pleasure in creating, of sense of self. The public schools—those "killers of

---

[10] *Crisis in the Classroom,* published by Random House in 1970, was Charles Silberman's report as director of the Carnegie Study of the Education of Educators.

dreams" to appropriate a phrase of Lillian Smith's—
are the kind of institutions one cannot really dislike
until one gets to know them well. Because adults take
the schools so much for granted they fail to appreciate
what grim, joyless places most American schools are,
how oppressive and petty are the rules by which they
are governed, how intellectually sterile and esthetically
barren the atmosphere, what an appalling lack of civil-
ity obtains on the part of teachers and principals, what
contempt they unconsciously display for children as
children.[11]

---

[11] *Crisis in the Classroom*, p. 10.

Chapter 8

Self-Inflicted Censorship

In the restrictive climate that prevails at most
schools, students who dare to rebel at censorship
policies know they face official punishment, a factor
which the Supreme Court has called a "chilling effect"
on the exercise of First Amendment rights and an unconstitutional restraint on the general press.

Such a chilling effect discourages most students and
results in the most pervasive form of censorship—that
imposed by the students on themselves. The result is
apathy and passivity. To survive as members of the
paper's staff, students know they must make no waves.
John Griffin, a student editor from Charlotte, N.C., described it this way:

It's just the way it's always been run, and the way
[the adviser] ... presents it. It's not that we're brain-
washed, it's just that we're ... filtered into a pattern
that we just kind of do it that way.

I sat in class last year with all these ideas in my head of how to make a really great paper, and as I watched, I saw that it just wasn't going to work out. There was going to be too much friction. I may get in, but I'm going to have a lousy year in here. So, I just kind of sat back and learned to accept it, figuring, when I get into college, I would have all the material background, you know.

The paper doesn't cover the issues. It's a very conservative paper. It deals with what's going on in school, and, you know, the clubs, stuff like this, sports, and it has editorials on the school, and that's what mainly puts it together.

Students quickly learn what is acceptable and what is unacceptable. Abraham Arevalo, a student editor from Robstown, Texas, explained to the Commission the reason his adviser could claim she had done little censoring was "because they knew what she was going to take out. So that is the reason that nobody ever wrote anything . . . because they knew what was going to be in and what wasn't. So if there was a controversial issue or something they probably would not write anything about it because they knew it was not going to be published."

Censorship of the student press is "mostly self-inflicted," Danny Segal, a student editor from New York, told the Commission. Rather than write stories that would cause "a little stirring," he said, students "go to the principal, and they ask if she would like a story printed, and if she says, 'Well, I would not like that story printed,' it won't go in, no questions asked or anything like that."

Segal said, "In a way, they're sort of playing into the administration's hands, even though the administration doesn't happen to be all bad. But the purpose of the paper—it's run by students—and it should be for the students, not for the administration."

Four New York student journalists—Alan Lipsky, Rod Hurley, Ami Ross, and Jeanne Cohen—canvassed twenty-five New York high schools on assignment by the Commission and reported finding widespread self-censorship.

Lipsky found "an unofficial school policy that you shouldn't deal with things that are . . . taboo, like talking about fights within the administration, or teachers' suspensions, for whatever reasons they were suspended, or obscene words, or a lot of things along this line; guidance counselors, talking about problems kids have with them, because this is sort of taboo. And even if you write the story, it just won't be put in because . . . the editor will say it's not good to cause dissension among the students and everything. . . ."

In Hurley's view, the students engaged in "self-censorship" which resulted in a newspaper that did not represent the interests of the student body.

A major reason for self-censorship is students' lack of knowledge of press law and of their own constitutional rights. Even where state law requires school publication guidelines consistent with the First Amendment, as in California, there is little evidence that young people are aware of the legal protections.

Nor is the picture much different in New York despite a series of court decisions and rulings from the office of the Chancellor of the City of New York bolstering the rights of students and the scholastic press.

Danny Segal, one of the most articulate students to appear before the Commission, said he was not familiar with the legal protections. Asked about First Amendment law, he replied, "I have discussed it with several members of my staff, and my friends, but we have not had it on a formal basis on the newspaper."

Where press law is taught, teachers often emphasize the restrictions on young journalists and ignore or downplay their rights. A case in point involved the 1972 convention of the Empire State School Press Association at Syracuse University.

The convention program listed a press law workshop on libel entitled, "It's tough to edit the school paper in a jail cell because you've libeled Miss McTavish." A crucial factor the lecturer failed to mention until questioned by a Commission staff member who attended the session was that New York has no criminal libel statute.

Describing her first classroom contact with press law, Jann Wesolek of South Bend told the Commission, "We didn't go into the First Amendment. We discussed libel and slander."

Although many students are complacent about their lack of knowledge of their own rights, a survey by the Commission also shows that many others are interested in learning about their rights. The survey showed that 51 percent of those polled were dissatisfied with subjects covered by the student press, and 55 percent of those who were dissatisfied cited inadequate coverage of student rights as a reason for their dissatisfaction.

Even more depressing is the professional journalists' lack of knowledge of—and concern for—student press rights and high school censorship problems. A survey of managing editors by the Commission indicated that 57 percent were unaware of federal court decisions favoring student journalists in censorship cases. Only 35 percent of the editors favored full First Amendment rights for student journalists and 46 percent were uncertain about whether such rights were exercised in their communities' high schools.[12]

---

[12] A summary of the survey appears in Appendix B.

Chapter 9

Kind of Material Censored

Articles that may be considered obscene, libelous, or disruptive of the school—factors that courts have cited as a legal basis for school publication guidelines— are seldom at issue in school censorship controversies. A review of court decisions reveals that only twice have "four-letter words" been at issue, and in no case has obscenity, libel, or disruption of the school been established.

Evidence compiled by the Commission overwhelmingly shows that school officials' censorship policies have focused on three categories of writing:

1. Controversial political issues, such as racism, students' rights, and, at one time, the Vietnam War.
2. Criticism of school administrations or faculty policies, or unfavorable images of the school, such as criticism of athletic teams or of school censorship policies.
3. Life styles and social problems, such as birth control and drug abuse.

School officials may consider such articles just as offensive in alternate school papers as in official school papers, of course, and may seek to suppress those papers, too. For example, there was the case of five San Antonio student journalists who distributed, off campus, the newspaper, *Awakening,* which printed information on marijuana and listed a free counseling service on venereal disease and other problems.

The material the administrators found objectionable included:

An estimated 23 million Americans have smoked marijuana, including 43 percent of all college students. Under existing laws all of them could go to jail. Smoking marijuana isn't the issue, unjust laws are. NORML (National Organization for the Reform of Marijuana Laws).

And

... For information and treatment of (A) V.D., (B) Birth control, (C) Food and Nutrition, (D) Medical treatment, (E) Psychological Aid, (F) Drug Counseling, (G) Draft counseling, call San Antonio Free Clinic, 733-0383.

The students involved with the paper were suspended from school. Calling this reaction "incredible," the U.S. Court of Appeals ordered that all records of the suspensions be expunged from the students' records and that school officials adopt publication guidelines that would respect the Constitutional rights of students.

As the material in this report of the Commission study shows, witnesses at each of the hearings corroborated what the Commission learned from the case law about the kind of material usually censored from the school press.

Even officials who are well aware of court decisions supporting a free high school press are prone to either ignore the court-approved standards for guidelines or apply them in such a way as to censor the paper. As James Cunningham, a student journalist for an alternate newspaper in South Bend, said, his school administration's attitude was that "anything that disrupts the school's *thinking* is disruptive to the educational process and should not be allowed."

Trudy Martin, a student editor from Mills High School in Millbrae, California, told of attempting to insert in her paper a student's column which declared it was undeniable that the school had a relatively high number of drug users. "That was the part that was censored and was not permitted to be included in the paper," she said. "It could not go out because the statement was inflammatory and detrimental to the school image, and to the image of the students. This was because of this fear the principal has regarding public pressure, and the climate at Mills High School in relation to the community and the kind of influence they have over what happens at the school."

To students sensitive about problems of their community, such censorship can be especially frustrating. Deborah Tillman, a student editor from Dunbar High School in Washington, D.C., told the Commission her school paper avoids criticism of the school and other controversial subjects because the adviser "won't allow it." She said:

We might be able to criticize the cafeteria or study hall, but not how the school is being run. And I think that's the only way students can find out about and evaluate school policies, through the school newspaper.

The Dunbar student newspaper staff is not allowed to cover the community issues either. We, as blacks, should cover the community. We have thought about the issues that touch our lives and those people in our communities—job cutbacks, housing—but we don't have a chance to write about them. We just cover football games and things like that.

The degree of overt censorship exercised depends largely upon the extent to which students attempt to deviate from the house organ concept of the paper.

Sam Mercantini, Indiana's former assistant superintendent of public instruction, told the Commission, "As long as you are expressing what the administration likes, be as free as you want. As soon as you get on any kind of touchy ground . . . restrictions are more stringent."

School administrators, Mercantini said, simply do not want to worry about what the school newspapers are going to be saying in every issue and are inclined to shut them down if the worry becomes too burdensome. "I do feel most all school authorities think of their . . . paper as a house organ, to be used when it can be used, and put on the shelf when it causes problems," he said.

The Commission's student survey disclosed that 53 percent of students polled believed their school papers were used to create a good impression of the school with outsiders; 27 percent disagreed and 20 percent had no opinion. Among newspaper staff members the finding was even more emphatic, with 60 percent saying yes, 27 percent no, and 13 percent with no opinion.[13]

Officials who insist on the house organ concept will stop short of banning or discontinuing the school paper if they can force that concept on the students. But the

---

[13] Summary of survey appears in Appendix B.

censored publication that results from such policies is a
newspaper in name and appearance only.

Censorship more than any other factor has a greater
adverse effect on the quality and relevance of high
school journalism. Good writing, editing, layout, and
production are important, but the essential purpose of
a newspaper is to communicate a message.

A mimeographed publication, such as the *Ram-Page*
of Ranson Junior High School of Charlotte, N.C.,
which prints school news of substance, including student problems and protests, is a newspaper in every
sense of the word. But most high school newspapers,
including many that repeatedly win national scholastic
press honors, emphasize appearance rather than substance and bear little resemblance to an actual newspaper.

Testifying as to why a group of students at Mac-
Arthur High School in San Antonio spurned the school
paper, *Brahma Tales,* and started an alternate newspaper, David Mulcahy, a senior, said, "The newspaper
in itself is tastefully organized and well presented pab-
lum. That is the full extent of it. All the information
on the Data Club and the German Club and how well
the Football Club is doing and an interview with the
coach and things like this, you know, new teachers. . . ."

The Commission's content analysis of high school
newspapers showed that 52 percent of the news coverage was devoted to sports and social news. All the high
school newspapers analyzed were primarily concerned
with those subjects.[14]

Similar profiles of high school newspapers showing
little news content of substance have emerged from
surveys in the past. A study by *Quill and Scroll,* for
example, showed that 75 percent of school papers
carried no news concerning suspension or expulsion of
students.

A 1972 survey of 59 high school newspapers in
Texas by Deason L. Hunt, Jr., found "little reporting
of significant issues in schools or education." Con-

---

[14] Summary of content analysis appears in Appendix B.

ducting the survey for his master's thesis at East Texas State University, Hunt found that 68 percent of the news space was taken up by news of organizations and activities, including sports. Curricular news took up 16 percent, individual achievements 12 percent, and community news 4 percent.

Nor is the subject matter covered the sole reason for the blandness of most high school newspapers. In-depth coverage of such subjects as sports, for example, could be informative and a useful exercise in journalism for students. But the Commission found that here, too, there are taboos that spring from the house organ concept of a school paper. One does not criticize the school team or its coaches. And one does not criticize special privileges that are sometimes accorded to athletes or the extraordinary financial support often enjoyed by athletic programs.

Criticism of cheerleaders can even cause problems. In 1973, Lori Clepper, editor of *The Viewer* of Mounds View High School of St. Paul, Minnesota, was fired from her post after she published an anonymous letter from another student without the approval of the adviser. The letter criticized the school's cheerleaders for demanding academic credit for their activities and the school for selecting an "elite" group of cheerleaders on the basis of beauty and personality. Clepper appealed her firing, but it was upheld by the school board.

In the final analysis the censored high school newspaper is exactly what most administrators and teachers want it to be—a house organ reporting only those things that give the school a favorable image.

Paul Growald, a professional journalist from San Francisco, told the Commission that he thought an expectation that school papers would do investigative reporting or print news of substance "is like expecting the Republican Party's campaign newspaper to have broken the Watergate story." He said:

It is just not something that I have seen happen in high school papers that I have read. I think that happens because any kind of mass communication media reflect the attitudes and values of the dominant institutions that they are reporting about. In this case they are reporting about the school institution, which, in most cases, is not the most open institution around. I think it is unfortunate but true that most high school papers are gossip sheets, and avoid providing useful information for their students, things like where to get contraceptives or what to do if you get pregnant or if your girl friend gets pregnant, or what to do if you are having even as simple a thing as a bad trip.

It is not only unfortunate, but unnecessary that so many high school papers are gossip sheets, as clearly shown by exceptions to the rule. A relatively free press can even flourish in a junior high school, as indicated by the example of *Ram-Page* of Ranson Junior High.

The Commission found cases where high school papers ignored student protests, sometimes on administration orders and sometimes through self-censorship. But the *Ram-Page,* in a 1973 issue, carried a long, dispassionate account of a student walk-out. Kim Holbrook, a ninth-grader, wrote an objective story in a simple narrative style that informed readers of both sides of the issue and included criticism of the principal as well as his comments on the matter.[15]

Enthusiastic students exposed to that kind of journalism at Ranson have gone on to high schools, however, and become disillusioned by what they describe as "heavy censorship." James Sills, the Ranson journalism instructor, told the Commission one of his former students "came back and talked to me about it, and to put it bluntly, their school paper was Mickey Mouse, they couldn't say anything that they wanted to say and everything had to pass through this censor's office."

That some students will make mistakes and perhaps abuse their rights of a free press if they are permitted to exercise them is undeniable, but the benefits of freedom are of paramount importance.

---

15 See Appendix C for reprint of *Ram-Page* article.

In an opinion in 1969 involving *Eisner v. Stamford Board of Education*, a U.S. District Court judge put it this way:

> The risk taken if a few students abuse their First Amendment rights of free speech and press is outweighed by the far greater risk run by suppressing free speech and press among the young. The remedy for today's alienation and disorder among the young is not less but more free expression of ideas. In part, the First Amendment acts as a "safety valve" and tends to decrease the resort to violence by frustrated citizens. Student newspapers are valuable educational tools, and also serve to aid school administrators by providing them with an insight into student thinking and student problems. They are valuable, peaceful channels of student protest which should be encouraged, not suppressed.[16]

---

[16] *Eisner v. Stamford Board of Education*. See Appendix A for discussion of case.

Specific Commission Findings: Censorship

1. Censorship and the systematic lack of freedom to engage in open, responsible journalism characterize high school journalism. Unconstitutional and arbitrary restraints are so deeply embedded in high school journalism as to overshadow its achievements, as well as its other problems.
2. Censorship of journalism is a matter of school policy—stated or implied—in all areas of the country, although in isolated schools students enjoy a relatively free press.

3. Censorship persists even where litigation or administrative action has destroyed the legal foundation of censorship; such decisions are either ignored or interpreted in such a way as to continue the censorship policy.

4. Repressive policies are used against school-oriented media published off campus as well as within schools; many of the several hundred alternate or "underground" papers that have sprung up in recent years have been actively opposed by school officials.

5. Although substantive and investigative journalism and controversial or image-damaging information are most severely censored, policies of censorship apply regardless of whether the material is substantive or controversial.

6. Even advisers or journalism teachers who in private favor a free student press often succumb to bureaucratic and community pressures to censor school newspapers.

7. As part of the day-to-day operation of high school journalism, censorship generally is accepted by students, teachers, and administrators as a routine part of the school process. This has developed into the most pervasive kind of censorship, that imposed by students upon themselves.

8. Self-censorship, the result of years of unconstitutional administrative and faculty censorship, has created passivity among students and made them cynical about the guarantees of a free press under the First Amendment.

9. Fear of reprisals and unpleasantness, as well as the lack of a tradition of an independent high school press, remain the basic forces behind self-censorship.

10. Censorship is the fundamental cause of the triviality, innocuousness, and uniformity that characterize the high school press. It has created a high school press that in most places is no more than a house organ for the school administration.

11. Where a free, vigorous student press does exist,
    there is a healthy ferment of ideas and opinions,
    with no indication of disruption or negative side
    effects on the educational experience of the
    school.

12. The professional news media does not take seri-
    ously the First Amendment problems of high
    school journalists and does little to help protect
    the free press rights of students.

PART II

Minority Participation

Chapter 10

"Three-fourths of One Percent—.0075"

> Woodrow Wilson High School is about 60 to 65 percent black and up until about two years ago black students just did not take journalism. —*Adolphus Thomas, counselor at Woodrow Wilson High School, San Francisco, California.*

> The school is 70 percent black, and the five editors, we're all white. —*Danny Segal, student editor, Erasmus High School, Brooklyn, New York.*

> Approximately 75 percent of the school population was Chicano and the Anglos had control of, well, the Student Council, the annual, and the paper staff. . . . —*Mario Trevino, student, Crystal City, Texas.*

Adolphus Thomas wanted his share of the American Dream, he told the Commission of Inquiry, and his dream was to be a great journalist. But when his family moved from Houston to San Francisco in 1944 and he entered high school, his counselor at the school advised him he could "make it in one of two areas, industrial art or music."

Since to him industrial art meant "something like sheet metal," he opted for music. Not that he particularly liked that either. "Some people can knock on a table and say that is E flat, and they are right," Thomas said. "They can hear a motor run and tell you what key it is running in. I wouldn't know one tune from another. . . ."

His primary interest was the school newspaper, but

he was blocked from joining its staff. Finally, in his last year, when he had an undeniable right as a senior to take one elective course, he got on the newspaper staff by selecting journalism.

Thomas became an instant success, a prolific writer of features and editorials. He won a *Quill and Scroll* award of the National Honorary Society of High School Journalism and was presented the award at a banquet which was publicized by the San Francisco press. He told the Commission:

> I received within the week two letters, one from the San Francisco *Call-Bulletin,* which was a daily newspaper that has just gone out of print, and one from the *San Francisco News* (also now out of print).
>
> So I went down with these letters in my hand, thinking I would receive a job, as offered, as a copy boy. This was the way you started when you worked your way up.
>
> When I went to the *Call-Bulletin,* I was told that the letter had been sent by mistake and that no such job was available to me, or to anyone, that there was no vacancy.
>
> I had another letter, so I went over to the *San Francisco News,* and there I was told frankly that they did not know I was Negro, and that, had they known, I would not have received the letter. Since they didn't think Negroes were taking anything like journalism, they had no possibility of even remotely dreaming that the letter would be addressed to a black person.

Now, more than twenty-five years since that incident, Thomas was telling the Commission of Inquiry that blacks and other minorities were still being excluded from journalism, beginning at the high school level.

Asked whether Blacks failed to participate in high school journalism because the opportunities were not open to them or because they were looking ahead and deciding journalism was not open to them as a career, Thomas said, "I think when you don't see the black or brown or yellow examples in your community, no one has to hit you on the head with a hammer to tell you ... that these positions perhaps are not available to you."

Since his early disillusionment with American journalism, Thomas had gone on to distinguish himself as a journalism teacher and had served as president of the Journalism Education Association of Northern California.

At Woodrow Wilson High School, where he was serving as counselor, black students "just did not take journalism" until two years ago even though the school was 60 to 65 percent black. He said he finally was able to recruit blacks by working through the Black Students Union and persuading them that "this is a thing that black students should relate to."

The Commission found, however, that Thomas is a rare exception to the rule. In the first place, there are relatively few faculty members—black or white—with his zeal for recruiting minorities for journalism. Also, there are relatively few black faculty members concerned with high school journalism even in predominantly black schools.

American newspaper editors are as conscious as any group in the United States of the press' traditional exclusion of minorities from its ranks. In April, 1972, an incident occurred at the American Society of Newspaper Editors convention in New York that reflected both the frustrations of minorities seeking access to equal employment opportunities and the fact that some editors have come to realize that their policies have been racist as well as exclusionary and that one place they should begin training minorities is in the high schools.

A chicano activist, Domínguez Reyes of the National Mexican American Anti-defamation League, seized a microphone in what he called a "hijacking" of the convention and proceeded to lecture the editors:

By excluding Chicanos as writers, editors, management, or as people worth noting, the American Society of Newspaper Editors exposes the racial-cultural prejudice that only blacks and whites are worth writing about or involving in the mass media. Chicanos and other people of Spanish descent have been denigrated and ignored by this mass media.

Although in his zeal he gave the media undue credit for involving and writing about Blacks, Reyes' complaint was valid as far as Chicanos were concerned. And Norman Isaacs, a former Louisville, Kentucky, editor who was presiding over the convention, admitted as much after Reyes relinquished the microphone.

Isaacs, a faculty member of the Columbia Graduate School of Journalism, announced the ASNE had conducted a survey that provided the first "reasonably accurate tally on minority news staff employees." It showed, he said, that nationally the figure on professional minority staffing by American newspapers is "three-fourths of one percent—.0075."

Of an estimated 40,000 reporters, writers, photographers, and editors, the ASNE survey had identified only 254 persons from minority groups—Blacks, Mexican-Americans, Puerto Ricans, Indians, Cubans, and those of Oriental descent. Evaluators of the survey arrived at the .0075 percentage by assuming another fifty minority group professionals were employed on smaller newspapers not reached by the survey.

Isaacs declared:

By numbers it is at least 100 less than I had originally guessed. It supports the assertion that we have, indeed, been racist in our employment practices throughout our years in the calling. I will be among the first to plead guilty. Even though my credentials as a crusader for civil liberties and for the equality of opportunity for all races were honorable in motivation through my first twenty-five years as an editor, I came to recognize that I was practicing a double standard. I thoroughly believed my contention that I was in truth color blind. Yet while I took many a long shot on white reporters, deskmen, and photographers, I somehow always thought it necessary to exercise the greatest of care when it came to hiring minority staffers. That is not at all to say that I now recommend the long-

shot method of hiring professionals. What I am saying
is that even some of us whom many of you regard as
starry-eyed visionaries were much less visionary than
we should have been—and as a result contributed to
holding back journalism.

Each of you who is sincerely interested in improving
the balance in your newsrooms is going to have to do
the most intensive work at your local high school
levels. This is where it all starts. The Committee on
Education in Journalism . . . discovered it is all too
clear that high school counsellors know next to nothing
about the opportunities in journalism, even for white
youth.

The ASNE survey had found "little evidence to indicate that more than a few editors" were moving with
vigor at local levels to produce acceptable trainees. And
despite the survey and Isaacs' stirring speech, in which
he urged editors to work with school superintendents,
principals, and counselors to increase minority participation, a year later ASNE reported little thrust
toward that goal.[17]

In fact, the 1973 report noted that general recruitment of minorities by newspapers had decreased and
that the sense of urgency for hiring minority journalists, that began with the urban riots of the 1960s,
had tapered off. The report declared, "Editors today
report no minority pressures being voiced and they are
taking their time in recruiting, reviewing more carefully
and moving much more deliberately."

The report urged editors to identify and encourage
aspiring minority high school journalists and to regularly examine high school counseling systems to make
sure journalism was not being played down as a career.

A survey of managing editors by the Commission of
Inquiry was similarly depressing. It disclosed that although 76 percent of the editors felt there were no
problems of minority access to high school journalism,
87 percent of them had never talked to teachers or
students about the subject.

---

[17] See Appendix C for *Editor & Publisher*'s report on the 1974
ASNE Committee on Minority Employment Report.

Chapter 11

Alternative Papers

On New York's East Side a young Puerto Rican, Fred González, found his high school paper suffered from "too much censorship" and a lack of identity with the Puerto Rican community. So after dropping out of school in his senior year he started a bilingual publication that became a success in his neighborhood. He told the Commission about the paper, the *Fourth Street I:*

> I find that there has to be more looking—of you people with the power—at us young people who are trying to achieve something. Myself, I have been through the whole school system up to high school. I had to leave high school, because I couldn't do my thing, and I found my thing is the *Fourth Street I.* Before, I did not do my thing. I could not read or write, but I have learned to . . . write and read better through *Fourth Street I* and also other brothers who are part of the staff have learned other skills with me, and this is without school.
>
> Now, I believe that we have done a great service in terms of our identity, and in terms of looking at ourselves for our brothers, who do not know who they are. . . .

In Texas, California, New York, and other states, minority students—Chicanos, Blacks, American Indians, and Puerto Ricans—have felt the same alienation from their high school newspapers. They have founded their own papers, frequently linking them to their communities as well as their schools. Often they have found unusual support in the community because the community itself has been ignored by the established media. For Chicanos and Puerto Ricans the alienation is

perhaps even sharper than for Blacks because of a
language difference. Testifying before the Commission,
Carlos Guerra, executive director of the Texas Institute
for Educational Development, a media and general
resource center for the chicano community in Southwest Texas, said that despite a heavy chicano population in South Texas, "by reading the paper . . . you
would see an entirely anglo society."

In San Antonio, where the Commission was holding
its third field hearing, the population was over 50 percent Mexican, he pointed out, and yet only six column
inches were devoted in a local newspaper to bilingual
news for Spanish-speaking readers.

Even in predominantly chicano school areas, he
said, Chicanos "unfortunately are still directed more
heavily toward printing than toward writing." Guerra
saw this as "part of the whole tracking system in vocational areas that we seem to be guided into," with the
result being a relative absence of Chicanos in professional journalism in Texas.

The ultimate result, Guerra told the Commission, is
"an Anglo perspective looking at a people that are—
oh, a number of words have been used—militant, foreign, quaint, and quite often criminal. I think this is
directly related to the massive failure of the educational
system with respect to Chicanos and specifically in
respect to Chicano journalism. Right now we have not
the ability to define ourselves but we are viewed as
somebody else would see us. We are foreigners in our
own land."

Although some Chicanos have successfully penetrated
the predominantly white world of high school journalism, Guerra and other activists have considered such
efforts so futile that they have turned to off-campus
community papers.

Chicanos trying to take part in high school journalism run into too many problems, he said, and find
themselves labeled militants and radicals. So instead
we "have gone to working with communities with the
same kids outside of the school. This way we can include the ones that have already dropped out and try
to start journalism endeavors there. This I think relates

much more realistically to the people as we are today
with . . . four out of five kids dropping out before they
finish high school."

One such paper supported by the Texas Institute for
Educational Development was *La Lomita de Libertad*
in Robstown, Texas, which was started following a
school boycott by chicano students. Abraham Arevalo,
a student journalist, told the Commission:

> We walked out because of the discrimination and we
> didn't have any books in Spanish or Mexican-Ameri-
> can. We didn't have any field trips or anything that
> we could determine from outside work and the paper
> they had there, I think last year they called it *El Chisme*
> [*The Gossip*]. They never said anything about the
> common student. They said something about the honor
> roll society and sports. . . . So after we walked out we
> decided to form our own paper with the help of the
> Texas Institute for Education Development. And we
> started it and I am proud to say that this next week is
> going to be our fifty-third issue.
>
> The circulation is 600 and we have approximately
> 3,000 readers. Every single one was taken by the peo-
> ple. We distribute to business places, stores, and so
> forth. The paper is self-supporting. We take in dona-
> tions. We only have volunteers on our staff. The only
> connection we have with the school is that the stu-
> dents help us in writing the paper and printing it and
> distributing the paper in the school. We cover all
> sorts of news, mostly news like discrimination in the
> school. Sometimes there are murders, car wrecks,
> school board meetings, utility meetings, etc. . . .
>
> No one working on the *La Lomita* has had any
> journalism classes or anything. We just decided we
> needed it and we need to communicate with our own
> Chicano people; so we decided to make our own.
> And sometimes in *La Lomita* there are typographical
> errors or misspelled words, but as long as the Chicano
> understands what we are trying to get across that is
> fine with us. . . .

Although *La Lomita* has proven to be a valuable
medium of communication, it is an exceptional case.

Few minority communities have organizations such as the Texas Institute for Educational Development to give such priority to communications.

Several witnesses in San Antonio attested to the fact that white society, including journalism, had failed to support biculturalism or bilingualism to help alleviate the problems of Chicanos. In fact, their testimony showed that in some predominantly chicano areas students and teachers who used their native language in schools met with punishment as well as disapproval. While that might seem incredible to many Americans, until recently state law in Texas forbade the use of Spanish in schools, except as a course in foreign language.

A boycott leader at a junior high school was spanked for speaking Spanish, testified Mario Trevino, a student journalist from Crystal City, Texas. "And there was a little boy who was in the second or third grade," Trevino said, "who was bruised so bad in the rear-end that he couldn't sit down for two or three days, because he was caught speaking Spanish."

A school administrator from Crystal City, Ángel González, told the Commission, "The first year I was there a teacher tried to make a point in Spanish to a student and he was reported and the sheriff came with a warrant for his arrest for teaching history class in Spanish. His class must have been 95 percent chicano."

Chapter 12

Journalism and the Integrated School

Lorraine Minor is a gifted black from Chicago's sophisticated Hyde Park area. After dropping out of the local public high school, Lorraine enrolled at St. Mary's Center for Learning, a private experimental school with an integrated student population of inner and outer city.

While still a freshman, Lorraine was encouraged to join the newstaff on the daily paper, the *Catalyst*. Lorraine spoke enthusiastically to the Commission:

> The first thing I got really interested in was the school newspaper because, when I first walked into the staff room I was amazed to know it. I said, "This is the staff?" I liked it a lot because there was so much freedom there I could express myself.
>
> The thing most important to me about the *Catalyst* is that it is made up of people who care about what they put in, and people who are not afraid to state an opinion and let you know their feelings on an article we have written. We welcome all kinds of feedback on every article we write, and we welcome ideas on what they would like to see and hear about.

Ruth López, a soft-spoken Chicana, hesitates before speaking to strangers. The slight frown that speaks of her nervousness gradually subsides as she warms to her subject and lets herself break out in a warm smile. Ruth told the Commission:

> I started working at the *Catalyst* first time in second semester. What got me interested was a girl friend going in there. When I walked in there, there was always a lot of laughing and talking, and nobody was sad or anything. So I just joined it. It was fun. It is a lot of fun because the articles we have to write on— I mean reports we have to make are mostly all interesting. The last one I had to do was on runaways. I had to go to the Police Station and ask what they do about it. At first I thought that I was afraid to talk to the police—to ask them. I thought they were going to be tough on us, so I was nervous to talk to them, but they made me feel free to talk to them and they asked me to come back again.
>
> I still get nervous when I have to interview people. I'll get out of it in a little while, I guess.

The current staff of the *Catalyst* has a balance of five Blacks, six Latins, and seven white students from a variety of backgrounds. The adviser, Micaela Conley, grew up with the chicano culture in Phoenix and maintains a fluency in Spanish. She encourages translations of important articles because the paper goes to many student homes every day. Parents know that the paper comes out every day and sometimes make a son or daughter return to school to retrieve the paper left behind.

In a paper to the Commission Micaela Conley offered opinions about staff minority balance based on her five years of experience in an integrated school and two years as a newspaper adviser:

> One of the factors in retaining a mixed racial and ethnic newspaper staff is a positive psychic environment. Journalism demands a great deal of discipline and, hence, the rewards have to be just as attractive. Publishing one's own work is a primary reward, yet the acceptance of others in the group, the sense of solidarity in working together, and a place or turf of one's own are more intangible, vital rewards.
>
> Integration is not solely a matter of race or culture. In fact, it is more important to me to attempt integration among students of varying intellectual backgrounds, for it is in this respect that virtually all high schools maintain segregation.
>
> Since the adult in the group, in this case the adviser, can be an important force in establishing and maintaining a positive environment, I find it necessary for me to call on far more than journalism skills or traditional professional competence. I need to recognize interaction patterns and to offer opportunities for emotional expression so that the feelings that might handicap the group's working together can be aired and channeled effectively.
>
> To encourage students of such diverse backgrounds to work in journalism is an acceptance and appreciation of their standards, interests, manner of approach and language style. It's a risk for anyone to put writing out for public consumption. As a result, I've found it necessary to offer a great deal of support and very little criticism to keep students writing. After they experience some initial success, they're ready to

struggle with their reluctance. I'm sure that editors on the *New York Times* would delight in the apt metaphors, the simple, direct style, and the amazing insights of my students to the point that they might soften the heavy editing pencil.

When given the chance, students are not afraid to open themselves to others. The result is truly exciting reading and an exchange of trust among members of the staff.

In the nation's capital, with a predominantly black population and an overwhelmingly black public school population, school journalism, with few exceptions, is dying. One of the exceptions, the *Black Voice,* at Browne Junior High School, covers community as well as school news.

With a staff of 87 students, the *Black Voice* not only encourages broad participation in journalism, but also has helped build writing skills and give students a sense of the value of a free press. Fletcher James, editor of the paper, told the Commission, "It's a student-run newspaper. The adviser does what he is trained to do, advise. I get the last decision and I discuss it with my executive staff. I still get the last decision."

The adviser, Ulysses Houston, blames the general lack of interest and support for journalism on the abandonment of Washington schools by whites in the wake of desegregation. He told the Commission:

Look, prior to 1954 there were two separate worlds in Washington, D.C., which still exist to an unfortunate degree, but was legal then. There was the white school system with its materials and its equipment; and then there was the old colored school system as it was called in those days which had literally the worn-out, hand-me-downs from the white system. I'll never forget my second year in high school, what a tremendous thrill it was for the teaching staff at Armstrong High to get Diesel generators. Here was a supposed technical high school and yet, for thirty years, they were operating without one Diesel generator in the entire school.

Well, in 1954 extensively that wall got broken down

and what happened was this. This isn't just Washington, this happened and continues to happen across the country. When integration struck, the whites looked up one day—good God! They took their trophies. They took their equipment. They took their expertise and vanished to the suburbs. The few that stayed had no use and have no use for black students. Their hatred, their fear is still there ... they couldn't care less whether these black students learn—that's part of the problem.

Commission hearings and surveys indicated that generally the percentage of minority students in a school population was a substantial contributing factor to the degree of access they had to student journalism.

The Commission found that not only in Washington, but in other schools where minority students constitute a large majority of the population, there tend to be fewer school papers or other journalistic media than in predominantly white schools; media outlets that do exist at these schools usually exhibit little relevance to the school experience.

Where minorities constitute a small number, apathy, powerlessness, and institutional discrimination result in minimum participation of minority youth. For example, in Charlotte, North Carolina, where the desegregation plan in effect required all schools to have approximately 30 percent black and 70 percent white students, the Commission found little effective participation of black students in high school journalism. A similar situation was found to exist in South Bend, Indiana, which had a minority student population of less than 20 percent.

The degree of minority access, while remaining low, appeared to increase slightly in schools where the number of minority students was roughly equal to the number of nonminority students. In those schools, the Commission saw a higher degree of minority participation in journalism and more awareness of the importance of journalism in political and cultural development.

The survey showed, however, that only 29 percent of minority students at racially balanced schools, compared to 66 percent for white students, find their papers representative of the range of student opinion.

Where minorities are over 60 percent of the school population, 64 percent said they believed their high school papers were representative.

Several witnesses testified about a tendency of white students to withdraw from journalism or other elective activities when confronted with a new and sizable minority interest. This has helped retard student journalism in some desegregated schools and has left blacks even more disillusioned with the white world of the media.

Wherever Blacks are given anything approaching equal access to student journalism, whites tend to shy away, Richard Navies, a teacher from Berkeley, California, told the Commission in recounting experiences of his school's paper, the *Jacket*. "I think the *Jacket*'s becoming predominantly Black is just like our attendance at our sports games . . . becoming predominantly Black, and all other social affairs," he said. "I think society is going to have to deal with that in terms of white students. They are going to have to educate white students, or we are going to have to educate them, to the point where they are not afraid of equal-access competition with Blacks, because that is what is really happening."

Chapter 13

Institutional Discrimination

Although in some cases members of racial, cultural, and ethnic minorities seeking to enter student journalism may run into overt barriers, more often they are confronted by subtle and invisible barriers.

The Commission found that factors contributing to subtle or institutional discrimination included:

- Methods of staff selection.
- Student journalism's poor coverage of minority news and opinion.
- The attitudes of nonminority journalism students toward minorities.
- Scheduling of journalism activities as an extracurricular and "after-school" activity.
- Financial problems that afflict schools with large numbers of minority students, together with systems of "tracking" that divert minority students from journalistic pursuits.
- High school workshops and summer training programs that recruit only a few minority students.

Staff Selection

The emphasis on grades and participation in journalism classes as a prerequisite to becoming a staff member of a newspaper has contributed to the scarcity of minority journalists and minimized journalism skills other than those measured by grades. This has placed a low priority on initiative, curiosity, and familiarity with significant issues, attributes considered essential for good journalists.

Moreover, this can result in class as well as racial or ethnic bias and in the creation of an elitist newspaper staff. School papers generally tend to be dominated by college-bound, middle- or upper-class students, with those of low income or a vocational bent participating in minimal numbers.

Howard Maniloff, a Charlotte, North Carolina, school administrator, said, "There is a very real problem in the fact that the high school newspaper is the reflection of what the college-bound students in that high school may be thinking. . . ."

The Commission's survey of advisers found that 64 percent of those who found their schools' papers to be unrepresentative of the schools thought the papers reflected only the views of the student staffs. Among students surveyed who also thought their papers were unrepresentative, 61 percent thought the papers reflected only the views of the staffs.

Danny Segal, the New York student editor quoted earlier, said, "Another problem is that in order to get onto the paper, you have to have, say, about a 90 average in English, because it's a course given by the English department, and because of that not many black students get in. In Erasmus, the top 10 percent of the graduating class, I would say, is about 90 percent white, and the school is 70 percent black, so you can see the contrast."

As Segal and another New York student journalist, Ted Cartselos, testified, the elitism of high school journalism goes beyond excluding minorities. Segal said the editors of his paper were "in like the top five percent of the . . . graduating class, and they gear the paper toward the people who are in the top 10 percent of the school, thereby cutting out the other students and there are 5,000 students at Erasmus."

Cartselos, a student at Bronx High School of Science, founded and edited an alternative paper, *The Gotham Herald*. He told the Commission he started the paper because he felt the regular school paper, *Science Survey,* had become "an intellectually elite paper from an intellectually elite high school and what did happen is that not only did they only publish their own specific views, which were basically middle class . . . white, et cetera, baloney, and what it came out to be was just completely tasteless and bland. . . ."

Just to be considered for a place on his newspaper's staff, a student must have a B average in English, Abel García, a student journalist from Cotulla, Texas, said. A student with a B average can enroll in a journalism course, he said, and if the adviser finds the student has the necessary writing skills, he may be selected for the paper. "As a result," García said, "there are about three . . . or four Mexican-Americans on the staff paper. However, there are numerous others who could or would express interest in writing who are not given the opportunity to write at all for the newspaper."

While the matter of skills and academic achievement is often cited as a reason that few minority students participate in journalism, some teachers see this as a special challenge and obligation to teach communication skills to young people.

James Garrick, a high school newspaper adviser from Keenan, South Carolina, said that while he thought generally white students have less trouble than blacks in reading and writing the English language, he sees journalism as an excellent opportunity for blacks to develop basic English skills and gain experience in writing. He also told the Commission:

> I think that we teachers are snobbish, and I do think that our standards are perhaps very high and we do think about journalism as a program for students of academic ability who can write when they come to us. I have heard many teachers say: "If the kid can't write he can't do me any good." And I think perhaps that I am too structured, and I perhaps share more of that opinion than I would like to . . . .

Another adviser, Micaela Conley of Chicago, Illinois, said the key to recruiting minority students for the newspaper staff is "really a desire to have them" and to encourage them to ask questions and express ideas and opinions. In her own case, she said, many minority students have served on the paper and disagreed with her on what should go in or be left out of the paper. "I think we pretty much have equal voice in that kind of situation," she said. "I am not, usually, too much of a heavy. If I get overwhelmed by the staff, I am overwhelmed and it goes."

Minority Coverage and Attitudes of Nonminority Student Journalists

The failure of high school media to cover minority issues is a result as well as a cause of the absence of minorities from the staff. And the tokenism that sometimes characterizes the desegregation of a high school newspaper staff solves neither problem.

Alan Lipsky, a student journalist and member of the Commission's New York student investigative group, said that the acceptance of a few black students on a paper's staff resulted in other staffers' giving "ourselves a pat on the back." He said, "If we go out and get black students, well, then we did a good deed, we were representing more of the school . . . it's not a matter of whether you can work with them or not, but just like . . . tokenism, saying, okay, we'll do it with black students, whether we can work with them or not, just that they're on the staff."

Even a sincere effort to give the paper a balanced staff may fall on deaf ears if there has been little or no minority coverage. Craig Dellemore, editor of the *Black Spectrum,* a newspaper within the Harlem community, funded by the *New York Times,* told the Commission about the paper in his white-dominanted high school:

> Our newspaper really had nothing to do with us, and just to open it and read it, there was no incentive to work for the paper.
>
> If only because you didn't really know what you can do, it took them close to a year to do a story on the black student union, and it had started under a storm of protest from a number of people, and you know, when they got around to it, they did . . . a small story, and so I didn't think there's that much encouragement on the part of the papers.

In cases where minority students break through the barriers and participate in high school journalism, they do not always find a favorable atmosphere in which to work because they often are still in a white-oriented, white-directed activity. Even in minority dominated schools, many administrators and advisers are white. Close administrative supervision of high school media leaves largely intact the perception that high school journalism is part of the power structure and reflects attitudes of school administrators unfavorable to minorities.

Fernando Gutiérrez, a professional journalist in San Antonio, told the Commission:

> First of all, high school journalism is not a distinct institution from the high school administration. . . . It is intimately connected with the school administration and institutional structure of education. And insofar as it is an institution controlled by Anglo-American

values, it has totally failed the Chicano in almost all respects. And in that sense I would like to say that I have a very pessimistic attitude about high school journalism. . . .

Racism in the high school newsroom also can be a problem. Danny Segal told of a black editor at his New York high school who "was fired because she was never there, and never did her work, and the reason for this is the atmosphere in the office would not make it so that a minority student could feel comfortable in there. I mean, it's . . . you might say racist, and it doesn't make for a pleasant environment."

Scheduling

Minorities as well as low-income whites who might otherwise be interested in high school journalism find that they cannot afford to participate because of the common practice of scheduling journalism as an extracurricular and "after-school" activity.

While such scheduling is traditional in many places and is not intended to discriminate, the results still effectively deny minorities access to journalism. Phyllis Lynch, a community organizer in Charlotte, North Carolina, testified that "in many instances" low-income students, especially among minorities, "had to work and could not afford to participate in a journalism class that was held at the end of the school day. So that intentionally or not intentionally, things were designed to exclude certain students."

Financial Problems and Tracking

Many schools with large numbers of minority students face financial problems so severe that they have little money available for media. Some predominantly black or chicano schools have no media programs at all.

Carlos Guerra, the chicano leader from San Antonio, pointed out this is a problem throughout the Southwest. He said, "School districts that have heavy chicano and black population also have low property values and often are taxed at a much higher rate, but yield much less money. The result is that Mexican-American and black students are often denied the same amount of money spent on the Anglo students in some of the richer districts."

Also, because of socio-economic factors, such as poverty and racial discrimination, many minority students are ill-equipped in communication skills. And because of systems of "tracking," they often are diverted into vocational or mechanical art studies and away from courses that would help them develop communication skills.

High School Press Workshops

Although there are workshops and summer programs that help train and encourage high school journalists, minority participation is minimal. Three factors are largely responsible for this: the relatively small number of minority students in high school journalism; the fact that many of those who do participate are not considered advanced enough to meet the workshop qualifications; and financial considerations that generally weigh more heavily on minorities.

The Northwestern Summer School of Journalism, which trains about ninety high school journalists a year, had worked at increasing the minority participation, but had been able to raise it to only 10 percent of total enrollment at the time of the Commission's 1973 hearing in South Bend. Professor Jack Williams, director of the school, emphasized the need for doing more, but explained:

> First, not too many minority students are involved in high school journalism at the level we would like to take them. I don't know how this problem can be solved. Second is a matter of money. We have raised our tuition now to the point that I don't think we can go any higher. It is a little less than $100 a week— $480 for a five-week term.

Recruiting

Although methods of staff selection, minority news coverage, scheduling, tracking, financing, and supplemental programs tend to work against minority access to high school journalism, the Commission found isolated but successful attempts to overcome this through intensive recruitment of minority journalists.

In some cases this was accomplished by the adviser or other staff members seeking consultations with minority student organizations, or simply by contacts with individual minority students.

One of the most successful examples of recruitment involved the *Daily Jacket* of Berkeley High School. Patti Fisher, who became adviser to the school's daily newspaper when the staff was predominantly white, told how she helped bring about greater black participation during a period of student unrest and strikes at the school.

During that time, she said, "students were on drugs. There were more out of classes than there were in classes. More teachers were absent during that year because they were depressed. I think for the first time they were going to have to deal with minority students' learning problems."

Fisher found that while her predecessor as adviser had helped turn out a "journalistically very well-written, beautifully laid-out" school paper, there had been little attempt to deal with minority problems either in the news columns or in recruitment for the staff. Having worked successfully with minority students in the past, she went to work in both areas and "accepted a lot of writing that I didn't think was that good." But the *Daily Jacket* became a success. She told the Commission:

In 1970 and 1971 my Journalism I classes became predominantly black, and by the next spring semester they were at least two-thirds, if not three-fourths, black students, and they were no longer just academically-oriented students. Out of the staff of eighteen kids on the *Daily Jacket*, I have two-thirds minority students.

Before, it used to be that you had to have an A or B in Journalism I before you could get on the *Jacket* staff. At this point, I do not make any grade requirement.

Another thing that I thought was very important in terms of encouraging black students to go into journalism is to make contacts with people who have succeeded—not only just black people who have succeeded specifically—but also other people who have succeeded, so that people get as close a contact as they possibly can to the field, and to people who have succeeded in spite of obstacles. And they have been very inspirational so far.

Most of the journalism advisers who appeared before the Commission expressed concern about both the lack of minority participation and the white-orientation of school publications. Fay Van Hecke, an adviser from Charlotte, North Carolina, said she was trying to solve the problems by having "a very capable one, or two, or three or four, however many I can get, black students whose by-lines are seen and who are read, and I feel that would open the doors. . . ."

Electronic Media

The Commission's study focused primarily on the printed media, principally because the high school newspaper which first appeared on the American scene in today's form about 1920, is by far the most common type of school journalism.

However, the Commission found that in recent years several school systems have developed innovative radio and television programs that some school officials believe offer minority students relatively greater access to high school journalism and to career opportunities as well.

One factor is that the broadcast media is a relatively recent addition to school curricula, it is not as traditionally white-oriented as newspapers.

The example of local television news programs in many cities with large minority populations also has stimulated the interest of minority students in broadcast journalism. While Chicanos still face problems breaking into television in the Southwest, there are many cities, such as New York, Washington, and

Atlanta, where television stations employ relatively large numbers of black reporters and newscasters.

David Brown, a teacher of broadcast journalism in New York, suggested that video uniquely addresses itself to the concern of minority access. He said, "On a professional level, television . . . is opening more and more job opportunities . . . to minorities, and we are certainly aware of that, and we are pushing that as far as instruction is concerned."

(Some of the electronic media programs in schools are discussed in Part III.)

Native Americans

If black Americans and Spanish-speaking Americans play a minor role in high school journalism, Native Americans play an even smaller part. And the absence of journalism is perhaps even more unfortunate for the Indian people whose conditions of life continue to be a national disgrace. The destruction of native American cultures in the schools they attend is part of that disgrace.

The Commission found, however, that in a few instances, especially where Indians control their schools and work to reinforce their cultural heritage, students have participated in media programs of value in building both their self images and communications skills.

One of the most dynamic media programs was initiated at Ramah, New Mexico, a small Navajo community west of Albuquerque, by the school principal, Abe Plummer, a Navajo, and the Navajo-controlled school board.

The school paper, *Singing Sands,* covers Indian community news, as well as school news, and is sold throughout the reservation. In addition, students also publish a magazine of Indian culture, *Tsá Ászi,* which includes student artwork, creative writing, and articles on Indian history and handicraft.

The adviser, Wendy Reyna, also a Navajo, said, "*Tsá Ászi* is relevant to the students because it is them: it's their culture, their past, their future, and the bridge in between."

At Ramah students also have been involved in broadcast journalism through a radio station with broadcast facilities in the school. The Office of Economic Opportunity established the station as a pilot program and students have used it to broadcast programs in Navajo and English. Because of federal government cutbacks in social programs, however, the future of the station, which was providing a vital service to the Navajo people, has become uncertain.

Commission staff members visited Pine Ridge, a reservation of the Sioux nation in southwestern South Dakota, in 1973 immediately after armed members of the militant Indian movement had ended their occupation of the nearby Wounded Knee community. The occupation had spurred some Indians at Pine Ridge and at other reservations to join in the militants' complaints about white destruction of Indian culture. Staff members observed that the atmosphere of the school was of a beseiged institution due to the Wounded Knee takeover. School had been closed sporadically and was a target for charges that white man's education is a tool for destruction of Indian culture. Only one Indian taught in the entire school. He taught the school's one course on Indian history.

Despite this atmosphere and the fact that the reservation's Oglala High School was being operated by the Bureau of Indian Affairs, students were involved in a literary magazine, *Hoyekiya,* and a newspaper, *Oglala Light.*

Hoyekiya was considered to be an important instrument for advancing self-awareness and cultural preservation, but the *Oglala Light* reflected an image much like that of most American high school newspapers with emphasis on sports, social activities, the faculty, and school administration policy.

Since the Commission began its study, *Hoyekiya* has gone out of existence, because of the departure of the adviser from the school. The *Oglala Light,* which operated with a different adviser, has continued to be published.

Another ill-fated project to bring Indian students into

the world of journalism was observed by the Commission at Little Big Horn High School in Chicago, a federally-funded institution controlled by the city school system.

The school's paper, *Talking Leaves,* contained school, community, and national Indian news and appeared to be read widely within the school. But in 1974 the paper was not being published—again because the adviser had departed and there was no one to replace her.

Specific Commission Findings: Minority Participation

1. Students who are members of racial, cultural, and ethnic minorities tend to face special problems in gaining access to high school journalism.
2. The barriers they face usually are subtle and invisible. They include methods of staff selection, student journalism's poor coverage of minority news and issues, scheduling of journalism activities as an extracurricular activity, systems of "tracking" that divert minority students from journalistic pursuits, and high school press workshops and summer training programs that attract only a few minority students.
3. Other factors adversely affecting minority access include financial problems of many schools comprised mostly of minority students, failure of schools to help minority youth develop reading and writing skills, and failure of high school journalism organizations and established media to promote minority participation.
4. Negative attitudes of racial minority students toward established and high school media also work against their participation in journalism. Such attitudes result at least partly from the established media's failure in many instances to

adequately and fairly cover minority news and opinion.

5. Largely because of these attitudes and subtle forms of discrimination, relatively few minority students have become involved in high school media.

6. The white orientation of school journalism and the lack of significant minority participation have resulted in minimal coverage of minority issues by the school media.

7. Where minorities constitute a small percentage of the student body, they face their greatest barriers to entering journalism.

8. Minority students enjoy their greatest degree of access in schools where their numbers are roughly equal to the numbers of nonminority students.

9. Where minority students constitute a large majority of the school, there tend to be fewer school papers or other journalistic media than in predominantly white schools.

10. In some school districts electronic media is being effectively utilized to bring minorities into journalism. Some teachers believe that because of widespread readership problems among minorities, radio and television may offer the best potential to bring minorities into journalism. Minority youth often demonstrate more familiarity with—and greater affinity for—electronic media as opposed to printed journalism.

11. The lack of multilingual and multicultural journalism in Spanish-speaking and Indian communities is a particularly severe and often-ignored problem. By ignoring the language and culture of large numbers of minority youth, the established media has alienated itself from them.

12. School newspapers generally are dominated by college-bound middle- or upper-class students, with those of low income or of a vocational bent participating in minimal numbers. This results in an elitism that excludes cultural and ethnic minorities as well as racial minorities.

PART III

Journalism and Journalism Education

Chapter 14

The Role of Journalism in the High School

The editorial page of the Keenan High School newspaper that was published just before the 1972 presidential election carried two provocative columns written by students.

One supported the Democratic nominee, Senator George S. McGovern of South Dakota, and raised questions about $10 million in anonymous contributions raised by the Committee for the Re-election of the President.

The other urged the re-election of President Richard M. Nixon and cited his support of the 26th Amendment, which gave eighteen-year-olds the right to vote, as well as his opposition to busing of schoolchildren to achieve racial balance.

The columns alone made the page a stark contrast to the usual chatty, gossipy items that characterize many high school newspapers. But even more significant, perhaps, was an editorial on racism on the same page. Keenan High School is in Columbia, South Carolina, an area where desegregation had been a hot issue for many years and where by the 1970s busing to achieve school desegregation had become an explosive political issue.[18]

In May, 1973, when the Commission of Inquiry heard testimony about Keenan during hearings at Char-

---

[18] See Appendix C for reprint of article.

81

lotte, North Carolina, the school was predominantly black—56 percent.

Blacks comprised only a third of the staff of the school paper, *The Sword and Shield,* although there was evidence of strong efforts to recruit Blacks. Moreover, all of the student journalists worked in one of the freest atmospheres observed by the Commission.

The school had the essential combination for good journalism education—a principal who strongly supported the program and an adviser-journalism teacher who gave highest priority to teaching students to report and express themselves on issues of substance.

The result was a newspaper that kept administrators, the faculty, and parents, as well as the student body, informed of student thinking on crucial issues.

The newspaper's young adviser, James W. Garrick, Jr., worked out a written policy statement in which the principal agreed there would be no censorship and *The Sword and Shield* staff agreed to exercise responsibility and to seriously consider suggestions and opinions of the adviser.

While good journalism education requires teaching students ethics and responsibilities, Garrick told the Commission, permitting them to make the ultimate decision on the contents of the newspaper also is essential.

Sometimes *The Sword and Shield* touched off controversies with reports about drug use among students or about disciplinary problems, which Garrick described as "one of those hot subjects in the Columbia public schools."

The reporting of controversial views by some teachers also created campus stirs. Garrick told about this incident involving a white teacher who was interviewed:

He made some comments . . . that these students who were not interested in learning should be turned out of the public schools and locked up in cages and something like that. A lot of the students felt that he was talking about black students and that this was blatant racism, and they were a little concerned about that.

Despite the controversies, the adviser has always had the backing of the principal. "He may not always be pleased with what we print," Garrick said, "but he does believe in the need for a paper that is an open channel of comunication, a paper that speaks what the students feel, what their ideas and opinions are."

But Garrick pointed up one of the perils a principal may face if he supports a free press and a problem a journalism teacher may face if his school's principal is transferred. Asked if a new principal would mean once again having to sell the idea of a policy of noncensorship for the school paper, he said:

> That's true ... the new principal would have to be worked with, and we have recently had a very conservative term in the school board in Richmond District One and I don't know that the principal's life in Columbia is going to be too long. He is much, much, much more liberal than the present school board, and I also don't know what they might dictate to him as to what he can allow in the school newspaper. . . .

The Keenan newspaper and many other high school papers are supported entirely by high school funds and are distributed without charge to students. But some better-financed and more sophisticated school papers pay all or part of their costs through subscriptions and advertising.

One of the most successful is the *Lion* (cited in Part I), a biweekly at Lyons Township High School in La Grange, Illinois, which in 1973 had a circulation of about 5,000, a subscription rate of $2.50, a $20,000 operating budget, and an advertising income of over $5,000—all extraordinary statistics even for a large school.

With strong official support, the *Lion* is a newspaper of substance that on many issues has had an impact on not just the school, but on the community, which is largely all-white, upper-income. One of relatively few school papers that do serious investigative reporting, the *Lion* gained considerable attention in the Chicago area in 1972 for its reporting of a murder case.

After a Lyons student was killed by an unknown assailant near campus in the fall of 1971, *Lion* reporters regularly reported on developments in the case. As the official investigation dragged on and finally appeared to have hopelessly bogged down, *Lion* reporters, in March, 1972, wrote a story that began, "Authorities say they know who murdered Alan Fredian '74 but are not ready to make arrests. Two Cook County state's attorneys investigators told *Lion* reporters . . . they are interested mainly in four south campus students."

The article touched off intense interest in the case by Chicago newspapers and radio and television stations and eventually was credited with causing new investigative leads and an accelerated investigation that led to an arrest in the case.

While murder is an unlikely subject for high school journalism, the *Lion*'s example of investigative reporting reflects the potential of student journalism when it operates in a free atmosphere with official support.

In a formal statement, the superintendent of schools in La Grange, Donald D. Reber, commended the *Lion* staff for its efforts to bring about justice in the case. "As is often the case in controversial issues of this type," he said, "certain risks and dangers exist. Students are free to choose the issue and to discuss it broadly and forthrightly with honesty and integrity. Where lines of communication with the administration are established, freedom can be fostered."

Lyons Township also operates a student-managed FM radio station, licensed under the auspices of the school district. In 1972, while the *Lion* staff was investigating the Fredian murder, Allan Loudell, student manager of Station WLTL-FM, was organizing high school stations throughout the suburbs to cover the election results. The resulting relay of students assigned to precincts throughout the suburbs allowed all of the student stations to scoop the commercial media and report on important congressional races.

Few school media programs are as well budgeted as

those of Lyons Township, of course. But even a skimpy
budget does not preclude a publication of substance if
the administration supports the principle of a free student press and there is an enlightened teacher.

In Ranson Junior High School in Charlotte, N.C.,
for example, an aggressive teacher who was concerned
more with substance than appearance involved a large
number of students in a journalism program that operated on a small budget, but produced large results.

In a school of 950 students, James Sills taught four
classes of journalism. He accepted all comers for his
media projects. He served as adviser to the newspaper,
the *Ram-Page,* as well as supervisor of a program of
tape-recorded interviews by students for a local radio
station contest. He arranged for his students to visit
newspapers, radio and television stations, including
media owned and operated by blacks.

The ratio of white to black in the student body was
70–30. So was the ratio on the newspaper staff.

Some of the students who enrolled in journalism were
advanced, but others were less motivated. Some, known
as "trouble-makers," fought, cut classes, smoked in the
woods, took things from the cafeteria, were "just little
hoodlums," Sills told the Commission.

But once they became interested in journalism and
using tape recorders for interviews and found they
could accomplish things in journalism, Sills said, disciplinary problems diminished.

Sills pointed out that while *Ram-Page* had won journalism awards, "the thing I was proudest of . . . was
not that we won, but that it wasn't the class of the
special ability kids that did it. It was the class of kids
that come from the tremendous cross-section of our
school population."

Discussing his philosophy as a teacher, Sills said:

> I just try to draw on their strengths instead of playing
> up the weaknesses that they have, and if they have any
> weaknesses they have probably heard about them in
> every other class all day long, and I just try to show
> them that they can do something; if they have any
> talent whatsoever it pretty soon comes out.

Two of Sills' students—Cynthia Cassidy and Melody Nienke—told the Commission they had had no interest in journalism until being motivated by Sills. Another student journalist, Chuck Jones, said:

> I guess I will have to go along with the pack because that's the same way I felt. I signed up for creative writing and didn't have any interest at all in journalism, and, well, when I got into this class, the way it was presented, the way that the teacher was with the class, it just floored me all of a sudden that journalism was something I would really enjoy!

Highly motivated teachers supported by school administrators also have helped turn out literary and cultural magazines of substance. An outstanding example is *Foxfire,* the brainchild of B. Eliot Wiggington, a high school teacher in the rural Appalachian community of Rabun Gap, Georgia.

Fresh out of college seven years earlier, Wiggington told the Commission he took a job as English teacher at the mountain school of 240 students and quickly found that the school's standard materials for his class left his students "bored, restless, unmotivated, disinterested."

Realizing he had "some serious disciplinary problems" on his hands, he "decided to shelve the whole business and start something new . . . the upshot of that was the founding of a magazine called *Foxfire.*"

Wiggington had to sell the school administration on the idea, then seek outside financing. He started the magazine with a small grant of $500, then secured another $750 from the same source on a matching-funds basis. Later he secured two grants totaling $19,400 from the National Fund for Humanities, an unusually large total grant for a school project. The grants provided for the purchase of a darkroom, darkroom equipment, videotape equipment, tape recorders, and other material and equipment.

His program was based on sending students out to research and report about their own culture in the belief they would learn skills and knowledge and, at the same time, benefit their school and community. Wiggington told the Commission about the kind of people the students interviewed:

> People who've had to build their own houses, make their own clothes, farm and raise their own food. The students went out in the community and located and still locate people who remember exactly how all these things were done. They find a man who was building a log cabin and they get him to show them specifically how to cut notches for the same out of a few logs. They find a woman who knows how to churn butter and learn how and get them to churn butter. They find people who know how to make wine wheels and they get them to make wine wheels again. And, as the people make these things, the students take a full set of photographs and take audiotape and videotape to document the entire process.

Foxfire quickly became a handsome and informative magazine with articles that are being reproduced in four volumes by Doubleday. The first book was published in 1972 and book royalties now pay for producing *Foxfire*.

In addition, *Foxfire* became a model for other cultural magazines founded on Indian reservations (including *Tsá Ászi* of Ramah, New Mexico, mentioned in Part III), and in black and white communities in Maryland and the Southeast. Wiggington and some of his staff members also consulted with interested groups in Jamaica, Alaska, and other places, and the idea that originated with *Foxfire* spread to other places with the help of Ideas Incorporated, of Washington, D.C., and a grant from the Ford Foundation.

Keenan, Lyons Township, Ranson, and Rabun Gap represent some of the most effective journalism experiences in the schools. The Commission found that in general, the entire area of journalism education suffers from the extremely low priority accorded it in the nation's schools.

Although most schools have some form of journalistic experience, relatively few programs enjoy the attention and support of their communities or of established media. In many cases, the financial support is minimal.

Journalism programs sometimes embrace literary and cultural magazines, as well as electronic media, but they most often focus on a newspaper.

So an important question is: What should be the role of a school newspaper in the secondary school? A former journalist, Howard Maniloff, assistant superintendent of schools in Charlotte, North Carolina, discussed that question in testifying about the problems of journalism education:

> I think we should ask what kind of learning experience a high school newspaper should provide, and for whom. . . . I don't think there is any doubt that the paper should be a learning experience. It is part of the school. Well, at this point I think the only learning that goes on is for those directly involved in the newspaper, and even there, that's a rather superficial learning. They might learn something about the clichés of journalism—the inverted pyramid; the Who, What, When, Why, How and Where. They might learn a little bit about things like basic layout. From reading high school newspapers—I'm not convinced that they are learning to stretch their minds, to try different kinds of writing techniques, or even to master basic ones. One kind of learning experience I think the newspaper is *not* is a learning experience for the larger community, the school community. The kind of information that is conveyed in high school newspapers, the manner of that conveyance could, I think, be just as well conveyed in a simple, short, clipped mimeographed bulletin.
>
> I think we have to ask whether high school newspapers can or should serve as a device for prodding students, teachers, and administrators into thought.
>
> I think we have to ask ourselves about a high school newspaper as a sounding board, a place for ideas to come into and go out of. . . .
>
> We have a lot of kids dropping out of high school. Now, I am not sure what the high school newspapers say to that. I am not sure about what the high school

newspaper does to let the people who are part of that high school community know about the problems of these kids, or the problems of kids who will get through high school, but without really having learned very much or developed very much.

Chapter 15

Journalism Teachers and Advisers

Given an atmosphere of relative freedom, quality journalism education depends more than anything else on teachers and advisers who are committed to the need for journalism in the high school. Even experience and training are not essential if a teacher is willing to learn and dedicated to a journalism program. James W. Garrick, Jr., the adviser of *The Sword and Shield* at Keenan High School, had a minimal background in journalism. So did B. Eliot Wiggington, the founder of *Foxfire*.

Unfortunately, surveys indicate that a majority of teachers and advisers not only have little or no journalism background, but have relatively little interest in taking their jobs in the first place.

Less than half the teachers surveyed by the Commission had either more than twelve hours of college preparation or experience in journalism. Only 32 percent of them had requested their assignments.

The fact that the nation's schools and departments of journalism at the university level have been primarily occupied with the training of professional journalists and not journalism educators has contributed to the dearth of qualified high school teachers. Most university departments do not have a sequence for undergraduates preparing for secondary school accreditation. Few have a close relationship with the campus school of education in the development of methodology courses or student-teacher programs.

If a high school graduate decides that he wants a career as a high school journalism teacher, he can find an acceptable program by searching schools in a broad geographic area, but during the boom years of teacher undersupply, students were counseled into teaching under two main headings—the sciences and the humanities—and not specifically into programs requiring special college choices.

Preparation of teachers in electronic media in the high schools is largely in the hands of the university's speech department or education (audiovisual) department where the emphasis is not likely to be journalistic. Throughout the hearings when student journalists were asked about the opportunity to apply their skills to videotape, the Commission drew a blank.

The lack of undergraduate programs has led to the pervasive band-aid programs in most states. English and business education teachers temporarily diverted into journalism are urged to enroll in summer journalism workshops, often cooperatively sponsored by the university journalism department and the state scholastic press association. Such teachers, understandably, are merely trying to keep their heads above water in dealing with basic layout and staff organization and are not expecting challenges in investigative writing or analysis of student rights issues.

Since the turnover of journalism teachers is as high as 60 percent annually in some states, follow-up programs are difficult to develop. But the problem is further compounded by the turnover of state scholastic press administrators who are commonly graduate assistants who move on when they complete their degrees. The mainstays, then, of most state and regional programs of teacher support are the veteran advisers who sustain long term roles in the state scholastic press associations and often set the priorities for seminars, conferences, and workshops for students.

With a lack of teachers trained in journalism, the job of journalism teacher often goes to an English teacher or any teacher who winds up as adviser to the newspaper. Fernando Piñon, a professional journalist from Laredo, Texas, said, "You will find there is very seldom a journalism teacher, somebody who had taken a degree in journalism, as the instructor. You will find that any English teacher or any other teacher who volunteers or who is drafted to sponsor the high school newspaper is the one who gets the job."

The Commission's survey of journalism teachers showed that schools with a predominantly minority student population have the largest ratio of inexperienced journalism teachers. One-third of them had no training or background before taking their positions, compared with 10 percent at schools with a predominantly nonminority population and 3 percent at racially balanced schools.

The lack of training is sometimes compounded by a uniformity of outlook and background. Carlos Guerra, the chicano community organizer from San Antonio who was quoted in Part II of this Report, said:

> Very often we find that journalism teachers are, first, people who have never worked on newspapers, people who have no real contact with what journalism is. They worked maybe with a college paper when they were in college. Secondly, they are almost entirely white Anglo-Saxon Protestants and very middle-of-the-road or conservative. They're a type of people who are keepers of the status quo and would certainly not rock the boat. They hide behind terms such as "professionalism" and "objectivity," neither one of which can be attributed to the press, in any respect.

The low priority usually accorded journalism by school administrators discourages teachers from participating and disheartens many of those who do participate. While athletic teams, bands, and pep squads rarely suffer from funding, high school media is in a constant financial squeeze.

Journalism teachers also frequently are required to bear unfair burdens of heavy scheduling, inadequate compensation, and—in cases where they buck the tide of censorship—job insecurity.

Patti Fisher, adviser at Berkeley High School, told about her schedule:

> At eight o'clock I teach Advanced Composition. At quarter to nine I teach Journalism I. The next two periods I have with the *Jacket* staff. I have a two-period lunch break, which is partly for preparation. Then I have the yearbook class, and then I have *Jacket* supervision and assist with the yearbook.
>
> I was at school until 10:15 last night, trying to get the yearbook out. I get no pay, no extra time, nothing. In fact, I have the roughest schedule of any teacher in the last ten years, which I intend to fight.

Unfavorable working conditions, including censorship problems, account in part for a high turnover of journalism teachers and advisers. A survey in California indicated that two out of three changed assignments yearly.

Advisers, even if trained and committed, usually face problems related to the low status of journalism education. In a paper prepared for the Commission, Jean Grambs, a Commission member and professor of secondary education at the University of Maryland, wrote:

> There is practically no budget and usually no special facility. If the paper is produced by the journalism class, then production time must be pirated from other parts of the day for both teacher and students to get it out. If it comes out of a journalism club, it may be wholly an after-hours operation. In either event, participating students need time after school, transportation, and the ability to pass other classes even when they are not in attendance. . . .
>
> The administration in most cases views the school paper as an unfortunate necessity; if funds disappear, then not even that. The general view of school students is that the paper probably is not terribly important; and the bigger the school, the more likely is this to be true. A look at a sampling of papers shows them to range from mediocre to awful. Where controversial matters are raised, the student views seem

to be conservative (as in the case of busing) or non-existent.

Another Commission member, Dorothy McPhillips, whose experiences as an adviser are cited in Part I, filed a report with the Commission saying the journalism program is "often considered the bastard child of the English Department and in many schools the adviser is placed in the same position." She wrote:

The English Department chairman may be the boss when it comes to the curriculum, the principal when it comes to school policy and public relations, and the vice-principal or activities director may control the finances. And at some point during the course of a year all three may disown the offspring.

Few school newspapers are without financial problems. The student body withholds financial support on grounds it is a classroom activity. On the other hand, curricular funding is either minimal or entirely absent because the traditional administrative viewpoint is that it is an extra-curricular activity. When advertising is the main financial support of a paper, it usually takes over as the primary learning activity for seldom does a high school paper draw enough advertising to support a balanced portion of news.

Overloading and underpaying a journalism teacher is unfair to the students as well as to the teacher for it means less time and incentive for good teaching and for producing quality media. Chet Hunt, an adviser in San Antonio whose school paper operates on an unusually large annual budget of $20,000, testified:

Another important thing about this program is that I am given a little bit of extra time and a little bit of extra compensation to do it. I think this is very important. You cannot overload the journalism teacher and give him five classes of English and two publications, a Journalism I course and everything except custodial duties and expect him to put out any kind of publication or teach any kind of journalism.

Another problem frequently faced by advisers and journalism teachers is the lack of a definitive purpose for their programs. If high school education is not aimless, it at least has few stated and recognized goals. Are those goals to train future journalists? To increase the general skills of students? To develop critical writing skills, based upon perception and investigation? Are they to sharpen the student's ability to write "good" term papers? To enhance the student's abilities to communicate ideas, opinions, and information? Or are goals so submerged by the low status of journalism that the subject winds up as an "add-on" course which students take to fill out schedules?

The Commission found that high school journalism may fit any one or a combination of those concepts, depending upon where one happens to drop anchor and observe. This seems to be both a reflection and a cause of the low priority given journalism education.

On one hand, disinterest in journalism education by school administrators, the established media, and the community at large means little pressure for establishing definitive purposes. On the other hand, the seeming confusion over the purpose of journalism education discourages interest in journalism programs.

Ideally, journalism education in high schools should be communication oriented, with emphasis on First Amendment freedoms as well as ethics and responsibilities of the media. The high school media can be—and in some cases is—a dramatic instrument to demonstrate to students the rights of a free press. Ironically, the media more often gives little voice to these rights and in some cases suppresses them. Moreover, even advisers who would like to change the situation often find themselves stifled by administrative controls.

Journalism Education Association

A nonprofit educational organization, the Journalism Education Association (JEA) was organized at Madison, Wisconsin, in 1924, as the American Association of Teachers of Journalistic Writing in Secondary Schools. Since then, the organization's name has been changed several times.

With high school censorship cases surfacing in increasing numbers in recent years, JEA has increased its services and its membership. During the 1973–74 year, JEA's membership increased by 30 percent. Another 30- to 50-percent increase was projected by JEA for 1974–75, which would bring total membership to about 2,000. Membership is not by school, but by individual teachers, although some organizations and libraries join in order to receive JEA publications. The chief publication is *Communication: Journalism Education Today (C:JET)*, a professional quarterly edited by Virginia Woodring, which emphasizes contemporary professional issues such as censorship and current research related to scholastic journalism.

Ten years ago JEA initiated a Curriculum Commission. The central thrust of the commission's research and creative interaction was summarized in *C:JET* by the commission's first chairman, Sister Ann Christine Heintz, who also served as a member of the Commission of Inquiry.

JEA services include:

• A "Hotline Service," which provides information and support to teachers involved in censorship controversies. Phone numbers of volunteers who have had experience in high school journalism problems are listed so that members may call representatives living nearest to them for advice. Postcards are sent to the "Hotline" coordinator, JEA's secretary.

• A "Press Freedom Fund," which JEA officers established in 1973 in response to the Don Patrick Nicholson censorship case. The fund's purpose is not to defend individual JEA members, but to educate the judiciary and the public on the need for scholastic press freedom, as well as professional standards.

• "Newswire," a professional newsletter that keeps members abreast of developments in the world of the scholastic press, including reports by JEA's Commission on the Freedom of the Scholastic Media and summaries of "Hotline" questions and answers. "Newswire" was published three times in 1973–74, but was scheduled to be published six times in 1974–75.

JEA local affiliates also have increasingly spoken out in opposition to censorship policies. In early 1974, for example, the Los Angeles Journalism Teachers Association was directing a campaign to end school policies which were so blatant that they endorsed censorship by that name. The Los Angeles Board of Education's handbook on student rights and responsibilities provided:

> Although a high degree of freedom is extended to the school newspaper staff, advisers and administrators retain the authority to censor when necessary. . . . In occasionally exercising censorship, the adviser is protecting the student's privilege to produce a newspaper.

The president of the Los Angeles Association, Mike Wiener, journalism teacher at Canoga Park High School, launched a campaign that drew the attention of the *Los Angeles Times* and other established media. Wiener's drive, aided by other JEA members, was aimed at forcing the rescinding of the censorship rule and at pressuring the city's schools to comply with the city board of education's own free-expression rule:

> A full opportunity must be provided for students to inquire, to question, and to exchange ideas. They should not simply be allowed but encouraged to participate in discussions in which many points of view, including those which are controversial, are freely expressed. Students should be provided with avenues for the research of ideas and causes which interest them and should be allowed to express their opinions.

At the time of this Report's issuance, the Los Angeles school board had not as yet acted on Wiener's request.

Chapter 16

Electronic Media

If the American high school paper is of relatively recent vintage, electronic media as high school journalism can be considered of almost modern origin.

And because, as journalism, electronic media still is rare in American schools, the Commission's study and its Report deal largely with print journalism, which is common to most schools. However, in both its hearings and its staff investigations the Commission heard evidence of outstanding electronic journalism programs and of the electronic media's potential for becoming a major force in journalism education.

Electronic systems are not new to most American schools. Over the years schools have used public-address systems and short documentary films, the former usually to make school announcements and the latter for instructional purposes.

What is relatively new is the creative use of electronic systems as communications media by students, ranging from rudimentary student-produced news programs on public-address systems to expensive and sophisticated closed-circuit in-school television broadcasts.

However, the fact remains that even in schools that have electronic systems there usually is limited student access to the systems for journalistic purposes. School administrators see such systems more as devices to instruct and to maintain control. Closed-circuit television, for example, is used predominantly for instructional and security purposes.

The Commission found outstanding challenges to that restricted concept of school electronic systems at St. Mary's Center for Learning in Chicago, an institute with a widely acclaimed video educational program.

At a special consultation session there, the Commission heard discussions by students, teachers, and administrators emphasizing the potential of video and audio journalism, including use of closed-circuit systems, such as public-address systems and low-wattage FM radio stations.

However, Sister Ann Christine Heintz, teacher and administrator at the center and a member of the Commission of Inquiry, pointed out that when electronic systems are used for school journalism, school control over free expression may be even more complete than it is over print journalism. In a paper prepared for the Commission she wrote:

> The theory of a free press in this country is essentially that of an independent press—a hybrid between libertarianism and social responsibility. Even the minimal public controls over broadcasting in the past five years have raised questions of the government destroying that independence, and a broadcaster's restraints arise because of his use of the *public* airwaves. How then can we expect a sixteen-year-old to function as an independent producer of media in a school when he produces on *public* property, normally uses *public* funds administered by a *publicly* appointed official and produces for an audience whose age is a cause for *public* shielding and protection rather than indiscriminant exposure?

Sister Ann noted a limited, but "hardly liberating," movement toward broadcasting in the nation's high schools. She wrote:

> About 100 FM stations in the country are owned by school districts, mostly suburban districts. Those that are operated by large metropolitan districts are managed by employees of the school board with some student talent. The suburban stations are largely mother-monitored, transmitting a combination of syndicated education tapes, student disc jockey entertainment, and some live newscasting and sportscasting. . . .
> Television broadcasting opportunities are still very restricted in the nation's high schools. Very few schools

have a total closed-circuit system for all-school broadcasting, but where a system exists there is evidence
that the system becomes a video P.A. system. Classes
or home-room groups are constrained in classrooms
to watch the monitors and assimilate the information.
To the extent that the P.A. systems have ever served
the role of watchdog, critic, and student opinion force
in the nation's schools, to that extent expect closed-
circuit video to do the same.

The answer to free expression for students through
electronic journalism may not be in the schools, Sister
Ann believes. "Should youth be able to express themselves freely?" she wrote. "If your sociological, psychological, pedagogical, constitutional, aesthetic, or journalist response is 'yes,' then it seems that you should
be concerned in your community about the development of expressive media opportunities for youth outside the school."

Where electronic journalism programs have succeeded in schools, however, there is optimism about its
impact on the future of journalism education. One of
the most persuasive witnesses to appear before the
Commission was David Brown, a teacher at Haaran
High School in New York, who testified that an extremely low level of reading ability and comprehension
in the New York public high school system enhances
the electronic media's potential. He said:

> What I'm suggesting, very frankly, is that perhaps one
> of the reasons for the apathy on the part of students,
> in terms of reading newspapers and whatever, is that
> they do not have the basic tools for reading.
>
> Electronic media, especially video, can be used to
> combat this.
>
> I think that we need to make a mammoth effort
> to upgrade reading instruction and writing ability on
> the part of youngsters, but I also think that at the
> same time, to be perfectly candid, and to be realistic
> about the situation . . . we need to take advantage of
> the fact that we do live in a highly visual society;
> I think students are very much turned on by tele-
> vision . . . and that while we are developing their

ability to read better and to be able to write better,
and report, and so on, we also need to investigate to
the fullest the potential of video as a way of developing these abilities.

... There is a tremendous transference of language
arts ability, as a result of involvement with video, and
specifically I'm thinking of youngsters who come to
us who are totally non-English speaking, and who at
the end of the semester are speaking well—not per-
fectly—but speaking well, because of the need to
transfer information verbally.

The teachers in English tell me that as a result of
video involvement they find that students are much
more curious, that they want to learn more, that they
want to talk more....

Students learning electronic communications, Brown
said, seem to catch on rapidly and become much more
curious and interested in issues of substance. He suggested that video journalism might develop programs of
more substance than high school print journalism.

In the area of video, he said, "We are deliberately
trying to ... get students to address themselves to questions that are of vital concern to them personally."
Many of the tapes they produce are broadcast into the
community by cable television and viewed by the students' parents and the community at large.

Brown said, "I see video instruction within the public
system as an alternative and perhaps a more viable type
of journalistic endeavor."

Another witness, Gilbert Ballance, a high school
broadcasting teacher since 1953, told about a unique
radio program he conducts with students at Garinger
High School in Charlotte. More than a serious journalism program, the broadcasting course began as a
gimmick to improve speech, he said. Then in 1968 it
went from a one-hour-a-day course to a full-time Vocational Broadcast Training Program. Ballance has been
teaching broadcasting full time ever since. He testified:

Our goal is to reach two kinds of students: one, the
kind who wants to be a disc jockey, program director,
station manager, or station owner, so our emphasis is

on commercial broadcasting. The other objective is to interest those students who are not interested in being broadcasters, but who are interested in social problems and would like to participate in programs such as discussion of racial problems among teen-agers, venereal disease, legalization of marijuana, the rights of the injured minority, things of that sort.

These are the students who may be lawyers, future doctors, journalists, people who have no interest in broadcasting, per se, so our program, I hope, appeals to widely different categories of students.

Some video programs for youths have little direct concern with journalism, but offer training and experience that could be useful in journalistic endeavors. An example is Videopolis, a program in Chicago supported by grants from the Wieboldt Foundation, the Illinois Arts Council, and the University of Illinois.

The program operates several projects for high-school-age youth. One is sponsored by the board of education and involves twelve "gifted" students, mostly black, in a ten-week project that includes studio work experience as well as filming and production.

Videopolis is also an example of limited, but creative use of video in alternative schools. It sponsors two programs of videotaping school operations. One program, conducted at Prologue High School, involves white students from Appalachia who are drop-outs from Chicago schools. The goal of the project is to document the life styles of Appalachians and American Indians in Chicago.

Equipment cost is a major problem facing expansion of electronic media programs in high schools. Costs range from $1700 for a videotape camera to $20,000 for a studio. Unfortunately, even schools that can afford such equipment sometimes fail to put it to maximum use.

Ms. Lilly Ollinger, a director of Videopolis, said, in an interview with a Commission staff member, that many Chicago public schools spent considerable money for video equipment and then were not sure what to do with it. The result, Ms. Ollinger felt, were programs that offered mostly technical instruction, with little guidance about varied uses of the medium. Students were not afforded an opportunity for self-expression, she said, but were mostly involved in videotaping a school play or a football game.

Despite the high cost of equipment, innovative programs with extensive educational benefits can be operated with a minimum of equipment. For example, at the East Chicago Media Center in East Chicago, Indiana, a parole officer, John Wasko, purchased a single videotape recorder with his own funds and worked with local youths in a journalism program highly regarded in the community.

Most of Wasko's parolees are drop-outs. They talked with him about their problems along the wharf area and in their neighborhoods where they got into trouble the first time and invariably got into repeated trouble after being paroled. Wasko suggested that they take the video equipment and capture that information on videotape. Later they edited the tape with equipment support from Governor's State University, adding their own narration:

The tape has been shown to local community agencies, the police, and the state parole board. The video "veterans" asked for the camera again to investigate local colleges and their attitudes toward high school drop-outs who want a second chance. Each investigation stems from the individuals' sense of need, but as is the case with good professional journalism, the individual's need proves to be the community's need.

Another community youth program which is not journalistically oriented, but which teaches skills necessary for a television journalist is conducted by the University of Notre Dame Station (WNDU) at South Bend, Indiana.

The WNDU program has been in operation since 1960 and since 1966 has produced a weekly television series, *Beyond Our Control.* Patterned somewhat after the network program, *That Was the Week That Was,* it is a satirical television show about television and American comedy and culture. It involves thirty-one high school students who produce the entire show:

writing, editing, filming, film editing, sound, lighting, and so forth.

Cable television, a method of distributing television signals through a coaxial cable rather than through the air, may offer the greatest potential for youth participation in electronic media.

The Federal Communications Commission requires that every cable TV company provide for a public access channel. The Commission of Inquiry, which has consulted with experts on the matter, believes that if the FCC standard on public access is enforced, youths will have no problem securing broadcast time.

Experts say that the cable TV system, which can carry up to 20 interference-free channels on one cable, will revolutionize the electronic media and make it accessible to almost every American citizen. Some communities already have taken advantage of it, establishing innovative programs of education and information.

In Reading, Pennsylvania, for example, the public library has become a workshop center where citizens learn video skills and check out equipment to use in creating their own broadcast messages for cable TV.

Reading schools include in their curriculum a course in understanding of citizen access to media. And other community agencies work jointly with a cable TV company and the video access center at the library to provide optimal use of video reporting.

Chapter 17

Alternative Journalism Education

As cases previously cited in this Report show, alternative journalism education projects often are more meaningful and educational than many of the standard programs sponsored by high schools.

Such projects include not only alternative newspapers supported entirely by students, but also intern programs sponsored by the established media, and in a few instances, media-sponsored newspapers.

Intern programs and media-sponsored newspapers are especially valuable because they bring students into contact with professional journalists and offer a more realistic sense of the problems and potentials of journalism. Such projects offer effective career preparation, but there are relatively few of them.

Students testified that the freedom of working on media-sponsored newspapers and the association with professionals made them attractive projects. Craig Dellemore, who edited a New York community newspaper sponsored by the *New York Times,* said, "You're not forced in a high school newspaper to do the kind of writing that you would have to answer to a community for . . . we have to gear our stories to our audience."

The paper's staff members who have attempted to go into journalism, Dellemore said, "have found it a lot easier than it could have been. . . . The basic thing that makes it a professional training ground is the professionalism of the people who train us."

In New York, Dr. Sharlene Hirsh, director of the Office of Educational Development, Department of Human Resources, has directed an extensive internship program with the public schools. Her office has placed interns in various media, including magazines, community newspapers, television stations, radio stations, and public information offices.

The quality of journalism education provided may vary with the internship and opportunities presented, she told the Commission. "In other words," she said, "we are not a classroom, providing classroom journalism education, but we are offering opportunities that open doors, on-the-job kind of experience."

An Urban Journalism Workshop conducted by the Washington, D.C., public school system also is career-oriented. Students who are released from school in the mornings attend the workshop and receive special training, as well as work on their own news magazine.

The Washington program emphasizes techniques in research, interviewing, and writing, Carolyn Jones, director of the Workshop said. "We bring in people already in the profession for the students to have mock interviews with. . . . It's a press conference-type situation . . . and they interview them and write up the stories."

Chapter 18

Journalism as Career Education

The potential for high school journalism to prepare students for careers is widely recognized. What is not as well known is the fact that with rare exceptions— some of which have been cited in this Report—it fails to live up to the potential.

The Commission's survey of professional editors showed that 93 percent of them felt that student journalism served as a useful tool in introducing students to the idea of journalism as a career and 49 percent believed it was useful training for future careers. Only 37 percent, however, felt current high school journalism programs were of little value.

On the other hand, the Commission developed substantial evidence that high school journalism seldom is career oriented and frequently distorts the scope and purpose of professional journalism, especially in the publishing of school newspapers.

Edward Cruttenden, former assistant to the State Superintendent of Education in Ohio, testified:

I think the time has come for us to face up to the fact that we might be a little bit hypocritical about our school publications. I think it is time for us to level with kids, and it is time for us to look kids right in the face and say, "The printing of a school newspaper has nothing to do with providing you with valid journalistic experiences. It has everything to do with P.R., for me and the image of the school administration, of the Board, or superintendent."

Some professional journalists also testified about the problem. One, Fernando Piñon of Laredo, Texas, a former high school journalism teacher and newspaper adviser, said school papers reflect the attitudes of administrators who fail to see the resources that a newspaper can provide. The attitude of using the papers as strictly a public relations venture, he said, was still prevalent throughout Texas.

Working on high school newspapers frequently gives students a warped sense of a professional journalist's role, according to Piñon. He said:

Another problem is that in many high schools the newspaper becomes a social activity. You will find that the Student Council president or the most popular girl becomes the editor of the newspaper. And you will find the students who are more popular are the ones that actually perform or take part in putting out a newspaper. . . .

People who take part in high school journalism under these conditions have the misconception that to be a journalist is to be very popular, very outgoing, being the nice guy, having people coming to you and telling you how great you are. Yet when you go into college you find out that popularity had no place in journalism. That it is definitely hard work. You don't get as much popularity or social acceptability just because you are with the newspaper. So you find many students who were very active in high school newspapers completely bombed out of journalism school because training and the proper attitude were not there.

Professional journalists who have taken high school journalism courses are acutely aware of its lack of career orientation. One of them, Sam Mercantini, former state assistant superintendent of public education in Indiana, said, "Journalism courses are ridiculous. I think I learned more writing obituaries for the newspaper than in any journalism course in high school."

Summer Workshops

A relatively large number of summer journalism workshops aimed at improving journalism skills of high school students are held throughout the country, but most of them last only a weekend or a few days. And they seldom deal with problems of censorship or minority access. Also, because of tuition requirements, they attract few minorities.

Two impressive exceptions are the Blair Summer School for Journalism, which operates a five-week program at the Blair Academy in Blairstown, New Jersey, and the five-week National High School Institute sponsored by Northwestern University. Both deal with press law and investigative reporting, in addition to more traditional courses in grammar, topic development, interviewing, and editorial writing. Both sessions are characterized by in-depth instruction and extensive writing assignments more comprehensive than would be possible in the usual weekend or week-long workshop.

Other impressive programs are conducted by the University of Wisconsin Extension at Madison and the University of Missouri at Columbus. Attended primarily by Wisconsin and Missouri high school students, these programs attract an extremely qualified teacher faculty and offer quality instruction to students.

Chapter 19

Scholastic Journalism Organizations

Although scholastic journalism organizations serve useful purposes, they are part of the status quo of a sick institution. They have failed to use their prestige and potential to be a force for reform.

They could serve as protective forces for students and teachers caught up in censorship controversies and they could help minorities gain equal access. However, they demonstrate a low level of consciousness of the problem of minority access and little awareness of the extent, forms, and pernicious effects of censorship.

The Commission realizes that at times the cry of censorship may be unjustified. Unquestionably there are occasions when an adviser who is trying to help a student with editing is wrongly accused of trying to censor the product. Still, the greater problem by far is censoring in the name of advising. Despite this fact, the scholastic press associations appear to put little emphasis on censorship. Charles O'Malley, director of the Columbia Scholastic Press Association (CSPA) in New York, testified at the Commission's New York hearing:

> Many of the students learned that there's a freedom of the press, and so many of the students have learned about students' rights and the First Amendment, and so on. They want to print or put in their paper the things that aren't good journalism, and it isn't in good taste, so when an adviser—an adviser is just what it indicates, it is someone who is there to help—tries to help them edit, immediately they scream censorship. . . .
>
> Actually, it would be difficult for [CSPA] to do anything about minority access other than . . . putting out as much propaganda as we can. There's not much else

we can do. We try to show the student who writes
what is going on around the country, so that if problems come up in this area maybe they can follow what
happened in another area, but there's not much we
can do. We would like to have everybody be on the
school publication, but there's not much we can do
about it. We can't set a policy for the schools. It
would not be in our realm.

Of particular concern to the Commission were the
contests and evaluation services sponsored by some of
these organizations. They do serve the purpose of providing journalism teachers and student journalists with
a visible means of success and they help justify financial
support from the school for the publication. At the
same time, they reinforce the administration's appreciation of journalism as a means of enhancing the image
of the school.

The criteria used for these awards and evaluative
services are weighted heavily in favor of style, composition, and technical skills, with much less significance attached to editorial or news substance.

Teachers must meet contest standards for their publications to receive an award, thus reinforcing current
norms of high school journalism, including rigid supervision by teachers and administrators.

The Columbia Scholastic Press Association's and the
National Scholastic Press Association's evaluation of
high school newspapers is based principally on form,
layout, and content coverage. The latter, however, deals
with the breadth of items covered, not the depth of
coverage. There seems to be little effort to encourage
in-depth reporting on issues or problems of major
importance to schools and communities.

The only part of CSPA's annual journalism contest
devoted to in-depth writing is a contest that is sponsored
not by CSPA, but by the American Newspaper Publishers Association.

Another scholastic group, Quill and Scroll, an international honorary society of high school journalists,
was organized on April 10, 1926, by a group of high

school advisers to encourage and reward individual achievement in journalism and allied fields.

To qualify for membership, students must not only excel in some area of journalism, but must be juniors or seniors in the upper third of their classes in general scholastic standing—a requirement that encourages staff "elitism" on school papers.

Over the years, Quill and Scroll, which is operated by Quill and Scroll Foundation at the University of Iowa's School of Journalism, has granted charters to more than 10,000 high schools.

The Chapter Manual of Quill and Scroll recommends a list of twenty-six suggested projects and activities, ranging from publishing a homecoming football program to handling school publicity and writing a visitor's guide to the community for the local chamber of commerce. The list includes no mention of First Amendment rights or suggestions that members engage in investigative reporting or other journalism of social significance.

Quill and Scroll's national services, projects, and contests include:

- An annual contest to reward schools that carry out exceptional programs in observance of National Newspaper Week.
- An annual contest of school journalism, with awards in the categories of editorial, feature stories, news stories, advertisements, photographs, and sports writing.
- A current events quiz prepared by the American Institute of Public Opinion, which produces the Gallup Poll. Every high school in the nation is eligible to participate.
- A newspaper evaluation service "which measures the success of the paper in terms of the services it rends a particular school."
- *Quill and Scroll* magazine, which includes articles by advisers and editors of school publications. In addition, Quill and Scroll publishes pamphlets and handbooks for advisers and staff members of school publications.

Winners of the Quill and Scroll writing contest and of the current events quiz are eligible to apply for $500 scholarships toward college journalism studies. Each year up to ten scholarships are granted. In addition to these general services, Quill and Scroll has been a source for special resource grants and emergency funds for teachers.

Specific Commission Findings: Journalism and Journalism Education

1. The great majority of high school journalism programs investigated by the Commission did not encourage free expression, independent inquiry, or investigation of important issues in either the school or the community. Most high school publications analyzed were found to be bland and often served as public relations tools for the schools.

2. The Commission found relatively few instances of community-based journalism developed by or substantially involving youth. Most community-based media programs developed by young people were short-lived and suffered from lack of financial support and serious journalism skills problems. In few instances did the Commission find that such media experiments were assisted by adults.

3. Generally, the Commission found that the nation's high schools accord journalism and journalism education low priority. This is reflected in the elective nature of the courses and assignment of teachers and advisers without special skills in the subject area. Often they are assigned against their preference, with relatively little or no compensation for long hours of extra work. The problem is

underlined by the fact that most media production, for budgetary and scheduling purposes, is
considered an extracurricular activity. In addition,
the Commission found that most teachers and
advisers had little experience in dealing with First
Amendment issues or minority access problems
associated with high school journalism.

4. The Commission found that in low-income areas,
problems of journalism were further exacerbated
by serious economic problems facing schools and
students. This was reflected in extremely small
publications budgets, a high rate of inexperienced
and "assigned" teachers and advisers in journalism programs, and in many cases, an alarming
absence of any media programs.

5. In general, the Commission found that professional organizations of journalism educators have
been slow to initiate change or support reform
in the field of scholastic journalism. However,
within the past year, the Journalism Education
Association has begun to support teachers and
students involved in controversies over the right
of free expression.

6. Awards programs, whether at a state or national
level, do little to encourage substantive reporting.
While form, layout, and variety of coverage
receive priority attention in judging high school
papers, there is practically no emphasis given to
in-depth and investigative reporting.

7. While the Commission noted some unusually good
summer workshops for high school journalists
(for example, Blair, Northwestern, University of
Wisconsin, and several of the Newspaper Fund's
Urban Journalism Workshops), it found that most
programs were of extremely short duration, did
not deal with what the Commission believes are
the basic issues in high school journalism, and had
very little minority participation.

8. The Commission found relatively little exposure
of high-school-age youth to electronic media instruction or production. Where access to equipment exists in the schools, relatively little creative

use has been made of it. Because of a variety of problems, including costs, low-income areas have had the least opportunity to experiment with media forms, including electronic media. Yet it was in those areas that the Commission felt some of the greatest potential existed for experimental use of electronic media. In a few instances, the Commission discovered young people creatively using electronic media in community-based programs, including experiments in cable TV. For the most part, however, youth involvement in community-based electronic media programs was limited.

PART IV

Established Media

Chapter 20

The Isolation of the High School Media

> I think you're carried away with the program. High
> school newspapers are a privilege granted by school
> authorities and supported by the taxpayers. As such,
> they should have no recourse to First Amendment
> protection. —*A Missouri editor.*

> High school newspapers can only be regarded as
> house organs subject to control of the organization
> paying the bills, the school district. —*A California
> editor.*

> All animals walk with assistance before they run.
> Only poisonous snakes are trusted with a venomous
> bite from birth. —*An Indiana editor.*

The above comments from managing editors answering a questionnaire from the Commission of Inquiry
underscore the alienation of high school journalists
from the established media.

The Commission's survey and staff studies found
little evidence that professional journalists are aware
of high school journalists' legal rights or are concerned
about their problems. In fact, the high school media is
so isolated that in most cases professional journalists
are not even aware that problems exist.

Fifty-seven percent of the editors surveyed were unaware of federal court decisions applying the First
Amendment to high school students in censorship cases.

Forty-six percent said they were uncertain whether
school publications in their areas were permitted to exercise First Amendment rights. Twenty-eight percent

117

said they were not permitted to exercise the rights and 26 percent said they were.

Perhaps the most important finding of the survey was the lack of strong support for a free high school press. Only 35 percent of the editors said unequivocally that First Amendment rights should apply to high school journalists. Another 52 percent favored First Amendment rights "only under certain conditions" and 10 percent were opposed to applying them at all, with 3 percent voicing no opinion.

By their comments many editors indicated they favored restraints because of the immaturity of high school students and because of the fact school media programs generally are financed by the schools. The comments were solicited with the understanding that they would not be attributed by name.

An Indiana editor commented:

> You can let any weed grow wild, but if you want a good, sound crop, you exercise the responsibility of discipline and control until the plant can stand on its own. With the right start, it can make a productive plant. Same goes for people. There is far too much yapping about freedom of the press among news circles, but those same circles produce a product which shows lack of responsibility and maturity in far too many instances.

Some editors indicated they had given the matter of high school journalism little thought before the Commission's survey, but were interested in learning more about the application of First Amendment rights. An Oregon editor wrote:

> As to First Amendment rights, I'm sure most school officials here don't know them and don't care whether students have them or not. There is censorship of copy of some of the papers for sure. I myself am unsure whether students should be able to print anything and everything they want in a school newspaper.
>
> The reason for my uncertainty is that I recognize the special setting of a school and the need for a certain amount of order to be necessary for the learning

process. The principal of . . . high school has asked me in the past to discuss with him this issue, and frankly I've not done it. It hasn't been a case of not caring to but I'm not sure what to propose to him. I'd like some help and a copy of those court decisions.

A Pennsylvania editor wrote that he felt strongly about the potential value of high school papers and suggested that local newspapers initiate projects "whereby professional newsmen who live in an area could 'adopt' a high school paper as a consultant-at-large or something to bring a measure of experience to the aid of the advisers/editors."

Another editor who expressed interest in reforming high school journalism wrote:

I am glad to know of your committee. In an effort to improve high school journalism in our area, my department heads and I talked months ago to a vocational education specialist with the county school office about trying to upgrade the quality of journalism instruction in our county and making the instruction more realistic and pertinent to the field of journalism. He agreed wholeheartedly, but when he brought the idea up to the school superintendents in the county he got a mixed response. A couple of superintendents were favorable and the others didn't seem to care.

What the vocational specialist and I proposed was that someone qualified and experienced in journalism be hired to teach high school journalism throughout the county through the county school office. That is, the person would teach a class at one high school for one or two hours, move to the next high school for the same duty and so on.

Another idea was that we set up a high school journalism workshop in the county on a once-weekly basis wherein those students who had genuine interest would come to work under experienced journalists—either members of my staff or those who have retired—and get some practical experience. This is something I am going to pursue, even though the school officials showed little interest initially. My feeling is that high school journalism is by and large a waste of time all around, as it's now set up.

Other editors also expressed a keen interest in the future of high school journalism. However, the general limited awareness of and support for the constitutional rights of student journalists indicated a failure to regard as serious either their abilities and aspirations or the problems of free expression in the schools.

Another factor in the gulf between student journalism and professional has been the established media's failure to adequately report on problems and issues in schools. Sports is by far the single greatest subject of media coverage of the high school world, with considerable time and resources spent by many newspapers and radio and television stations to cover and analyze sporting events. In some cases students are employed as "stringers" or junior reporters to assist in the coverage of high school sports.

Even the sports coverage, for all the money and energy spent on it, is relatively superficial, seldom going beyond the reporting of athletic events and interviews with coaches. The questioning of budgets or priorities for sports is practically unheard of.

The media also usually covers school board meetings, school bond issues, and if they are dramatic enough, instances of student unrest or protests. But for the most part, professional journalists rely heavily on the official version as pronounced by a school board or handed out by spokesmen for the board or the school administration. Rarely are the views of students sought out.

Nor does the media do much about investigating or criticizing regressive educational policies. The views held by many educators that technical competence and socialization of students are principal purposes of schools usually go unchallenged.

Seldom is there significant news coverage of such issues as free expression or the handling of school disciplinary problems. Censorship problems may get some attention in those rare instances where students or advisers resort to litigation. But those problems—and more particularly problems of minority access and the quality of high school journalism—are generally ignored. In fact, they are seldom perceived as problems, certainly not as problems worthy of the media's attention.

In the final analysis, the media mirrors a basic attitude of American society: that the schools are best left to professional educators, that high-school-age youth are still "kids," and that the educators must know best because of their training and experience.

Testifying before the Commission, Lynn Ludlow, a professional journalist in San Francisco, spoke to that point. "I think, generally speaking, newspapers don't see themselves as being in the social service business," he said. "They sort of leave that to the schools or they think they have left it to the schools."

Although a substantial number of newspapers have some form of contact, however limited, with high school journalism programs, the Commission found that the contacts tend to be self-serving and designed to enhance the public image and business purposes of the sponsoring papers rather than to help high school journalists and publications with their problems. Not surprisingly, such programs usually are directed by the newspaper's public relations or promotion departments, with little or no direct involvement of the news and editorial departments.

Field studies by the Commission showed the most common programs involve tours of newspaper offices, award banquets, speaking engagements by reporters in journalism classes, and publication of student articles in the daily paper.

The Commission's survey of editors showed 86 percent had had some contact with high school journalism, although it was minimal in most cases. The most common form of contact, according to the survey, involved student journalists who wrote articles for the local paper (70 percent), followed by consultations with teachers and students (62 percent), which often means sporadic speaking engagements at the local high school.

Editors reported fewer programs involving more sustained contact. For example, 46 percent reported their papers sponsored workshops and 47 percent reported internship programs.

Only 24 percent of the editors said their newspapers supplied funds or equipment to aid student journalists.

The Commission found that articles written by students for local newspapers generally are as noncontroversial and as social or sports oriented as those written for school papers. Since the articles seldom deal with substantial problems facing the school or surrounding community, the contact in these instances do little to encourage meaningful journalism or to acquaint the students with the world of professional journalism.

Although the Commission did not take a formal poll among the electronic media, field studies indicated that here, too, there has been relatively little sustained contact with high school journalism and apparently little interest in establishing such contacts.

Professor Jack Williams, director of the summer high school journalism program at Northwestern University, told the Commission of writing 2,000 letters to members of the Radio Television News Directors Association requesting scholarship aid for minorities attending the Northwestern program and to urge more participation by broadcasting media in conjunction with local high schools. He said he received only one positive response—from WTCI in Hartford, Connecticut.

Again, however, there are outstanding exceptions to the rule. Among them are the program of Gilbert Ballance, the broadcasting teacher at Garinger High School in Charlotte, North Carolina, and the internship program in New York directed by the Office of Educational Development, Department of Human Resources. Both programs were discussed in Part III of this Report.

Ballance, in a report to the Commission on March 1, 1974 wrote:

> One of the most important factors in broadcast training at Garinger High School is the cooperation of professional broadcasters from Charlotte as well as from nearby towns.
> Since 1953, when broadcasting became a part of the curriculum ... commercial broadcasters have helped in many ways. In 1969, educational broadcasters began to help.

Cooperation includes talks by staff members of various radio and television stations, help on advisory groups, and arranging a tour of network facilities in New York.

During the 1972–73 school year, more than 30 announcers, writers, producers, and executives met with the classes.

Later the production head of one of the radio stations held a weekly workshop in which students learned production techniques. Another station's general manager and operations manager worked with the school to produce a weekly series of discussion programs, each involving an adult guest, two student panel members, a student announcer, and a student producer.

Still another group of broadcasters, involving executives from a number of stations, are now working to establish a broadcast center, which would include facilities not only for radio but for television and motion picture training.

Another ambitious project is live summer broadcasting from the school's studios through the facilities of WCGC, eleven miles from Charlotte. Students broadcast a Top 40 program featuring music, news, and public service announcements. A station in Charlotte furnishes free news copy from its teletype service.

Chapter 21

Substantive Contacts Do Help

A number of cases observed by the Commission demonstrated that substantive contacts between high school journalism and the established media can help alleviate problems of censorship and minority access.

Consider, for example, the *South Bend Tribune* (discussed in Part I), which publicly encouraged high school students to submit uncensored copy for publication in its "High School Page" section. The *Tribune* is

published in a community notable for some of the most
severe repression of student expression observed by the
Commission, yet it withstood school administration
pressures to censor the students' articles.

The Black Spectrum, an alternative newspaper that
was sponsored by the *New York Times* and produced
by minority youth in the Harlem community, was a
project that dealt with the problem of career training
as well as minority access. Journalism professionals on
the *Times'* staff helped train the students. Unfortunately, the *Times* decided in the fall of 1973 to dis-
continue the program, a move a *Times'* public relations
man said was caused by "lack of funds."

Teachers who have managed to establish good rap-
port with the local media consider this relationship a
vital part of their program. Mrs. Fay Van Hecke, adviser at Olympic High School in Charlotte, North Carolina, told of bringing *Charlotte Observer* reporters to
her school to discuss the coverage of stories of substance, from the problems of massage parlors to the
plight of the poor and the hungry. She told the Commission she also had brought in women who had become editors "so that my girls can see that girls are
being promoted now to editorships and this kind of
thing. . . ."

(Although there has been no evidence that women
lack access to the high school media, with some notable
exceptions, the established media is still largely a man's
world.)

In several instances, the Commission noted important
contacts between student journalists and professional
journalists working for publications founded as alternatives to a community's established media. This was
most often the case where minorities started alternative
publications because of inadequate local news coverage
of minority problems.

In areas of heavy Chicano population, language
problems have spurred the founding of such community
publications. Fernando Gutiérrez, editor of *Magazin* in
San Antonio, Texas, told the Commission that Chicano
students who had been unable to express themselves in
other publications had been stimulated into self-expres-

sion by bilingual papers. "For the anglo students," Gutiérrez said, "journalism seems to be a leisure activity. For us, it is a necessity."

The Commission's findings show that in its own self-interest if nothing else, the nation's established media should concern itself with problems that cripple high school journalism. For censorship in the high school educates young people into acceptance of repression as a normal way of life, eroding support for freedom of the press. And the failure of student journalism to include significant numbers of minorities does nothing to help alleviate the problem of minority exclusion from the established media.

Since surveys have shown that students, especially minorities, increasingly turn to television as their source of news, newspapers would seem to have a particular stake in making efforts to bring about better high school journalism programs to increase interest in newspapers.

Even junior high school journalism programs can help develop newspaper reading habits as well as aid students with reading problems. For example, Richard Rubin, adviser to the school paper at Shore Junior High, an all-black school in Washington, D.C., told the Commission a major benefit of the paper was stimulation of students to read. He said:

> There's no secret that reading is a problem for these students. It is the major problem children still come to the seventh, eighth, and ninth grade and they can't read and I've seen in my reading classes students who buy the newspaper and in fact, there's one girl who can't read very well at all, yet she is always one of the first people to come in and buy the newspaper.
>
> It's building a habit with her that she's going to turn to a newspaper and she's going to feel that it is an essential part of life. Many other students just don't have access to newspapers or magazines or even dictionaries at home.

The relative lack of confidence in newspapers on the part of many young people is another reason the established press should take greater interest in high school

journalism. A November, 1970, national youth survey
by Louis Harris and Associates, showed that magazines
and television were more highly regarded than newspapers for coverage of news and public events.

The survey showed that 68 percent of the youths
thought magazines did a good or excellent job of "edu-
cating the public to important issues," while 28 percent
thought they did only fair or poor. Television rated
second in credibility with percentages of 64 and 34,
with newspapers trailing at 57 and 41.

In the category of "responsible interpretation of today's events," 64 percent rated magazines favorably
and 31 percent rated them unfavorably. Television rated
second with percentages of 61 and 36, followed by
newspapers with 53 and 44.

Other polls have shown that newspapers lag far behind television as a believable news medium. For example, a November–December, 1972, poll by the
Roper Organization indicated that 48 percent of American adults considered television the most believable
news medium among newspapers, magazines, radio,
and television. Twenty-one percent of those polled
chose newspapers first on the issue of credibility, while
magazines drew 10 percent, and radio 8 percent.

Chapter 22

Programs and Organizations

The Commission reviewed the work of a number of
high school journalism programs involving various seg-
ments of the established media. Some of the programs
dealt with the crucial problems of censorship and
minority access, but others ignored them.

The Newspaper Fund, for example, has conducted an

outstanding program, while the American Newspaper Publishers Association has paid little attention to high school journalism except for promoting the use of newspapers in classroom teaching.

The Newspaper Fund

Founded in 1958, The Newspaper Fund is supported by Dow Jones & Co., Inc., publisher of *The Wall Street Journal, The National Observer, Barron's National Business* and *Financial Weekly*, the twelve local newspapers in the Ottaway Group, and the Dow Jones News Service.

A nonprofit organization based in Princeton, New Jersey, its chief purpose is to encourage talented young people to enter the newspaper profession.

Although much of the Fund's work focuses on college students, it also assists high school journalism programs, providing training and information for students and teachers and sponsoring programs designed to recruit minority students for journalism careers.

The Fund, spurred by studies in the 1950s that indicated few high school newspaper advisers had training in writing and even fewer were able to teach journalistic writing effectively, established a training program for advisers and journalism teachers in 1959. The Fund reports that since then, it has brought nearly 6,000 inexperienced advisers back to college campuses for practical journalism training.

The Fund also has provided incentives and recognition for exceptional performance to hundreds of high school journalism teachers. Through its Special Awards Program, outstanding teachers receive grants to establish Journalism Learning Centers in their schools.

The Fund's "Newsletter" is mailed regularly to high school newspaper advisers. It discusses scholastic journalism events and reports on issues in the profession at large, relating them to their impact on scholastic journalism.

Another Fund publication, *These Struck Our Fancy*, informs teachers and students about current topics and methods of writing and reporting in various high school newspapers by the reprinting of articles from high school papers.

The Fund also has pioneered in recruiting and training minorities in high schools for journalism programs and careers through Urban Journalism Workshops. Each of the workshops are conducted with the assistance of local newspapers and journalism schools.

Grants by the Fund for the workshops are matched by local sponsoring newspapers. And if the 1973 experience is any indication, newspapers are not as concerned about the minority problem as they were in the immediate preceding years. In 1972, 180 students participated in eight different workshops.

In 1973 the program involved only sixty-eight students at six workshops held at the University of Southern California, Los Angeles; University of Minnesota, Minneapolis; University of Missouri, Columbia; University of Wisconsin, Milwaukee; Ball State University, Muncie, Indiana; and Blair Academy, Blairstown, New Jersey. Another workshop had been scheduled at Temple University, Philadelphia, Pennsylvania, but was canceled, the Fund reported, "due to lack of promised financial support from local co-sponsoring newspapers."

The Fund also initiated a pilot program in 1973 to bring minority journalism students in contact with minorities who are professional journalists. The program, which operated in Los Angeles, Atlanta, and Philadelphia, has three goals: to encourage minorities to consider newspaper work as a career by demonstrating to them that minorities do work for newspapers and are succeeding in their careers; to provide professional direction to students in techniques of writing and editing their school newspapers; and to provide for journalism teachers and newspaper advisers some professional direction in teaching writing and editing skills.

The Minneapolis Star

Among the more innovative programs involving joint ventures by local newspapers and school systems is

"Metro Newsbeat," a cooperative project of the *Minneapolis Star* and the city's schools.

Created in 1973 with federal assistance, "Newsbeat" involved thirty-two students from twelve schools in a bureau that prepares news for the city's high school newspapers. The students work under the supervision of professional journalists.

The program is aimed at increasing minority access as well as improving the general quality of high school journalism. Support for it has come from Title III, Innovative Programs, of the Elementary and Secondary Education Act of 1965.

Bill Greer, a veteran member of the *Star* news staff, directs the program, supervising the students in coverage of such stories as school vandalism and its relationship to the work of school repairmen; the impact of the women's movement on school sports; and how and where tax money is collected and spent for schools.

The American Newspaper Publishers Association Foundation

The nation's newspaper publishers, concerned about mounting attacks on the press by government officials and polls showing a low credibility rating for newspapers, launched a broad program in 1971 aimed at strengthening public support for the press. However, except for promoting the use of newspapers in classroom teaching, the program hardly addresses itself to high school journalism.

The American Newspaper Publishers Association Foundation appropriated $10 million for the 1970s to 1) advance the professionalism of the press; 2) develop and strengthen public understanding of the press and of freedom of speech and press; and 3) develop informed newspaper readers.

Part of the ANPA program involved extending its fifteen-year-old Newspaper in the Classroom program "in an effort to help insure that all young people can read daily newspapers effectively."

Basic issues of high school journalism, including censorship and minority access, are ignored by the ANPA program.

Sigma Delta Chi

The professional society of journalists, Sigma Delta Chi (SDX), which has more than 25,000 active members also has failed to address those basic issues.

SDX's main activities concerned with high school journalism have involved providing educational material on career opportunities. It reports that since 1963 it has distributed more than 300,000 copies of various journalism careers publications to high schools and colleges, individual students, vocational counselors, teachers, and SDX members and chapters.

The failure to perceive censorship and minority access in high school journalism as problems probably has been a major reason for the lack of SDX programs in those areas.

The Minnesota professional chapter of SDX, for example, quickly resolved to take action on the high school front once it learned the nature of findings the Commission of Inquiry was preparing to make in this Report.

The chapter passed a resolution pledging support to high school journalism programs, and Lew Cope of the *Minneapolis Tribune*, chapter president, said, "We intend to be of help to school journalism in whatever way possible. We are willing to make phone calls, supply speakers to schools, help arbitrate disputes on press freedom—anything to give the teachers and students some support."

The Reporters Committee for Freedom of the Press

In March, 1970, a group of reporters gathered at Georgetown University in Washington, D.C., to discuss their growing concern over threats to a free press, especially a U.S. Department of Justice policy of subpoenaing reporters to try to force them to disclose names of confidential sources.

Out of that meeting came The Reporters Committee

for Freedom of the Press, a Washington-based organization that sponsors a legal defense and research fund for reporters whose First Amendment rights are threatened.

The Committee quickly became a national clearinghouse for information and legal help for reporters around the country. In 1973 it extended its program of collecting and disseminating information to include the college and high school press.

First Amendment cases involving high school journalism became a regular part of the Reporters Committee's Press Censorship Newsletter. Among the cases cited in the November–December, 1973, issue, for example, was one from Gresham, Oregon, about Marilyn Schultz, who was relieved as adviser to the paper at Centennial High School when she refused to endorse the paper's code of ethics drawn up by the school administration. "Ms. Schultz lost an appeal to the school board and now plans to file a suit challenging her dismissal from the journalism job and the legality of the newspaper code," the Newsletter reported. "The code's 20 points include a ban on inclusion of 'offensive' material, 'suggestive' language and 'unkind references about individuals.' Among other things, Ms. Schultz plans to argue that the code is unconstitutionally vague."

The Reporters Committee plans to expand its high school journalism activities. In March, 1974, after consultation with the Commission of Inquiry and the Robert F. Kennedy Memorial, the committee established a goal of creating at the earliest possible time a special high school and college press project.

Dedicated to an independent and responsible student press, the project would establish a legal defense and research service that could offer legal information on case developments, files on reported instances of high school censorship, and legal information to attorneys litigating student press cases.

The work of the Reporters Committee and the Newspaper Fund suggests that the established media will recognize a special responsibility when it perceives the problems of high school journalism.

The interest expressed by the Reporters Committee,

the Fund, the Minnesota chapter of Sigma Delta Chi, and other organizations in the work of the Commission of Inquiry also suggests the established media may be on the threshold of a better perception of those problems.

To conclude this section of its Report, the Commission asked three of the nation's most distinguished newspaper editors to write brief statements on high school journalism: Thomas Winship, editor of the *Boston Globe;* Eugene C. Patterson, editor of the *St. Petersburg Times,* and Tom Wicker, associate editor of *The New York Times.*

THOMAS WINSHIP

Freedom of the press should be one of the most valued rights provided by the constitution on which this nation is based.

Over the decades many people have tended to ignore the importance of this crucial freedom. Lately, the press has been battered with heavy, unfair political criticism. Recent Supreme Court decisions suggest the press should feel some restraints.

I am not advocating an irresponsible press. I am advocating the need for a well-educated public, which understands the essential role the press plays in keeping the people informed about their community and their public leaders. An uninformed public cannot form the base of a healthy community. No one agrees with everything a newspaper prints. But disagreement is no grounds for censoring the press. It is important that the press has the freedom to challenge the powers that be, to argue—when the need arises—for different policies than those offered by the communities' leaders.

High school is the ideal place to instill the value of a free press. The four high school years usually offer students a chance to work on the newspaper and to come into contact with the same issues of honesty and fairness, the need to speak out, that confront the nation's press. Here students have a chance to grasp the meaning of the First Amendment to the constitution.

Helping educate students to the meaning of a free press is important for the nation as a whole. These young people may never become journalists as adults. But they will join the adult world, as newspaper readers and voters, with a better understanding of the press' need for freedom and the dangers of suppression.

Another part of this educational experience is the insight high school administrators can gain in trying to support students. They must recognize that this student work is like a microcosm of the real world. They should expect good quality and fairness from the students. However, they should avoid the instinct to censor and repress, which must be as abhorrent in high school journalism as it is in journalism around our world today.

EUGENE C. PATTERSON

I believe high school faculties are missing something essential if they fail to teach the full meaning of freedom of expression in America, and that includes encouraging the practice of it in high school newspapers.

A free press creates difficulties for bureaucracies, whether they are educational or governmental. That is all the more reason for encouraging students to speak and write freely—responsibly, because responsibility goes along with rights.

Freedom is a difficult art. To teach it, one must practice it. Students are quick to identify lip service. And if a school administration forces timidity, conformity, insincerity, and hypocrisy on its student editors, they are going to grow up thinking that is the way America works, or else they are going to take a cynical view of American freedoms as being empty words.

Surely it is worth a lot of worry and inconvenience on the part of school administrators if they can educate the young in the full meaning of the First Amendment. Only by teaching freedom can they begin to bring home to young minds the full meaning of responsibility for the words one writes or says.

Curt censorship of high school newspapers amounts to an education in authoritarianism and I do not believe that is a wise direction for schools to take in a democratic society.

TOM WICKER

About thirty years ago I was the industrious editor of a mimeographed high school newspaper inaptly called *The Sandspur*. There were a lot of sandspurs lurking in the grass around Hamlet, North Carolina, to prick the bare feet of schoolboys, but if whoever thought up that name for the school paper meant to suggest that it would ever get under anyone's skin, he was sadly disappointed.

The Sandspur in my day reported badly on sports, club meetings, homeroom news, the senior play, war stamp sales, and reputed romances; then it filled out the ample remaining space with corny jokes. Its staff had no trouble with school officials because nothing was ever printed that could have caused anybody any trouble; it had no political content because high school students in those days, at least in the smalltown South, had no more politics than the universal belief that the good old U.S.A. was the greatest country on the face of the earth and always would be.

It may come as a shock to those of my generation and beyond, who remember their own *Sandspurs* and all those hot items about Joe Doe holding hands at the Bijou with Jane Plain, that things have changed in the high school press room. Young folks who've been through Vietnam and the sex revolution, just to mention two counts of the indictment, and who've been brought up on television, don't bear much resemblance to Harold Teen and Andy Hardy. Besides, affluence has had its influence; it was hard to be political when all a budding Winchell had to work with was four mimeographed pages, but now that there's money around to finance elegant offset production; young editors are likely to make the most of it.

In short, some—not all—high school newspapers have gone political, whether about the principal's latest disciplinary rulings or the nation's latest war. Even where the school newspaper remains a poor jokebook, sometimes school organizations or individual students organize rallies, pass out leaflets, picket the school board. So the issue of First Amendment ___ has appeared in high schools, with the predict-___ ___ that teachers, administrators, and parents

again some, not all—are outraged and cracking
down. To the extent that the matter has reached the
courts, as matters almost always do in America, the
results have been mixed.

Why should that be? Do constitutional rights begin
at age eighteen? Or maybe twenty-one? Where does it
say so in the Constitution? The fact is that high school
students have—or should have—as much right to free
speech, free press, and free assembly as anyone else,
and subject only to the same kinds of common-sense
restrictions that apply to everyone else—you can't
shout "fire!" in a crowded theater or during school
assembly, and there's no more right to hold an antiwar rally during French class than in the subway at
the rush hour.

Look into most restrictions on high school students'
exercise of what everyone else can do as a constitutional right and you will generally find that an administrator has made a ruling for the convenience of
administration; it is probably easier for a principal
not to have students picketing outside the school, and
not to have some fiery editor writing that the principal
is a fascist beast or a male chauvinist pig. But the
Constitution is not supposed to be suspended for anyone's convenience, as even Presidents of the United
States are beginning to learn.

But if a school board finances a school newspaper,
can't the school board control what goes into it? If
that were true, there surely would never be anything
printed critical of the school board; so there goes the
First Amendment right away. Better constitutional
scholars than I might say that a school board doesn't
have to finance a school newspaper at all, and maybe
that's true; but if it does, surely it has no right to
demand that it be a school or school board propaganda sheet, or to dictate the editor's politics, or that
they have no politics.

This report goes far more deeply into these issues
than I can, in this small space. My point, anyway, is
not so much to argue the matter myself as to suggest
that there is an argument to be made, and a good one;
and that no one ought to be more interested in it than
professional journalists. High schools right now are

full of youngsters who ought themselves to be professional journalists someday—our successors; and if
we care half as much as most of us say we do about
the profession itself, and its importance in American
life, we ought to be as concerned for it in the future
as in our own times.

Yet, a lot of these young journalists are being taught
today, not that a free press is constitutionally obligated to publish and let the chips fall where they may,
but that the press is an instrument of policy for school
administrators and school boards, that the courts will
permit that view, and that First Amendment rights
therefore are only for some people some of the time.
All too many of these high school editors and reporters may well conclude, from hard experience, that
freedom of the press is as bad a joke as the ones
school boards would like for them to print in place
of news and opinion; and holding that cynical view
they are far more likely to become doctors, engineers,
or politicians than reporters. If they do become reporters, having felt the knife so early, they are not
likely to stick their necks out in the name of the First
Amendment.

Besides, if courts can rationalize themselves into
upholding administrators who quash *anybody's* First
Amendment rights, then *everybody's* First Amendment
rights are to some extent endangered. So, fellow journalists, the next time your local principal cracks down
on a kid editor who shows some gumption, send not
to know for whom the bell tolls; it's not much of a
jump from there to an injunction against the Pentagon
Papers.

Specific Commission Findings: Established Media

1. Despite the established media's obvious vested interest in encouraging youth journalism and student support for freedom of the press, the Commission found little indication that media—print or electronic—saw either an opportunity or a challenge to encourage high school journalism or to develop a youth constituency supporting the First Amendment.

2. In surveying newspaper editors, the Commission found that the majority are unaware of basic issues facing high school journalism, including student consciousness about freedom-of-speech issues and serious violations of First Amendment rights. In fact, among editors surveyed, many indicated that they favored restraints on First Amendment rights as they applied to high school journalists.

3. Some editors, while admitting general ignorance of the condition of high school journalism, indicated a desire to learn more about the situation and help in the general upgrading of high school journalism.

4. The Commission found that, except for reporting on sports, bond issues, school board meetings, and school crises of immediate community concern, established media has generally avoided news reporting on school conditions. Generally, the media "leaves education to the educators," taking the position that young people in schools are children best left to the authority of professional educators.

5. With a few exceptions, established media has done little to encourage minority participation in high school journalism. Despite the American Society of Newspaper Editors stated concerns about problems of minority training for and access to jobs in the media, and its assertion that contact with minorities must be made in the junior and senior high schools, little sub-

stantive effort has been made by established media in
this area. Even media controlled by minorities have
failed in this respect. It should be noted, however, that
the Commission did see a few encouraging programs in
this area, such as The Newspaper Fund, which sponsors programs to upgrade journalism education and to
bring more minority youth into scholastic journalism
programs.

PART V

Toward Action

Recommendations of the Commission

I. *On Censorship Issues*

General Statement The student staff should have ultimate authority over and responsibility for high school media, which means the right to know and to produce and disseminate information free of interference or restrictions.

The Commission recommends that:

A. Full discussion of First Amendment law be made a part of school curriculum. Students should know the full extent of their rights as well as any limitations.

B. First Amendment rights of high school journalists be fully observed. Only material that is legally obscene or libelous or likely to cause immediate and substantial disruption of the school should be prohibited in the school media.

C. Out-of-school media produced by students must be accorded the same First Amendment protections.

D. Student journalists remain alert to First Amendment issues, protect gains made in First Amendment areas for future journalists, and assist students in other schools to gain similar rights.

E. Student journalists and teachers routinely seek advice and support from organizations in the community traditionally concerned with the protection of First Amendment rights and that a national channel be created for those who cannot find local support.

F. The established media keep special vigilance to protect First Amendment rights of youth journalists.

G. There be widespread distribution and discussion of guidelines to protect free expression of student journalists.

H. Student journalists, teachers, and administrators make special efforts to share successful experiences, based upon the development of equitable guidelines and procedures for the protection of First Amendment rights of youth journalists.

II. *On Minority Participation Issues*

General Statement   The Commission emphasizes the value of media and communications programs reflecting the cultural pluralism so integral a component of American life. Toward this end the Commission recognizes the need for full participation of youth minorities, whether racial, ethnic, cultural or economic in school-based and out-of-school media programs.

The Commission recommends that:

A. Teachers and current journalism staffs make special efforts to understand the racial, cultural, ethnic, and economic diversity of their communities and to mirror this pluralism in the content of their media.

B. Teachers and student journalism staffs undertake active recruitment of minority youth for in-school media programs.

C. Community-based organizations concerned with minority rights recruit minority youth for in- and out-of-school media.

D. Established community organizations show greater leadership in augmenting media resources available to minority youth, with special emphasis on the development of community-based youth media enterprises mirroring special minority concerns.

E. Special media projects and summer journalism programs undertake more active recruitment of minority youth. Where necessary, scholarships should be provided for minority youth.

F. Schools encourage the operation of multiple media with simple production capabilities for groups who are presently screened out of media programs because of tracking or traditional methods of staff selection.

III. *On Journalism and Journalism Education Issues*

General Statement   The ability to communicate effectively is a vital function of education in a democracy. Journalism can be an integral part of that education if it upholds the right of free expression, encourages inquiry and investigation, and builds communications skills. Generally, journalism and journalism education for youth fall far short of these goals. The quality and general availability of journalism experience in the schools should be dramatically improved. Since education transcends the school, the Commission emphasizes the need to open up similar opportunities within the larger community.

The Commission recommends that:

A. Schools recognize the unique opportunities offered by media experience. Consistent with their importance, media programs should be given full consideration in budget and curriculum planning, with academic credit given for participants of in-school media programs. Journalism teachers and advisers should be selected on the basis of interest and ability and provided with sufficient time and compensation for their efforts.

B. Schools offer academic credit for work done by students involved in out-of-school media programs, including work in community newspapers, broadcasting, or alternative media.

C. Journalism teachers and students develop contacts with established media in order to increase their understanding of professional journalism as an institution.

D. Schools investigate costs of various printing methods and use any cost savings to support alternative media opportunities for students.

E. Local, state, and national scholastic awards programs be revised to include consideration of content as a major criterion in judging youth media.

Solicitation of entries should include community-
based as well as in-school media. Schools should
give serious thought to the standardizing influence
of such programs and create their own evaluation
norms that are consonant with the unique purpose
of each medium in the school and community.

F. Established media, civil rights organizations, and
other community institutions concerned with youth
development and their First Amendment rights take
a much more active role in helping young people
gain access to media experiences, including the development of their own media programs.

G. Journalism education be broadened in concept beyond traditional publications programs to the central curriculum so that all students will have the
opportunity to elect courses that deal with the
significance of media in contemporary society and
that offer opportunities for free media expression.

IV. *On Established Media*

General Statement   It is the responsibility and in the
immediate self-interest of established journalism to increase the numbers of citizens knowledgeable about,
committed to, and effectively practicing the right to free
expression. Likewise, the Commission believes that the
freedom, competency, and growth of youth journalism
are largely dependent upon support from strong community institutions. As such an institution, American
journalism could perform no greater service in the interest of free expression than to encourage free and
effective expression among young people generally and
youth journalists in particular.

The Commission recommends that:

A. Locally, established media fully evaluate the state
of youth journalism, focusing attention on the consciousness of youth and youth journalists' rights and
responsibilities posed by the First Amendment, the
extent to which youth media is receptive to minority
concerns in its community, and the general quality
of youth journalism and journalism education.

B. Cooperating with school authorities, where possible,

established media provide students with information on the history and meaning of the First Amendment. Professional journalists should participate in discussions of those rights within school classrooms.

C. Established media use its voice and prestige to support youth journalists seeking their First Amendment rights; help protect these students and supportive school personnel against arbitrary and punitive actions by others; and, where necessary, provide advice and resources in cases of prolonged negotiation and litigation.

D. Established media act quickly and affirmatively on recommendations of the 1972 report of the American Society of Newspaper Editors calling for encouragement of minority participation in school journalism and greater efforts to recruit members of minority groups into the journalism profession. The Commission further urges media controlled by minorities to make aggressive efforts to support freedom of expression in youth media programs, with full access to minority youth.

E. Established media make itself more available to youth journalists as a laboratory for gaining important experiences common to professional journalists. This should be done through such activities as short-term internships, regular consultations with youth, journalism projects, and financial support and professional expertise to enrich and broaden student participation in summer workshops.

V. *Action Programs*

Beyond setting forth general recommendations, the Commission believes it has a responsibility to recommend specific courses of action. Here the Commission suggests eight major action proposals and a vehicle to press for their implementation. It supplements these proposals with additional action suggestions illustrative of those recommended by concerned citizens during the life of this inquiry.

A. The Commission recommends establishment of a National Youth Journalism Project (hereafter re-

ferred to as The Project) to encourage the widest
possible discussion of this Report; serve as an information clearinghouse for information on youth
journalism issues; and advocate and support initia-
tives at the local, state, and national levels to expand freedom of expression, encourage youth in
serious inquiry and reporting, increase minority
youth participation in journalism, and foster development of communications skills in all youth.

B. The Commission recommends that The Project give
immediate attention and support to eight major actions:

  1. *Regional Workshops*   The Project should con-
     vene at least five regional workshops, bringing
     together youth journalists, representatives of
     established media, legal consultants, and mem-
     bers of the education profession (teachers, ad-
     ministrators, school board members, and repre-
     sentatives of state departments of education) to
     review and discuss this Report in the light of
     youth journalism locally, to plan improvements
     in existing programs, and to develop new pro-
     grams, where appropriate. The Project should
     help conferees implement action recommenda-
     tions coming from these workshops.

  2. *Freedom for Youth Media*   A national center
     advocating First Amendment guarantees for
     youth journalists should be established as part
     of an existing organization sympathetic to those
     rights, or as a new entity. The center should
     circulate information on rights of free expres-
     sion, receive and refer complaints to local ad-
     vocates, and generally make every effort to
     encourage a consciousness and use of those
     rights among youth journalists. In this capacity
     it should work with students, teachers, and ad-
     visers to support the efforts of each in behalf
     of First Amendment freedoms for youth jour-
     nalism.

  3. *Work with the Established Media, Including
     Minority Media, to Develop Programs That
     Encourage Minority Youth to Consider Careers*

in Journalism In select localities, The Project should encourage established media to sponsor internships in established media operations on a part-time basis during the school year and full-time during the summer months, offer scholarships to existing media workshops, and encourage and support youth-developed media programs in the community.

4. *Encourage Action by the American Society of Newspaper Editors on Its Recommendations for Recruiting Minorities into Journalism and Journalism Education Programs* The Project should offer to explore with ASNE ways it might more successfully act on its own recommendations (formulated in the 1972 ASNE annual meeting) to encourage minority participation in journalism and journalism education in both junior and senior high schools.

5. *Local Associations of High School Editors* As a series of national demonstrations, The Project should help establish local groups of high school editors to assess and then act in ways increasing the integrity and quality of youth journalism. Small, independent budgets and professional consultants should be made available to these groups.

6. *Established Media Support for Excellence in Youth Journalism* An initial group of at least five major daily newspapers or electronic media stations, or both, should be encouraged to sponsor programs honoring exemplary youth reporting on issues of school and community importance.

7. *Recognizing the Importance of Content in State and National Youth Journalism Awards Programs* State and national awards programs should be encouraged to give priority to content as well as form of journalism entries. Only if such efforts fail should The Project consider ways to develop alternative awards programs at the state and national levels.

8. *Workshops with School Administrators* The

Project should make every effort to arrange workshops in cooperation with local and regional associations of school administrators in order to discuss youth journalism and journalism education in ways highlighting First Amendment issues, the content of youth media, breadth of student participation in media programs, and the variety of experiences which might increase communications skills.

C. Supplementing actions recommended above are others suggested to the Commission and its staff by concerned individuals and groups. Illustrative, but not inclusive, are the following:

1. Local bar associations should form special committees to inquire into the state of First Amendment rights of youth journalists.

2. Local constitutional rights organizations, such as the American Civil Liberties Union and Legal Defense Fund should help young people establish "hot lines" to report violations of free speech and seek procedural advice.

3. With the cooperation of student journalists, local rights organizations should establish committees to negotiate with schools written guidelines outlining rights and legal limitations on freedom of expression, and develop procedures for negotiating First Amendment issues. These committees should assist in the continuing education of students, teachers, and administrators on freedom-of-speech issues.

4. Local and state teachers associations should establish coalitions with organizations specifically concerned about the protection of First Amendment rights in order to build more support for free expression by youth journalists and to protect those teachers, advisers, and others who advocate full use of these rights.

5. Along with students, local community organizations representing minority interests should develop special advocacy projects to establish policies of bilingual media presentation where

bilingualism is common to the local youth population.

6. Local colleges and universities with journalism departments should establish "Upward Bound" programs to reach youth journalists, particularly those representing racial and ethnic minorities. Such programs could kindle the interest of minority youth in journalism careers.

7. Universities with journalism departments should create community media resource centers as part of their community relations programs. These centers should contain print and electronic media equipment consultants to work with both adults and youth on community media projects. University extension divisions are especially suited for work in this area.

8. Local public libraries should establish media resource centers available to young people. Centers should include print and electronic equipment, facilities for their use, and professional consultants.

9. Local community organizations should form coalitions to aggressively represent community interests in cable TV franchise negotiations, including the sponsorship of programs developed by youth.

10. Community and neighborhood newspapers should include news sections on youth affairs, soliciting from young people both editorials and special reports on issues of youth and general community concern.

11. City-wide and metropolitan media should establish a regular policy of publishing editorials and special reports authored by youth, using youth consultants in this process.

12. Local philanthropic foundations concerned with youth development should make small grants to youth for special inquiries and investigative reports of public value. Such grants could be used to defray transportation and communications costs and support significant journalism over summer vacations.

Appendix A

1. A Legal Guide for High School Journalism

This section is provided as a legal guide to students, teachers, school officials, and community groups. The Commission has also included at the end of Appendix B a list of organizations that may be helpful should you become involved in a censorship controversy.

The Commission feels obligated to warn both students and advisers that exercising one's rights can involve risks. The case histories of the students and advisers outlined in Part I of this Report are evidence enough of that fact. Some school officials openly defy the law. In other cases, reasonable people might disagree in specific situations as to whether the expression of views is "substantially disruptive." You may be acting within your rights, but you also may have to go to court to prove it.

Freedom of expression exercised by an uncensored press has long been established as an essential element of our Bill of Rights. These rights are no less important for students than adults. The existence and free exercise of First Amendment rights by students in schools is in accord with a primary purpose of public schools, the development of an informed and concerned public capable of active participation in community life. The Supreme Court has commented on the special responsibility placed upon our schools.

The vigilant protection of constitutional freedoms is nowhere more vital than in the community of American schools. The classroom is peculiarly the marketplace of ideas. The Nation's future depends upon leaders trained through wide exposure to that robust exchange of ideas which discover truth out of a multi-

tude of tongues, rather than through any kind of au-
thoritative ˙selection.[1]

The First Amendment and Official School Publications

That the First Amendment applies to high school students is no longer in question. The Supreme Court, in
Tinker v. Des Moines Independent School District,[2] has
held that students do not lose their right to free expression
under the First Amendment to the Constitution when they
enter school. The *Tinker* case involved an attempt by
school officials to prevent students from wearing black arm
bands to protest the Vietnam war. The Court stated:

> Students in school as well as out of school are persons
> under our Constitution. . . . In our system, students
> may not be regarded as closed-circuit recipients of
> only that which the state chooses to communicate.
> They may not be confined to the expression of those
> sentiments that are officially approved. In the absence
> of a specific showing of constitutionally valid reasons
> to regulate their speech students are entitled to free-
> dom of expression of their views.[3]

Tinker does not apply merely to the wearing of arm
bands. Other courts have applied the legal principles set
forth there to such forms of expression as newspapers,
leaflets, buttons, and political clubs.

Notwithstanding *Tinker,* many school officials claim
the authority to fully control the content of school publications. A major obstacle facing high school journalists
(and often their advisers) is the asserted administration
position of the *school as publisher*. The argument set forth
by these officials is: "We finance the paper, therefore we
rightfully control its content."

This argument has been consistently rejected by the
courts.[4] A federal judge in Massachusetts has summed up
the financing issue in this way:

> The state is not necessarily the unrestrained master of
> what it creates and fosters. Thus in cases concerning
> school supported publications or the use of school
> facilities, the courts have refused to recognize as per-
> missible any regulation infringing on free speech when

not related to the maintenance of order and discipline within the school.[5]

Consequently a principal cannot limit content because he finds it unpleasant or controversial. The First Amendment guarantees students the right to report on and editorialize about controversial topics and events in the school, community, nation, and world. It is, in fact, the discussion of controversial issues, the Supreme Court said, which is "the basis of our national strength and of the independence and vigor of Americans who grow up and live in this relatively permissive, often disputatious society."[6]

Principals are no more free to control advertising than they are to control news stories. Thus when school officials prohibited an anti-Vietnam war advertisement, a federal court confronted the educational and legal arguments of content control. The students argued that the official school paper was "to provide a forum for the dissemination of ideas and information by and to the students of the school."[7] School officials countered that "The publication is not a newspaper in the usual sense, but is a beneficial educational device developed as part of the curriculum and intended to inure primarily to the benefit of those who compile, edit and publish it."[8]

These school officials maintained that it was their policy to limit content to matters pertaining to the school and that this ban on expression applying to subjects not related to the high school was necessary to prevent the paper from becoming dominated by news unrelated to the school.

The court rejected all arguments of the school authorities and stated:

> If the paper's contents were truly as flaccid as the [school officials'] arguments imply, it would indeed be a sterile publication. Furthermore, its function as an educational device surely could not be served if such were the content of the paper.[9]

Supporting the student editorial board's view that the school's prohibition was a constitutionally invalid abridgment of their First Amendment rights, the court held:

> It is unfair in the light of the free speech doctrine, to close [the school newspaper] as a forum to this specific

idea. . . . It would be both incongruous and dangerous for this court to hold that students who wish to express their views on matters intimately related to them, through traditionally accepted non-disruptive modes of communication, may be precluded from doing so. . . .[10]

Legal Limitations

However, student journalists, editors, and writers must observe certain legal restrictions imposed upon all citizens and the established media. Thus students must refrain from publication of material which is obscene, libelous, or creates a clear and present danger of the immediate material and substantial physical disruption of the school.

School officials have also been given the clear authority to set reasonable regulations as to the time and place of distribution of printed material.

Where material does not fall within one of the three limitations listed it cannot be prohibited because it is "unpleasant" or in "bad taste" or too controversial. While a variety of court decisions have affirmed this position, it is worth quoting in this regard a school administrator, the Chancellor of the New York City public schools, Harvey Scribner.

So long as the publications do not exceed or go beyond the carefully noted and narrowly drawn exceptions . . . the policy of the Board of Education is to permit dissemination of any view, regardless of whether it is critical of the school system or its administration, raises social issues, or is a viewpoint of a minority within the school. . . . Material which does not exceed these standards must be permitted to be distributed, regardless of how controversial or unpleasant its content may be to some readers.[11]

The Legal Restrictions Analyzed

"Obscenity"[12] is a complex legal term that refers to the content of an entire writing, not the specific language used. When school officials claim that a publication is obscene they usually mean that it contains "dirty words." Dirty words are not obscene unless the document as a whole meets three tests of obscenity as established under recent

Supreme Court decisions referring to literature about sex:

(1) predominantly appeals to prurient, shameful interests of minors;
(2) patently offends community standards regarding suitable sexual materials for minors;
(3) taken as a whole lacks serious literary, artistic, political or scientific value for minors.[13]

To be illegal it must meet all three tests. Political and social literature and most other writings appearing in the student press meet *none* of these tests. There are no court decisions holding that dirty words as used in any high school newspaper or undergrounds have amounted to obscenity.

A federal court in New York, in a case involving censorship of a student publication because a story contained "four-letter words as part of a vocabulary of an adolescent and . . . a description of a movie scene where a couple 'fell into bed,' " held that student publications could not be banned as obscene unless they satisfied the above three tests.

The magazine contained no extended narrative tending to excite sexual desires or constituting a predominant appeal to prurient interest. The dialogue was the kind heard repeatedly by those who walk the streets of our cities, use public conveyances and deal with youth in an open manner. It was not patently offensive to adult community standards for minors as evidenced by comparable material appearing in respected national periodicals and literature contained in the high school library.[14]

Often school officials will object to language that is commonly found in reputable books and magazines widely read by students and often located within the same school's library. One court faced with such a situation attacked school officials' objections to student literature as being "arbitrary and unreasonable" and labeled their actions "rank inconsistency."[15]

While the use of most language that school officials will label obscene is not illegal, dirty words are often unnecessary and students will save themselves a great many problems by substituting other language. A battle in the courts is usually a long one and the time delay, expense and energy necessary to mount such a suit may not be worth the use of this type of language.

The Supreme Court has held that to **libel** a public figure the material printed must be known by the author to be false or printed with reckless disregard of whether it was false or not.[16] If what you write is libelous, you can be sued for money damages. If your criticism concerns school policies and you have good reason to believe what you say is true, the statements will not constitute libel even if you are not able to prove that they are true or even if what you write later turns out to be false.[17] Nothing that you say that is true is libelous.[18]

These policies were developed by the Supreme Court to support the constitutional principle that the public interest in having free and unhindered debate on matters of public interest is so great as to outweigh potential harm to individuals. Since some incorrect statements are inevitable, the "malice," and "reckless disregard of the truth" standards were felt necessary to avoid self-censorship by journalists fearful of legal attack.

Sound educational policy dictates that young people be encouraged to inquire about and report on all issues confronting them as students and citizens. In reversing the suspension of Troy, New York, high school students for criticizing school officials, New York State Commissioner of Education Ewald Nyquist wrote:

> The student press can be a valuable learning device and an important educational resource. Its effectiveness, however, would be substantially impaired if student editors were forced to function under imminent fear of discipline for errors in judgment. The right of freedom of expression carries with it the right to make mistakes on occasion. This, too, is an essential portion of the learning process.[19]

To justify the censoring of a student publication on the grounds of its **disrupting the school,** the censoring official must reasonably forecast that publication will in fact cause disruption.[20] As the Supreme Court noted in *Tinker:*

> Any word spoken, in class, in the lunchroom, or on the campus, that deviates from the views of another

may start an argument or cause a disturbance. But our Constitution says we must take this risk.[21]

In several situations courts have upheld peaceful actions of students even though students holding opposing views became angry.

When school officials attempted to ban distribution of a student newspaper because of the hostility of other students, a Texas court said that if the student was acting in an "orderly, non-disruptive manner, then he should not suffer if other students, who are lacking self-control, tend to over-react thereby becoming a disruptive influence."[22]

Similarly, where the publications adviser and principal maintained that an article on planned parenthood in the school newspaper would offend and cause disruption in the community and therefore could not be printed, a federal court reversed school officials and ordered that the article appear.[23]

A word of caution is necessary. Some school officials would prefer to censor and then fight in court. They know that carrying a case to court will delay the publication of the material and they will try to "wait-out" students. In a recent Ohio decision a principal's suppression of an article was upheld on the grounds that it was potentially disruptive.[24] The article in question in this case was intended for inclusion in the October, 1971, school paper. The decision was rendered in December, 1973, an appeal has been taken by the Ohio ACLU and will not be decided until late 1974. Needless to say, none of the students are still in high school.

Underground Papers

Student publications produced independent of school resources or personnel enjoy all of the same rights that apply to the official school papers discussed above. The standards that control these publications are those of *Tinker*. They may be prohibited only if obscene or libelous, or if they present a clear and present danger of the immediate substantial and material disruption of the school.

Some school boards have attempted to limit student expression on controversial topics by banning both sides of the issue. Such policies prohibiting the use of school facilities for all partisan political activities have been held to

violate the First Amendment rights of students.[25] A similiar
state law prohibiting distribution on school property of any
material of a "sectarian, partisan or denominational character" or the purpose of which is to "spread propaganda"
was held to be unconstitutional by a federal court in California.[26]

Special Problems of Undergrounds' Prior Review

A major issue confronting underground journalists is
school requirements that students submit literature to a
principal prior to distribution.

Two federal appeals courts have held that no such prior
review can be required since such a rule would violate the
First Amendment prohibition of censorship.[27]

Courts that have allowed the requirement of prior approval have demanded that the school board adopt specific procedural rules, such as one clearly stating what
literature must be submitted and to whom.[28]

Most importantly, if prior approval is required, the
school must set a definite and brief time within which a
decision has to be made, so that the principal cannot in-
definitely delay the distribution.

Finally, the school may be required to provide an opportunity for students to present their point of view at a hearing. If a decision disapproving their literature is made, students must have available to them "an expeditious review
procedure of the decision of school authorities."[29]

Even without a court order, such large school districts
as Philadelphia and New York have decided on their own
to prohibit prior review regulations.[30] This policy is better
in that it allows students to preserve their anonymity and
thus prevents school officials from punishing those who
distribute controversial literature.

Whether or not school officials require students to submit articles for review, since *Tinker* applies to undergrounds, school officials may not withhold approval of
literature without evidence that it is libelous, obscene, or
capable of creating substantial and material disruption of
the school.

Sale on School Grounds

In the only decision ruling directly on this point, the
Seventh Circuit Court of Appeals held that students could

not be barred from selling literature unless under the *Tinker* test there was evidence of disruption.[31]

In two cases where courts broadly upheld the right to distribute underground newspapers on school property, the papers were either sold or contributions solicited.[32]

Comment

In the last year an Ohio federal court was called upon to respond to a high school student's complaint of being suspended from school for wearing an arm band to commemorate the shooting to death of four students on the Kent State University campus.

The student's conduct was identical to that which the Supreme Court had unequivocally upheld four years earlier in *Tinker* as being protected by the First Amendment. The Ohio court responded by holding school officials personally liable and awarded the student money damages for the deprivation.[33]

While the court's response was the first of its kind, the action of school officials in directly defying a Supreme Court decision was not an isolated instance.

It is the Commission's hope that school officials will support the First Amendment rights of students and in so doing respect and promote the rule of law in this country's schools.

Where those officials continue to abuse young people's constitutional rights, it is our hope that students, teachers, professional journalists, attorneys, parents, and other citizens will join together to hold school officials accountable for such actions and bring them to an end.

Notes

1. *Keyishian v. Board of Regents*, 385 U.S. 589, 594 (1967).
2. 393 U.S. 503 (1969).
3. *Tinker* at 511.
4. *Trujillo v. Love*, 322 F. Supp. 1266 (D.Colo. 1971); *Antonelli v. Hammond*, 308 F. Supp. 1329 (D.Mass. 1970); *Dickey v. Alabama State Board of Education*, 273 F. Supp. 613 (M.D.Ala. 1967). See also *Scoville v. Board of Education of Joliet Township*, 425 F. 2d 10 (7th Cir. 1972).
5. *Antonelli v. Hammond*, 308 F. Supp. 1329 (D.Mass. 1970), opinion of Judge Garrity citing *Dickey v. Alabama State Board of Education*, 273 F. Supp. 613 (M.D.Ala. 1967). See also *Lee v. Board of Regents*, 306 F. Supp. 1097 (W.D.Wis. 1969).
6. *Tinker* at 508.
7. *Zucker v. Panitz*, 292 F. Supp. 102, 103 (S.D.N.Y. 1969).
8. *Zucker* at 103.
9. *Zucker* at 103.
10. 299 F. Supp. 103 (S.D.N.Y. 1969). For an excellent discussion of this case see Trager, *Freedom of the Press in College and High School*, 35 Albany L. Rev. 1971.
11. *Matter of Williams*, decision of the Chancellor, New York City Public Schools (March 30, 1971).
12. Much of this section and portions of the following ones are excerpted from *The Rights of Students*, Avon Books, New York 1973, an American Civil Liberties Union Handbook written by Alan H. Levine, N.Y.C.L.U. staff attorney and a member of the Commission, with Eve Cary and Diane Divoky.
13. *Miller v. California*, 93 S.Ct. 2607 (1973); *Paris Adult Art Theater v. Slaton*, 93 S.Ct. 2628 (1973); see *Ginsburg v. United States*, 390 U.S. 629 (1968).
14. *Koppell v. Levine*, 347 F. Supp. 456 (E.D.N.Y. 1972). *See also, Jacobs v. Board of School Commissioners of Indianapolis*, 349 F. Supp. 605 (S.D.Ind. 1972), *Aff'd* —— F.2d —— (7th Cir. Dec. 14, 1973).
15. *Vought v. Van Buren Public Schools*, 306 F. Supp. 1388 (E.D.Mich. 1969).
16. *New York Times Co. v. Sullivan*, 376 U.S. 254 (1964).
17. See *Rosenbloom v. Metromedia Inc.*, 91 S.Ct. 1811 (1971); *Monitor Patriot Co. v. Roy*, 401 U.S. 265 (1971); *Time, Inc., v. Hill*, 385 U.S. 374 (1969); *Curtis Publishing Co. v. Butts*, 388 U.S. 130 (1967).
18. *Time, Inc., v. Hill*, 385 U.S. 374 (1969).

19. *Matter of Brociner,* 11 Ed. Dept. Rep. 204 (New York State Commissioner of Education 1972).
20. See *Tinker, accord Burnside v. Byars,* 363 F. 2d 744 (1966); *Blackwell v. Issaquena,* 363 F.2d 749 (1966); *Quarterman v. Byrd,* 453 F.2d 54 (4th Cir. 1971).
21. *Tinker* at 507.
22. *Sullivan v. Houston Independent School District,* 307 F. Supp. 1328 (S.D.Tex. 1969).
23. *Wesolek v. The Board of Trustees, South Bend Community School Corporation,* Civ. No. 73S101 (N.D.Ind. 1973).
24. *Hannahs v. Endry,* Civ. No. 72–306 (S.D.Ohio 1973). This decision is currently on appeal.
25. *Sanders v. Martin,* 72C. 1398 (E.D.N.Y. 1972).
26. *Rowe v. Campbell Union High School District,* Civ. Action No. 51060 (N.D.Cal. Sept. 4, 1970) (3 judge court).
27. *Riseman v. School Committee of Quincy,* 439 F.2d 148 (1st Cir. 1971); *Fujishima v. Board of Education,* 460 F.2d 1355 (7th Cir. 1972). See also *Poxon v. Board of Education,* No.S1894 (E.D.Cal. Aug. 31, 1971).
28. *Eisner v. Stamford Board of Education,* 440 F.2d 803 (2nd Cir. 1971); *Shanley v. Northeast Independent School District,* 462 F.2d 960 (5th Cir. 1972); *Quarterman v. Byrd,* 453 F.2d 54 (4th Cir. 1971).
29. *Shanley v. Northeast Independent School District,* 462 F.2d 960 (5th Cir. 1972).
30. Both school districts' policies are cited in *Sullivan v. Houston Independent School District,* 307 F. Supp. 1328 (S.D.Tex. 1969). *See also, Matter of Williams,* decision of the Chancellor, New York City Public Schools (March 30, 1971).
31. *Jacobs v. Board of School Commissioners of Indianapolis,* 349 F. Supp. 605 (S.D.Ind. 1972), *Aff'd* —— F.2d —— (7th Cir. Dec. 14, 1973).
32. *Sullivan v. Houston Independent School District,* 307 F. Supp. 1328 (S.D.Tex. 1969). In addition, the Commissioner of Education of New Jersey upheld the right of students to sell a newspaper inside the school building. *Burke v. Board of Education of Township of Livingston,* N.J. 1970 School Law Dec. 319.
33. *Borenstein v. Jones,* Civil Action No. 72–188 (S.D.Ohio 1973).

2. Model Guidelines for Student Publications

It is undeniable that students, both on and off public school campuses, are protected in their exercise of freedom of expression by the First Amendment to the Constitution of the United States. Accordingly, it is the responsibility of the school district and its staff to assure the maximum freedom of expression to all students.

The following guidelines are intended to aid students, advisers, school officials, and school districts in drafting their own guidelines for both official school publications and off-campus publications.

Official School Publications

Content School journalists may report on and editorialize about controversial and crucial events in the school, community, nation, and world. However, school editors and writers must observe the same legal responsibilities as those imposed upon conventional newspapers and news media. Thus, school journalists must refrain from publication of material which is:

(a) obscene, according to curent legal definitions;
(b) libelous, according to current legal definitions, or
(c) creates a clear and present danger of the immediate material and substantial physical disruption of the school.

In determining the type of material that violates the above restrictions, it must be noted that the dissemination of matorial that invites or stimulates heated discussion or debate among students or in the community does *not* constitute the type of disruption prohibited.

Censorship of Content Student publications may not be subjected to prior restraints or censorship by faculty advisers or school administrators. Accordingly, the responsibility for the contents of the student publication shall be that of the student staff and not the school administration or district.

Restrictions on Time, Place, and Manner of Distribution The school district may adopt reasonable restrictions on the time, place, and manner of distribution. For example, distribution may be restricted to periods of time in which students are not in classrooms—e.g., before school, lunch time, and after school—and may be restricted in a reasonable manner so as not to substantially interfere with the normal flow of traffic within the school corridors and entrance ways. Limitations that effectively deny students the opportunity to deliver literature to other students may not be imposed.

Advertisements If commercial advertisements are permitted in school publications, political advertisements may not be prohibited.

Access by Non-staff Members Access must be provided for opinions that differ from those of the publication staff, particularly when there is only one school paper available.

Unofficial School Newspapers

The constitutional right of freedom of expression guarantees the freedom of public school students to publish newspapers other than those sanctioned by the school. Such publications, however, may be restricted by reasonable regulations relating to time, place, and manner of distribution. The prohibitions against obscenity, libel, and material which causes the immediate material and substantial disruption of the school are also applicable.

Any system of prior review is inconsistent with the traditional guarantees of the First Amendment. Students may not be required to submit unofficial school publications to school authorities prior to distribution.

Sales The school must permit the sale of all publications, including student originated or distributed publications.

Anonymity Students may publish and write anonymously and school officials have no right to require the identification of the author of any article or editorial.

Appendix B

1. List of Hearing Sites and Consultation Meetings

Hearing Sites

Charlotte, North Carolina	May 13–14, 1973
New York, New York	June 1–2, 1973
San Antonio, Texas	April 13–14, 1973
San Francisco, California	March 23–24, 1973
South Bend, Indiana	April 6–7, 1973
Washington, D.C.	April 28, 1973

Consultation Meetings

April, 1973 —Robert Maynard, Nick Blatchford, Professional journalists
Commission members present:
Jean Grambs
Douglas Still
Karen Blank
Trilla Ramage

April, 1973 —Eliot Wiggington, originator of Foxfire idea
Duncan Alling, Steve King, Blair Summer School for Journalism
Commission members present:
Jean Grambs
Douglas Still
Trilla Ramage

May, 1973 —Indian Consultations
Ramah, New Mexico
Commission member present:
Suzanne Martinez

Pine Ridge, South Dakota
Commission member present:
  Tillie Walker
Chicago, Illinois
Commission member present:
  Karen Blank

May, 1973   —Electronic Media Consultations
Commission members present:
  Ann Heintz
  Karen Blank
  Dorothy McPhillips

June, 1973   —Missouri Scholastic Press Association Consultation
Commission member present:
  Jean Grambs

August, 1973—Alternatives to In-School Media Consultation
Commission members present:
  Alan Levine
  Charles Silberman

2. Student Survey Analysis

(Survey conducted April 26–May 16, 1973)

At the request of the Commission of Inquiry into High School Journalism a survey was made of public high school students throughout the United States. The survey was a crucial part of a nationwide study of the problems and potential of high school journalism.

Forty-two high schools were selected for the survey. The schools are distributed throughout thirty states. (See Appendix I.) Thirty-nine schools returned their questionnaires. In thirty-eight of the thirty-nine schools a student newspaper is regularly published, in the remaining case a student magazine in lieu of a newspaper. All but three of the schools offered high school journalism courses.

During April 26 to May 16, 1973, a total of 2,775 questionnaires were mailed to student coordinators at the forty-two schools. The number sent to each school was in direct proportion to the number of students attending the school. Student coordinators were asked to attempt to achieve reasonable balance among student respondents in terms of sex, grades in school, and race. They were cautioned as well against concentration on student cliques and asked to try to represent all identifiable student groups. By late June a total of 1,789 completed questionnaires were returned. Of these, only 1,630 forms could be processed. Of these 1,630 questionnaires less than 2 percent of the answers were rejected as incomplete or contradictory on any particular question.

The distribution of school size was as follows:

Number of Students

1000 or less	1001–2000	2001–3000
7	16	9

3001–4000	Over 4000
2	5

The distribution of schools by location was:

Large City (over 150,000)	Small City or Suburb	Rural
16	15	8

The following is a breakdown of minority students included in the survey: 284 Black Americans, 98 Spanish-speaking Americans, 104 American Indians, and 39 Asian Americans. The distribution of schools by percent of minority students was as follows:

Minority Enrollment

Under 40 Percent	Balanced (40–60 Percent)
25 schools with 271 minority students	6 schools with 70 minority students

Over 60 Percent
8 schools with 187 minority students

Three of the eight minority schools were located in the Southwest, where Mexican-Americans dominate two of the schools and Indians one. Included in the survey were 474 journalism students and 312 students who serve on their school publication staff.

The questionnaire (see Appendix II) contains four sections of questions. The first section provides factual data about the student. The second section asks the student his opinion on various aspects of his high school publication. The last two sections of the questionnaire are addressed to journalism students and to the students serving on the school publication staff.

The opinion of the students was directed to the following questions:

1. Is their school publication representative of student opinion?
2. Are issues or topics adequately covered by your school's publication?*
3. Is the publication used to create a good impression outside of school?
4. Does the publication accurately reflect everyday school life?
5. Do you enjoy reading the publication?

In addition the students were asked what barriers existed to working on their school publication.

The students were asked the range of topics most frequently covered by their publication. The following table gives the breakdown of answers.

Table I
Range of Topics Covered

	Percent of 1,630 students
School sports and extracurricular activities	84
School social news	60
Local educational problems and issues	34
Local community issues	22
National and international issues	13
Other	8

This table indicates the most widely covered topics are sports, extracurricular activities, and social news.

Table 2 gives the overall distribution of responses on the

---

* The original question is the negative of this one. However, the wording and answers have been modified to be consistent with other opinion questions for comparative purposes.

Table 2
Opinian Questions (Percentages)

	Representative of Range of Student Opinion			Provides Adequate Coverage of Issues of Topics			Used to Create a Good Impressicn Outside Schocl		
	Yes	No	Don't Know	Yes	No	Don't Know	Yes	No	Don't Know
Overall Survey	55	30	15	28	51	24	53	27	20
Nonminority	54	32	14	28	53	19	52	28	20
Minority	57	24	19	28	46	26	55	25	20
Specific Minorities:									
Black American	58	26	16	23	53	24	57	25	18
Spanish-speaking American	54	26	20	27	43	30	47	28	25
American Indian	57	21	22	39	38	23	59	20	21
Asian American	64	13	23	31.5	31.5	37	54	26	20
Publication Staff	62	30	8	27	61	12	60	27	13
Readers	53	30	17	20	57	23	51	27	22

Table 2 (con't.)
Opinion Questions (Percentages)

	Accurately Reflects Everyday School Life			Enjoy Reading		
	Yes	No	Don't Know	Yes, Read With Interest	Indifferent, Read With Little Interest	Don't Read It
Overall Survey	46	42	12	49	41	10
Non-minority	45	43	12	46	43	11
Minority	47	41	12	56	37	7
Specific Minorities:						
Black American	49	40	11	54	38	8
Spanish-speaking American	41	47	12	44	45	11
American Indian	45	41	14	62	32	6
Asian American	51	34	15	77	20	3
Publication Staff	49	43	8	64	33	3
Readers	45	42	13	46	43	11

five opinion questions. Also shown are comparisons of the distribution of answers between minority and nonminority students and comparison of the responses of the specific minority groups. The last two items on Table 2 compare the percent responses for those students on their publication staff and for the readers of the publication, i.e., the rest of the students.

It is interesting to note that among those students who express an opinion, over 50 percent are favorable about their publication except in the category of adequate coverage. There were 816 students who felt their publication failed to provide adequate coverage. These students were then asked to specify what areas needed more coverage. A clear cut majority, 55 percent, felt students' rights issues needed more coverage, with college and career-oriented subjects second at 43 percent. Table 3 gives the detailed breakdown of answers.

Table 3
Issues or Topics not Adequately Covered

	Percent
Students' rights issues	55
College and career-oriented subjects	43
National and international issues	37
Local community issues	32
Local educational issues	25
Other	12

The reasons cited by the 476 students for the publications' failure to be representative are listed in Table 4.

Table 4

	Percent
Publication represents only the views of the student staff	61
Staff are not permitted to deal with serious issues of concern to students	32
Other	22
Publication represents views of principal and administration	19
Publication represents views of faculty	18

By far the greatest complaint was that the publication reflected the student staff's personal point of view.

Table 2 also gives the distribution of opinions by specific

Table 5

Opinion Responses by Minority Composition of Schools (Percentages)

	Representative			Adequate Coverage			Good Impression			Accuracy			Enjoy Read		
	Yes	No	Don't Know	Yes	No	Don't Know	Yes	No	Don't Know	Yes	No	Don't Know	Yes	Indifferent	Don't Read
Minority School															
min.	64	18	18	29	45	26	59	22	19	52	34	14	66	30	4
nonmin.	56	35	9	31	57	12	47	38	15	44	45	9	46	47	7
Balanced School															
min.	29	50	21	12	62	26	60	21	19	33	54	13	41	53	6
nonmin.	66	26	8	28	55	17	58	27	15	53	39	8	61	33	6
Nonminority School															
min.	55	25	20	30	43	27	47	29	24	43	46	11	47	40	13
nonmin.	52	32	16	28	53	19	51	28	21	44	44	12	44	44	12

minorities. It is interesting to note that the thirty-nine Asian American students expressed a more favorable impression of their school publication than any other group. Also a greater proportion of these students actually read their publication than other groups.

Only the ninety-eight Spanish-speaking Americans in the survey express a majority dissatisfaction with the accuracy of their publications. This group also has the largest proportion of minority students who fail to read their publication.

Table 5 gives a breakdown of the student opinion based on the percent racial balance of their schools and also whether or not the students are minority members. In the balanced schools, minority students show a marked dissatisfaction with their school publication. Only in the category of the impression outside the school do these students express a favorable opinion. In the category of accuracy the students who are in the minority in their particular schools show dissatisfaction with their publication. In the balanced schools the minority students also show dissatisfaction about their publication. In terms of enjoyment the nonminority students in minority schools and the minority students in balanced schools do not read their publication with real interest. The 817 students who answered that they don't bother to read their publication or they read it with little interest were asked the reason for their lack of enjoyment. The following results were found:

Table 6
Reason for lack of enjoyment

	Percent
Subjects covered are not of interest	52
Publication is rather irrelevant to my concerns	43
Articles and editorials are written poorly or in an unappealing style	20
Some other reason	17
System of circulation is poor	13

This table would indicate that a wider range of topics should be covered. This result corresponds to the answers on topic adequacy given earlier.

A cross tabulation between the categories of enjoyment and the other opinion subjects in Table 7 reveals some interesting highlights. On the average 105 students who did

Table 7
Cross Tabulation (Percentage)

	Representative			Adequate Coverage			Good Impression			Accuracy		
	Yes	No	Don't Know	Yes	No	Don't Know	Yes	No	Don't Know	Yes	No	Don't Know
Read with real enjoyment	40	6	5	20	20	14	29	12	7	32	12	5
Read but with little interest	15	19	7	7	26	8	20	12	10	12	24	5
Don't bother to read	2	4	3	1	5	4	4	2	3	2	6	2

Note: There is a 1 percent roundoff error in some of the above figures.

not bother to read their publication expressed definite opinions about their publication. Except for the question about creating a good impression, these students were three to one dissatisfied with their publication. Of particular interest is that twenty-one of those students taking journalism and ten actually working on the publication do not even bother to read their publication. Seventeen of these journalism students and eight staff members attend balanced schools.

The questions on barriers to serving on the publication staff produced the greatest number of answers in the "don't know" category. Overall, 35 percent of those polled did not know if one must be taking journalism to work on their publication staff. Forty-four percent did not know if there were other barriers to working on the staff. If you examine the answers of the publication staff, a far greater awareness of existence or lack of barriers is found. Only 5 percent did not know about journalism course requirements and 13 percent did not know of other barriers. These results are:

(Percentages)	Must a student be enrolled in a journalism course to serve on the publication?			Are there any other barriers?		
	Yes	No	Don't Know	Yes	No	Don't Know
Publication Staff	48	47	5	24	63	13
Consumers	32	26	42	16	32	52

Of the students with definite knowledge more than 50 percent indicated enrollment in a journalism course was a definite requirement, but the majority indicated no other barriers existed. In Table 8 the distribution of other cited barriers are given.

This breakdown indicates that "clique control" is the biggest barrier. The fact a student is a member of a minority group does not in general prevent him from serving on the publication staff.

Journalism Students and Publication Staff

The 474 journalism or ex-journalism students were polled on specific questions related to their journalism courses.

Table 8

Other Barriers to Serving on Publication Staff
(based on 278 students)

	Percent
The publication tends to be controlled by one clique of students	36
A certain average is required	33
Other reasons	31
Students who disagree with the school administration tend to be excluded	28
Teacher favoritism is a factor	22
Minority groups tend to be excluded	16

Among this group were 128 minority members. The following is the distribution of answers on the single most important factor used in the selection of students for journalism courses. The major reason listed is interest of students.

	Percent
Interest of students	61
Don't know	10
Order of applications	9
Teachers' or administration's choice	8
Grades	7
Other	7

The single most important reason for the student taking the journalism course was:

	Percent
Learn journalism skills	38
I enjoy writing	35
No particular reason	16
I enjoy reading	3
Easy course	3
I enjoy the company of journalism students	3
I like the journalism teacher	2

The distribution of journalism course technical content was:

	Percent
All subjects below equally	39
Writing skills	38
Technical skills	12
Reporting skills	6
Editorial skills	5

The percent indicating that the following topics were discussed:

	Percent
Freedom of the press as it relates to student journalism	55
Censorship in general	45
Freedom of the press and the First Amendment in general	44
Role of the communications media in a democratic society	40
None of the above	24

The following responses were given by the 312 school publication staff for the indicated questions. There were 88 minority members in this group. The distribution of minority responses was the same as for all staff members.

Number of semesters of journalism taken

	Percent
None	13
One semester	17
Two semesters	39
Three semesters	3
Four or more semesters	28

"Are any written guidelines used to help staff decide what material is appropriate for school publications?"

	Percent
Yes	40
No	42
Don't know	18

"How is the editorial policy of the publication determined?"

	Percent
By students, with supervision of faculty adviser	58
Solely by students	18
By the faculty adviser	11
Other	7
By school publication	6

"Are you satisfied with your publication as presently established?

	Percent
Yes	45
No	47
No opinion	8

In addition, a comparison on the opinion questions of the second section of the survey was made between the consumer or reader of the school publication and those who publish it. The results are shown in Table 2. In general, the publication staffs had definite opinions about their publications. Except for topic adequacy they were considerably more favorable about their publication than the consumer. A larger percentage of the consumers expressed a "no opinion" response to these questions.

List of High Schools Participating in the Survey

Region I
Montclair High School
Montclair, New Jersey
Taylor Allderdice
  High School
Pittsburgh, Pennsylvania
Brockton High School
Brockton, Massachusetts
John Dewey High School
Brooklyn, New York
Kennebunkport High School
Kennebunkport, Maine
Long Beach High School
Long Beach, New York
South Philadelphia
  High School
Philadelphia, Pennsylvania

Region II
Pearl High School
Nashville, Tennessee
Parkdale High School
Riverdale, Maryland
Welch High School
Welch, West Virginia
Prestonsburg High School
Prestonsburg, Kentucky

Region III
Calloway High School
Jackson, Mississippi

Lower Richland
  High School
Columbia, South Carolina
John F. Kennedy
  High School
New Orleans, Louisiana
Miramar High School
Hollywood, Florida
Douglas High School
Atlanta, Georgia

Region IV
Hillsdale High School
Hillsdale, Michigan
Cass Tech. High School
Detroit, Michigan
Shortridge High School
Indianapolis, Indiana
Woodstock High School
Woodstock, Illinois
Lyons Township
  High School
LaGrange, Illinois
Washington High School
South Bend, Indiana
Roosevelt High School
Dayton, Ohio

Region V
South East High School
Wichita, Kansas

Norton High School
Norton, Kansas
Beaver Dam High School
Beaver Dam, Wisconsin
Webster Grove
  High School
St. Louis County, Missouri
West High School
Davenport, Iowa

Region VI
Valley High School
Sanders, Arizona
Alamo Heights
  High School
San Antonio, Texas
Crystal City High School
Crystal City, Texas
Memorial High School
San Antonio, Texas

Region VII
Palmer High School

Colorado Springs, Colorado
Box Elder High School
Box Elder, Montana
Kuna Senior High School
Kuna, Idaho

Region VIII
Washington High School
San Francisco, California
Toppenish High School
Toppenish, Washington
Oakland High School
Oakland, California
Churchill High School
Eugene, Oregon
Nathan Hale High School
Seattle, Washington
Mirabest High School
Palos Verdes, California
Santa Rosa High School
Santa Rosa, California

Student Survey Questionnaire

Section A: Preliminary Questions

Every student should fill out this section.
1. In which grade are you now?
  a. 9th grade ....☐
  b. 10th grade ....☐
  c. 11th grade ....☐
  d. 12th grade ....☐
2. Which sex are you?
  a. female ....☐
  b. male ....☐
3. Do you consider yourself to be a member of one of the
following minority groups: Black American; Mexican-American or Chicano; Latin American or Latino; Puerto Rican
American; American Indian or Native American; or Asian
American?
  a. yes ....☐
  b. no ....☐
If "no," go to question #5.

4. If "yes," which one?
    a. Black American .... ☐
    b. Mexican American or Chicano .... ☐
    c. Latin American or Latino .... ☐
    d. Puerto Rican American .... ☐
    e. American Indian or Native American .... ☐
    f. Asian American .... ☐

5. What are your educational or career plans after high school, if any? (Please check one response)
    a. undecided .... ☐
    b. college .... ☐
    c. get a job .... ☐
    d. other (please specify) .... ☐

Section B: General Questions

To be answered by every student participating in the survey.

1. What publications do students produce at your school? (Please check as many as apply)
    a. newspaper .... ☐
    b. magazine .... ☐
    c. alternative, officially sponsored publication ...... ☐
    d. other (Please specify) .... ☐

2. Is there a course in journalism offered at your school?
    a. yes .... ☐
    b. no .... ☐
    c. don't know .... ☐

3. Do you feel that the contents of your school's news publication (paper or magazine) are representative of the range of student opinion?
    a. yes .... ☐
    b. no .... ☐
    c. don't know, no opinion .... ☐

If "Yes" or "Don't know, no opinion," go to question #5.

4. If "No," why do you feel this way? (Please check as many as apply)
    a. The publication represents only the views of the students who produce it. .... ☐
    b. The publication represents the views of a faculty adviser, or of teachers generally. .... ☐
    c. The publication represents the views of the principal and school administration. .... ☐
    d. Student reporters and editors are not permitted to deal with serious issues of concern to students. ... ☐
    e. Other (please specify) .... ☐

5. What is the range of topics most frequently covered by your school's publication? (Please check as many as apply)
    a. school sports and extracurricular activities ...... ☐

b. school social news .... ☐
c. local educational problems and issues .... ☐
d. national and international issues .... ☐
e. local community issues .... ☐
f. other (please specify) ....,............... ☐

6. Do you feel that there are issues or topics which are not adequately covered by your school publication?

a. yes .... ☐
b. no .... ☐
c. don't know, no opinion .... ☐

If "No" or "Don't know," go to question #8.

7. If "Yes," what issues or topics are not adequately covered by your school publication? (Please check as many as apply)

a. local educational issues .... ☐
b. local community issues .... ☐
c. national and/or international issues .... ☐
d. students' rights issues .... ☐
c. college and career-oriented subjects .... ☐
f. other (please specify) .... ☐

8. Do you feel that your school publication is used to create a good impression of school life among parents and members of the local community?

u. yes .... ☐
b. no .... ☐
c. don't know, no opinion .... ☐

9. Do you feel that your school publication accurately reflects everyday school life?

a. yes .... ☐
b. no .... ☐
c. don't know, no opinion .... ☐

10. Do you enjoy reading your school publication?

a. yes; read it with real interest .... ☐
b. indifferent; read it but without great interest ..... ☐
c. no; don't usually bother to read it .... ☒

If "Yes," go to question #12.

11. If "No" or "Indifferent" why? (Please check as many as apply)

a. subjects covered are not interesting .... ☐
b. articles and editorials are written poorly or in an unappealing style .... ☐
c. publication is rather irrelevant to my concerns ... ☐
d. system of circulation is poor .... ☐
e. some other reason (please specify) .... ☐

12. Must a student be currently enrolled in a journalism course in order to serve on the publication staff?

a. yes .... ☐

    b. no ....□
    c. don't know ....□

13. Are there any other barriers to becoming involved in writing or producing your school's publication?

    a. yes ....□
    b. no ....□
    c. don't know ....□

If "No" or "Don't know," go on to question #15.

14. If "Yes," what are the barriers? (Please check as many as apply)

    a. a certain academic average is required ....□
    b. teacher favoritism is a factor ....□
    c. minority groups tend to be excluded ....□
    d. students who disagree with the school administration tend to be excluded ....□
    e. the publication tends to be controlled by one clique of students ....□
    f. other (please specify) ....□

_____

15. To the best of your knowledge, which (if any) of the following media are available to students at this school as part of school programs or activities? (Please check as many as apply)

    a. printing (as in news publication) by students ....□
    b. broadcasts by students via the public address system ....□
    c. radio broadcasts by students ....□
    d. production by students of educational T.V. programs ....□
    e. production by students of other video tape programs ....□
    f. film making by students ....□

16. Is there an "underground" newspaper distributed at your school?

    a. yes ....□
    b. no ....□
    c. don't know; not certain ....□

17. If "Yes," do you enjoy reading it? (Please check one response)

    a. no; don't read it or the school paper ....□
    b. no; prefer the school paper ....□
    c. yes; read it and the school paper ....□
    d. yes; enjoy the underground paper more than the school paper ....□

        Thank you very much for your valuable help in answering these questions.

Section C: Journalism or Ex-journalism Students Only

Please answer this section only if you are or have been enrolled in a journalism course at this school.

1. What is the single most important factor used in the selection of students for journalism courses? (Please check only one response)
   a. grades ....☐
   b. interest of the students themselves ....☐
   c. order of applications (first come; first served) ...☐
   d. teachers' or administration's choice ....☐
   e. some other factor; please specify ....☐
   _____
   f. don't know ....☐

2. What is the single most important reason for your taking the journalism course? (Please check only one response)
   a. I enjoy writing ....☐
   b. I enjoy reading the school paper ....☐
   c. I enjoy the company of journalism students .....☐
   d. It's a fairly easy course ....☐
   e. I wanted to learn the skills of journalism ......☐
   f. I like the journalism teacher ....☐
   g. no particular reason ....☐

3. Which one of the following areas of journalism receives the most attention in the course you are taking? (Please check only one response)
   a. skills necessary for media production (technical skills) ....☐
   b. writing skills ....☐
   c. investigative reporting skills ....☐
   d. editorial skills ....☐
   e. none of these more than any other ....☐

4. Which of the following topics are discussed in your journalism courses? (Please check as many as apply)
   a. freedom of the press and the First Amendment in general ....☐
   b. censorship in general ....☐
   c. freedom of the press as it relates to student journalism ....☐
   d. the role of the communications media in a democratic society ....☐
   e. none of the above ....☐

Thank you very much.

Section D: School News Publications Staff Only

Please answer this section only if you are <u>involved</u> in the publication of a school news publication.

1. How many semesters of journalism have you taken at this school, including this current semester?
    a. none .... ☐
    b. 1 semester .... ☐
    c. 2 semesters .... ☐
    d. 3 semesters .... ☐
    e. 4 semesters or more .... ☐

2. Are any written guidelines used to help the staff (and/or the faculty adviser) in deciding what material is appropriate for the school publications?
    a. yes .... ☐
    b. no .... ☐
    c. don't know; not certain .... ☐

3. How is the editorial policy of the publication determined? (Please check only one response)
    a. solely by students .... ☐
    b. by students, with supervision of a faculty adviser .. ☐
    c. by the faculty adviser .... ☐
    d. by the school administration .... ☐
    e. other; please specify .... ☐

4. Are you satisfied with your publication as presently established?
    a. yes .... ☐
    b. no .... ☐
    c. no opinion .... ☐

5. If "No," why? (Please check as many as apply)
    a. it is too restricted in topics covered .... ☐
    b. there is excessive faculty or administration censorship .... ☐
    c. inadequate facilities .... ☐
    d. lack of interest and support by faculty and/or administration .... ☐
    e. the staff is dominated by one clique or individual .... ☐
    f. lack of interest and support by students .... ☐
    g. minority viewpoints are not represented .... ☐
    h. other; please specify .... ☐

Thank you very much.

3. Faculty Adviser Survey Analysis

(Survey conducted April 26–May 16, 1973)

From lists provided by the Journalism Education Association and the National Council of the Teachers of English, 700 faculty advisers and 700 journalism teachers were randomly chosen to be part of a nationwide study of the problems and potentials of high school journalism. Though these roles often overlap in the schools, two distinct surveys were mailed. On certain related questions there are obvious parallel responses received, but the faculty advisers' survey was primarily directed to the school publication and the journalism teachers survey to the journalism curriculum in the school.

Based on adviser and teacher response to preliminary question number 3, the schools are categorized as nonminority, balanced, or minority schools. The latter category means the study body is predominantly minority. In the journalism teachers survey the breakdown went 84 percent nonminority schools, 9 percent evenly balanced, and 7 percent predominantly minority. Similarly, the faculty advisers survey offered 86 percent nonminority, 8 percent evenly balanced, and 6 percent predominantly minority.

The data contained in the 388 advisers' surveys returned can be categorized as opinion material as well as factual material. The factual material includes responses concerning: 1) the adviser's background, 2) requirements for students serving on their publication, 3) any relations with scholastic press associations, and 4) the types of student media and the frequency and process of publication. The opinion poll includes the following three questions:

1. Is your publication representative of student opinion?
2. Does your publication adequately cover topics of interest?
3. Is your publication used for public relations outside the school?

The following table gives the results of the faculty advisers opinion poll on these three questions.

Percent

	Representative			Adequate			Public Relations		
	Yes	No	Don't Know	Yes	No	Don't Know	Yes	No	No Opinion
Minority schools	70	26	4	14	82	4	52	44	4
Balanced schools	88	12	0	32	58	10	66	31	3
Nonminority schools	68	24	8	29	64	7	49	46	5

These results correspond to those of the student survey in that the faculty advisers consider their papers representative of student opinion and also that their papers are public relations vehicles. As in the student survey the advisers also consider the range of topics not adequate.

Of the eighty-five advisers who felt their publication was not representative the following distribution of reasons are given.

	Percent
Publication represents only the views of the student staff	64
Other	26
Student reporters and editors are not permitted to deal with issues of concern to students	19
Publication represents only the views of the Administration	14
Publication represents only the views of the faculty adviser	13

Again the most prevalent reason for the publication not being representative is the same as in the student survey. The range of topics most frequently covered by the school publications are given below.

	Percent		
	Non-minority	Balanced	Minority
Sports and extracurricular	93	100	88
Local educational problems and issues	66	78	63
School social news	65	53	83
Local community news	49	69	33
National-international issues	36	47	13

In comparison to the student survey the advisers in non-minority and balanced schools indicated that the topics of local educational problems and issues occurred more frequently than school social news. However, in the minority schools the pattern follows that of the student survey. The percentage of advisers listing each topic is consistently higher than in the student survey.

There were 237 advisers who indicated that topics were not adequately covered. The following table gives the items not adequately covered.

	Non-minority	Percent Balanced	Minority
National-International news	58	39	50
Local community issues	52	33	20
Controversial student issues	51	44	23
Local educational issues	48	11	67
College or career-oriented subjects	43	22	39
Other	5	6	6

Faculty Advisers' Background

The faculty advisers are found to have the following backgrounds.

	Non-minority	Percent Balanced	Minority
Working experience	57	56	33
Journalism courses in college over 12 hours	57	56	42
Journalism workshop	44	69	54
Journalism courses in college under 12 hours	27	28	88
No background	18	18	38
Other	12	6	13

These responses indicate the advisers in minority schools have fewer qualifications for the position than the others surveyed. There is a larger percentage of advisers attending workshops in the balanced and minority categories.

The survey indicates the following reasons why the advisers hold their position.

| | Percent | | |
| | Non- | Bal- | Mi- |
	minority	anced	nority
Asked to take position	46	54	72
Applied when hired	41	23	28
Applied while teaching	10	23	0
None of the above	3	0	0

The most interesting result here is that in balanced and particularly in minority schools the majority of advisers were asked to take their position.

It was found that the faculty advisers were able to accommodate their duties as follows:

| | Percent | | |
| | Non- | Bal- | Mi- |
	minority	anced	nority
Most work in class time	31	40	32
Carry a full load but received extra salary	31	27	9
Relieved of some teaching load	25	23	50
Carry a full load and volunteer your time for publication	7	3	5
None of the above	6	7	4

The faculty advisers were asked to indicate what requirements were needed to serve on the publication staff, credit received for such work, and restrictions and guidelines given the students.

"How many semesters of journalism are required to join the paper?"

| | Percent | | |
| | Non- | Bal- | Mi- |
	minority	anced	nority
None	56	53	70
One	23	16	21
Two	21	28	9
Three or more	0	3	0

"Must a student be currently enrolled in a journalism course in order to serve on a publication staff?"

| | Percent | | |
| | Non- | Bal- | Mi- |
	minority	anced	nority
Yes	42	54	30
No	58	46	70

"Is credit granted for work done on publications?"

	Percent		
	Non-minority	Balanced	Minority
Yes	69	84	76
No	31	16	34

These results indicate less stringent requirements for publication staff in minority schools.

Eighty-one percent of those polled indicated that their editorial policy was set by the students with supervision of the faculty adviser. To the corresponding question on the student survey, 58 percent of the student journalists gave the same response. But responses to the following questions indicates "supervision by faculty advisers" is fairly extensive.

"Who in school has final right of approval of articles to be published in the paper?"

	Percent		
	Non-minority	Balanced	Minority
Publications adviser	64	87	74
Student editor	18	0	17
School administration	18	13	9

"Do you place any limitations on subject areas covered in the paper?"

	Percent		
	Non-minority	Balanced	Minority
Yes	36	45	44
No	64	55	56

"Does school administration place any limitations on subject areas?"

	Percent		
	Non-minority	Balanced	Minority
Yes	29	33	35
No	71	67	65

The percentage of advisers indicating their publication staff belongs to any scholastic press association is as follows:

	Percent
Nonminority	81
Balanced	97
Minority	83

To the questions "Has the paper been entered in any contests?" and "Has the paper won any commendations or awards?" the following responses were obtained:

| | Entered | | | Won | | |
| | | | Don't | | | Don't |
	Yes	No	Know	Yes	No	Know
Nonminority	79	15	6	74	15	11
Balanced	88	9	3	88	6	6
Minority	82	18	0	82	14	4

These are significant responses since it would tend to indicate advisers in all three types of schools feel it is important to enter these contests and appear to be successful.

The faculty advisers responded that the following types of media were available in their schools:

| | Percent | | |
	Non-minority	Bal-anced	Mi-nority
Printing by students	45	47	46
Filmmaking	45	25	20
Broadcasts by students (PA)	42	38	29
Production by students of video tape	40	31	12
Radio broadcasts by students	21	19	8
None of the above	18	28	33
Programs of educational TV	11	9	21

The balanced schools have far less filmmaking media than nonminority schools, and the minority schools have significantly less filmmaking, videotape, and radio broadcasts than the other schools. Thirty-three percent of the minority advisers indicated they had none of the listed media available in their schools. This result is suspect as these are supposed to be faculty advisers to a publication. "Printing by students" was probably misinterpreted to mean actual mechanical printing of the paper.

The types of printing used for school publication are

given in the next table. Offset is by far the most commonly used method. Minority schools do use mimeographing more frequently than the other categories of schools.

	Percent Non-minority	Bal-anced	Mi-nority
Offset	81	74	77
Mimeographing	9	13	18
Flatbed	8	13	5
Rotary	2	0	0

As shown below, in nonminority schools 78 percent publish every two weeks or monthly, with the greatest portion publishing every two weeks. This trend is reversed in balanced schools with the majority publishing monthly. In the minority schools, however, it should be noted that the publication is more likely to be published less frequently than in other schools.

Frequency of Publication	Percent Non-minority	Bal-anced	Mi-nority
Every 2 weeks	45	28	22
Monthly	33	50	48
Weekly	13	13	8
Less than monthly	8	9	22
More than once per week	1	0	0

The distribution of publication size is:

	Percent Non-minority	Bal-anced	Mi-nority
1–4 pages	44	38	48
5–10 pages	46	56	48
Over 10 pages	10	6	4

The minority schools are more likely to have smaller publications. The advisers in all categories indicated that on the average 27 percent actually did their own printing and 73 percent farmed the printing out.

The following table gives methods of funding the school publication.

	Percent		
	Non-minority	Bal-anced	Mi-nority
Proceeds from sale or advertising	65	75	58
Fund from school	42	41	33
Mixture	19	25	29
Fund raising efforts among students/community	15	25	33
None	3	3	1

In minority schools the paper is less likely to receive school funds and more likely to depend on fund-raising drives.

Faculty Adviser Questionnaire

Preliminary Information

1. Which of the following approximately describes your school's setting?
   - a. city, with a population of 150,000 or more ...... ☐
   - b. smaller city or suburb, with a population of less than 150,000 .... ☐
   - c. rural or consolidated school district .... ☐
2. How many students are enrolled at your school?
   - a. 1 to 1000 .... ☐
   - b. 1001 to 2000 .... ☐
   - c. 2001 to 3000 .... ☐
   - d. 3001 to 4000 .... ☐
   - e. 4001 to 5000 .... ☐
3. What is the approximate minority/nonminority breakdown of the school student population?
   - a. predominantly minority .... ☐
   - b. predominantly nonminority .... ☐
   - c. roughly even balance .... ☐
4. Which of the following categories fits your school with respect to journalism courses provided and student publications? (Please ignore other publications such as yearbooks)
   - a. there is a journalism course, and a newspaper is published .... ☐
   - b. there is a journalism course, and a news magazine is published .... ☐
   - c. there is a journalism course, and both a newspaper and a news magazine are published .... ☐
   - d. no journalism course, but a newspaper is published .... ☐
   - e. no journalism course, but a news magazine is published .... ☐

f. <u>no</u> journalism course, but <u>both</u> a newspaper <u>and</u> a
news magazine are published . . . . □

General Questions

1. Which of the following media are available to students at
this school as part of school programs or activities? (Please
check as many as apply)
  a. printing by students . . . . □
  b. broadcasts by students via the public address sys-
    tem . . . . □
  c. radio broadcasts by students . . . . □
  d. production by students of educational TV pro-
    grams . . . . □
  e. production by students of other video tape pro-
    grams . . . . □
  f. filmmaking by students . . . . □
  g. none of the above . . . . □
2. What publications do the students produce? (Please check
as many as apply)
  a. newspaper . . . . □
  b. magazine . . . . □
  c. other news publication . . . . □
  d. other non-news publication . . . . □
For the following questions, if there are both a magazine and
a news publication at the school, please answer in reference
to the newspaper. If only one publication (other than a yearbook) is produced please answer in reference to that publication. Please do not consider yearbooks.
3. How frequently is the publication published? (Please
check only one response)
  a. more than once per week . . . . □
  b. weekly . . . . □
  c. bi-weekly . . . . □
  d. monthly . . . . □
  e. less often than monthly . . . . □
4. How many pages does the publication normally have?
(Please check only one response)
  a. 1–4 pages . . . . □
  b. 5–10 pages . . . . □
  c. more than 10 pages . . . . □
5. How is the publication printed? (Please check only one
response)
  a. mimeograph . . . . □
  b. flatbed . . . . □
  c. rotary . . . . □
  d. offset . . . . □

6. Is the publication printed within the school?
   a. yes .... ☐
   b. no .... ☐
7. How many semesters of journalism are required for a student to join the publication staff? (Please check only one response)
   a. none .... ☐
   b. 1 semester .... ☐
   c. 2 semesters .... ☐
   d. 3 or more semesters .... ☐
8. Must a student be currently enrolled in a journalism course in order to serve on the publication staff?
   a. yes .... ☐
   b. no .... ☐
If "Yes," go to question #10.
9. If "No," how many students on the publication staff this semester are not enrolled in a journalism course? (Please check only one response)
   a. none .... ☐
   b. less than half the staff members .... ☐
   c. approximately half the staff members .... ☐
   d. more than half the staff members .... ☐
   e. all the staff members .... ☐
10. Is credit granted for work done on the publication?
   a. yes .... ☐
   b. no .... ☐
11. How is the publication funded? (Please check as many as apply)
   a. funds from school administration .... ☐
   b. proceeds from sales and advertising .... ☐
   c. fund-raising efforts among students and/or community .... ☐
   d. a mixture of the above .... ☐
   e. none of the above .... ☐
12. Do you feel that the contents of your school's publication are representative of the range of student opinion?
   a. yes .... ☐
   b. no .... ☐
   c. no opinion .... ☐
If "Yes" or "No opinion," go to question #14.
13. If "No," why do you feel this way? (Please check as many as apply)
   a. The publication represents only the views of the student staff .... ☐
   b. The publication represents the views of the faculty adviser .... ☐
   c. The publication represents the views of the principal and school administration .... ☐

d. Student reporters and editors are not permitted to deal with issues of concern to students .... □
e. Other; please specify .... □

14. What is the range of topics most frequently covered by the school's publication? (Please check as many as apply)
    a. school sports and extra-curricular activities ..... □
    b. school social news .... □
    c. local education problems and issues .... □
    d. national and international issues .... □
    e. local community issues .... □
    f. other; please specify .... □

15. Do you feel that there are issues or topics which are not adequately covered by your school publications?
    a. yes .... □
    b. no .... □
    c. don't know, no opinion .... □
If "No" or "No opinion," go to question #17.

16. If "Yes," what issues or topics are not adequately covered by your school publication? (Please check as many as apply)
    a. local educational issues .... □
    b. local community issues .... □
    c. national and/or international issues .... □
    d. controversial student activities .... □
    e. college and career-oriented subjects .... □
    f. other; please specify .... □

17. Do you feel that the publication is used as a public relations sheet for the school?
    a. yes .... □
    b. no .... □
    c. no opinion .... □

18. Are any written guidelines used to help the faculty adviser and/or student staff in deciding what material is appropriate for the school publication?
    a. yes .... □
    b. no .... □
    c. not certain .... □

19. If "Yes," by whom are these guidelines set? (Please check only one response)
    a. within the school, by faculty .... □
    b. within the school, by administration .... □
    c. by county or local Board of Education .... □
    d. by State Board of Education .... □
    e. elsewhere; please specify .... □

20. Who determines the editorial policy of the publication? (Please check only one response)
    a. solely by students .... □
    b. by students, with supervision of a faculty adviser .. □
    c. by the faculty advisor .... □

    d. by the school administration .... ☐
    e. other; please specify .... ☐

21. Who in the school has final right of approval of articles to be published in the paper? (Please check only one response)

    a. the student editor .... ☐
    b. the publications adviser .... ☐
    c. the school administration .... ☐
    d. none of the above .... ☐

22. Do you place any limitation on the <u>subject areas</u> covered in the paper?

    a. yes .... ☐
    b. no .... ☐

23. Does the administration place any limitation on the <u>subject areas</u> covered by the paper?

    a. yes .... ☐
    b. no .... ☐

24. Does the publication staff belong to any scholastic press associations in the following categories? (Please check as many as apply)

    a. local .... ☐
    b. state .... ☐
    c. national .... ☐
    d. other .... ☐
    e. none of the above .... ☐

25. Has the paper ever been entered in any contests?

    a. yes .... ☐
    b. no .... ☐
    c. don't know, uncertain .... ☐

26. Has the paper ever won any commendations or awards?

    a. yes .... ☐
    b. no .... ☐
    c. don't know, uncertain .... ☐

27. What preparation did you have for the position of faculty publications adviser? (Please check as many as apply)

    a. no background specifically in journalism .... ☐
    b. journalism workshops .... ☐
    c. journalism courses in college—up to 12 semester hrs .... ☐
    d. journalism courses in college—more than 12 semester hrs .... ☐
    e. working experience in journalism .... ☐
    f. other; please specify .... ☐

28. How did you come to be faculty advisor in this school? (Please check only one response)

    a. you applied for the position when you were hired .... ☐

    b. you applied for the position while teaching another
       subject ....□
    c. you were asked to take the position ....□
    d. none of the above ....□

29. How is your responsibility as faculty adviser accommodated into your teaching schedule? (Please check only one response)

    a. you are relieved of some teaching load ....□
    b. you carry a full teaching load apart from the publication work, but receive extra salary ....□
    c. most of your work on the publication is done during class time ....□
    d. you carry a full teaching load and volunteer your time for publication work ....□
    e. none of the above ....□

4. Journalism Teachers Survey Analysis

(Survey conducted April 26–May 16, 1973)

From lists provided by the Journalism Education Association and the National Council of Teachers of English, 700 journalism teachers were selected for a crucial part of a national study to determine the problems and potentials of high school journalism. Of those selected, 363 returned the questionnaire. The journalism teachers were found to teach in the following types of schools: 84 percent non-minority schools, 9 percent evenly balanced and 7 percent in predominantly minority schools.

The journalism teachers were found to have the following background:

	Non-minority	Percent Balanced	Minority
Working experience in journalism	57	58	46
Journalism courses in college; more than 12 semester hours	48	42	38
Journalism workshops	42	55	50
Journalism courses in college; less than 12 semester hours	24	36	4
Other	12	7	17
No background	10	3	33

202 CAPTIVE VOICES

This table shows 33 percent of the teachers in minority schools have no journalism background, but 50 percent have attended workshops.

The journalism teachers were found to have obtained their positions in the following manner:

	Non-minority	Percent Bal-anced	Mi-nority
Applied for position when hired	49	38	24
Asked to take class	32	45	76
Applied while teaching other subjects	14	17	0
None of the above	5	0	0

In minority schools the majority of journalism teachers, 76 percent, were asked to take their classes.

Of particular interest were the results of how outside sources—i.e., universities and the commercial press—contributed to the high school journalism classes. The following results were obtained.

Contribution by University Journalism Departments to Journalism Classes

	Non-minority	Percent Bal-anced	Mi-nority
Workshop sessions	60	68	50
No visible contributions	30	23	38
Materials, teachers' aids	24	32	29
Guest speakers	22	23	8
Other help	19	26	13
Courses and curriculum	10	13	17

The predominant contribution by university journalism departments is to hold workshop sessions. Thirty-eight percent of the minority school teachers indicated no contribution.

Contribution by Commercial Press to Journalism Classes

	Non-minority	Percent Bal-anced	Mi-nority
Publication of student articles in local press	54	39	25
Guest speakers	49	58	33

No visible contribution	25	16	42
Scholarships	23	16	8
Workshop sessions	19	23	25
Internships	7	7	8

A high percentage of teachers in minority schools, 42 percent, felt that the commercial press made no visible contribution to their classes.

The following information from the survey was learned about the courses offered in the schools.

The distribution of content in the journalism courses was:

	Non-minority	Percent Balanced	Minority
All the below items equal	42	48	29
Writing skills	41	39	37
Media production	9	13	13
Investigative reporting	7	0	13
Editorial skills	1	0	8

The distribution of number of semesters of journalism offered was as follows:

	Non-minority	Percent Balanced	Minority
4 or more semesters	49	68	46
2 semesters	30	22	38
1 semester	15	10	12
3 semesters	6	0	4

This table indicates that the greater percentage of all the schools offer at least two years of journalism courses.

Number of Students Enrolled in Any One Semester

	Non-minority	Percent Balanced	Minority
1–25	42	32	58
26–50	28	39	25
51–75	15	13	13
75–100	10	13	0
Over 100	5	3	4

In minority schools fewer students are enrolled in journalism class than in the nonminority and balanced schools.

The single most important factor used in the selection of students for journalism courses was as follows:

	Percent		
	Non-minority	Bal-anced	Mi-nority
Interest of students	83	87	71
Some other factor	5	0	0
Order of applications	4	0	13
Grades	4	10	0
Teacher's choice	3	3	12
Don't Know	1	0	4

In the student survey 61 percent of the students indicated that "interest of students" was the prime reason for selection of students. However, a larger proportion of journalism teachers give this reason.

The following items were discussed:

	Percent		
	Non-minority	Bal-anced	Mi-nority
Censorship in general	83	84	79
Freedom of the press/First Amendment	80	84	67
Freedom of the press as it relates to student journalism	84	90	79
Role of media in democracy	80	81	71
None of the above	4	—	13

These results would indicate that a great majority of the journalism teachers discuss these items. However, on the student survey only 55 percent indicated the lead item was covered.

"Do you feel that the student publication in your school provides an adequate outlet for your students' interest in journalism?"

	Percent		
	Non-minority	Bal-anced	Mi-nority
Yes	77	79	62
No	20	17	28
Don't Know	3	4	10

"How would you assess ability range of your journalism students?"

	Percent		
	Non-minority	Balanced	Minority
Diverse mixture	62	61	79
Mostly high achieving	35	39	17
Mostly low achieving	3	0	4

"How would you assess motivation of journalism students toward journalism class activities?"

	Percent		
	Non-minority	Balanced	Minority
Diverse mixture	51	41	81
High motivation	45	55	14
Low motivation	3	4	5

Journalism Teacher Questionnaire

1. What is the single most important factor used in the selection of students for journalism courses? (Please check only one response)
   a. grades ....□
   b. interest of the students themselves ....□
   c. order of applications (first come; first served) ....□
   d. teachers' or administration's choice ....□
   e. some other factor; please specify .....•........□
   f. don't know ....□
2. What contributions to these classes are made by university journalism departments, either independently or via H.S.P.A.'s? (Please check as many as apply)
   a. guest speakers ....□
   b. materials, teacher aids ....□
   c. courses and/or curricula ....□
   d. workshop sessions ....□
   e. other help or advice ....□
   f. no visible contributions ....□
3. What contributions to journalism classes are made by the commercial press? (Please check as many as apply)
   a. guest speakers ....□
   b. funds for materials, etc. ....□
   c. workshop sessions ....□
   d. publication of students' articles in the local press ....□
   e. internships ....□

f. scholarships ....☐
g. no visible contributions ....☐

4. How many semesters or equivalent courses of journalism are offered at your school? (Please check only one response)
    a. 1 semester ....☐
    b. 2 semesters ....☐
    c. 3 semesters ....☐
    d. 4 or more semesters ....☐

5. Approximately how many students are enrolled in journalism in any one semester? (Please check only one response)
    a. 1–25 students ....☐
    b. 26–50 students ....☐
    c. 51–75 students ....☐
    d. 76–100 students ....☐
    e. over 100 students ....☐

6. Which one of the following areas receives most attention in the journalism course or courses used? (Please check only one response)
    a. media production skills ....☐
    b. writing skills ....☐
    c. investigative reporting skills ....☐
    d. editorial skills ....☐
    e. none of these more than any other ....☐

7. Which of the following subjects are discussed as part of the course? (Please check as many as apply)
    a. freedom of the press and the First Amendment in general ....☐
    b. censorship in general ....☐
    c. freedom of the press as it relates to student journalism ....☐
    d. the role of the communications media in a democratic society ....☐
    e. none of the above ....☐

8. How would you assess the ability range of journalism students? (Please check only one response)
    a. a diverse mixture ....☐
    b. mostly high achieving ....☐
    c. mostly low achieving ....☐

9. How would you assess the motivation of journalism students toward journalism class activities? (Please check only one response)
    a. a diverse mixture ....☐
    b. mostly high motivation ....☐
    c. mostly low motivation ....☐

10. What preparation did you have to teach journalism in particular? (Please check as many as apply)
    a. no background specifically in journalism ....☐
    b. journalism workshops ....☐

    c. journalism courses in college: up to 12 semester
       hrs ....☐
    d. journalism courses in college: more than 12
       semester hrs ....☐
    e. working experience in journalism ....☐
    f. other; please specify ....☐
11. How did you come to be teaching journalism in this
school? (Please check only one response)
    a. you applied for a position as a journalism teacher
      when you were hired ....☐
    b. you applied for the position while teaching another
      subject ....☐
    c. you were asked to take the journalism class .....☐
    d. none of the above ....☐
12. Do you feel that the student publication (newspaper,
news magazine, etc.) in your school provides an adequate
outlet for your students' interest in journalism?
    a. yes ....☐
    b. no ....☐
    c. don't know, no opinion ....☐
If you answered "Yes" or "Don't know," stop here. If you
answered "No," go on to the next question.
13. If not, why not? (Please check as many as apply)
    a. coverage of subject matter is unduly restricted ...☐
    b. school policy does not encourage full presentation
      of students' views and opinions ....☐
    c. format is dull and uninteresting ....☐
    d. facilities are inadequate to publication needs ....☐
    e. other reason; please specify ....☐
       Thank you very much for your valuable help
      in answering these questions.

5. Managing Editor Survey Analysis

(Survey conducted April 26–May 16, 1973)

From lists of U.S. daily newspapers published in *Editor
and Publisher*, a random sample of 465 managing editors
was selected for a crucial part of a national survey to determine the problems and potential of high school journal-

ism and its relationship with the commercial press. One
hundred and eighty usable survey forms were returned.

The managing editors were distributed as follows: 63
percent from towns of less than 50,000 population, 21 percent from towns of between 50,000 and 150,000 population. The following table gives the distribution average
daily circulation of the newspapers.

Number of Newspapers	Percent
5,000–25,000	54
25,000–100,000	26
1–5,000	11
100,000–300,000	7
more than 300,000	2

These numbers reflect the fact that most of the editors
surveyed were from smaller towns. Thirty-nine percent of
the papers belong to newspaper chains, 61 percent are
independent.

The number of professional journalists on the staffs were
as follows:

	Percent
1–10	48
11–25	25
26–50	14
More than 50	13

The years of experience of the managing editors is as
follows:

Years experience of editor as a professional journalist	Percent
21–30	30
11–20	28
more than 30	22
6–10	12
0–5	8

Eighty percent of the editors have had more than eleven
years experience in journalism.

It was found that 98 percent or 177 editors indicated

there were high school newspapers or other media in their area. Of these high schools 86 percent indicated they had contact with the publication staff. The following distribution shows the type of involvement:

	Percent
Student articles published in their paper	70
Periodic consultations with students or teachers	62
Student interns on your newspaper	47
Workshop sessions or lectures	46
Award programs	32
Scholarships for students	28
Funds or equipment supplied for student use	24

These percentages would indicate a high degree of involvement by the managing editors; however, journalism teachers gave much lower figures. Only 54 percent of them indicated the leading item, with the other items to a much lesser extent. Fifty-six percent of the editors indicated they attempted to arrange further contact between their organizations and school journalists. The following barriers were indicated:

	Percent
Lack of interest among teachers or school administrators	48
Lack of funds or time available	41
Lack of interest in students	33
None of other statements	21
Lack of talent among students	15

The 44 percent who indicated they did not attempt to make further contact with high school journalism gave the following reasons:

	Percent
Have no facilities for training high school students	51
None of the stated answers	44
Have no money available to use for high school students	33
Have no confidence in high school students' abilities in professional setting	0

Ninety-three percent of the editors felt that high school journalism was useful in introducing students to the idea of journalism as a career; 49 percent indicated it was useful training for future careers in professional journalism; and 46 percent felt it provided a forum for discussion within the school.

Sixty-six editors, or 37 percent, felt high school journalism is currently of little value. Fifty-nine percent of these indicated reasonable changes would make high school journalism of value. This figure of 66 editors answering the question makes suspect the results of responses in the preceding paragraph. Obviously, these editors do not consider introducing students to journalism to be of great value.

"Do you believe that minority students in your area have equal access to journalism in high school?"

	Percent
Yes	76
No	6
Uncertain	18

"Have you talked to any teachers or students in high schools in your area about minority access problems in high school journalism?"

	Percent
Yes	13
No	87

Although 76 percent of the editors felt that there are no barriers to minority students, only 13 percent had discussed the matter with teachers or students. This makes suspect the figure of 76 percent and the basis the editors had for indicating minority students had equal access.

First Amendment Issues

"Are students in most schools in your area permitted to exercise First Amendment rights in the production of school publications?"

	Percent
Yes	26
No	28
Uncertain	46

"Have you discussed First Amendment rights for high school students with any teachers or students from high schools in your area?"

	Percent
Yes	35
No	65

"Do you consider that First Amendment rights *should* apply to high school students producing school publications?"

	Percent
Yes	35
No	10
Under certain conditions	52
No opinion	3

"If other than 'yes,' are students in most high schools in your area allowed enough editorial freedom in choosing the content of their publications?" (only 117 should answer but 126 did)

	Percent
Yes	44
No	10
Uncertain	46

"Are you aware of the recent court decision in favor of high school students in censorship cases, e.g., *Tinker v. Des Moines*, etc.?"

	Percent
Yes	43
No	57

"Do you think school teachers and administrators in your community are aware of such decisions?"

	Percent
Yes	7
No	48
Uncertain	45

"If 'yes,' do you think they act in accordance with the First Amendment when decisions are necessary on content of school publications?"

	Percent
Yes	20
No	12
Uncertain	68

"Do you believe that high school students are aware
of the importance of a free and vocal press in their
communities?"

	Percent
Yes	30
No	36
Uncertain	34

"Do you believe that high school students are aware
of the importance of a free and vocal press in their
schools?"

	Percent
Yes	25
No	30
Uncertain	45

Of the above questions with an "uncertain" answer available, 41 percent of the editors answered uncertain on the
average. The result would appear to indicate that despite
considerable contact with high school journalism, the editors are unaware of and unclear about the application of
First Amendment issues in high school publications.

Editor Questionnaire

Information derived through this survey will be totally anonymous, and will be used for statistical purposes only.
Please answer each question by checking the <u>box</u> opposite
the appropriate response.
1. Which of the following best describes the size of the town
or city where your newspaper is published?
    a. city, with a population of 150,000 or more ......☐
    b. smaller city or suburb, with a population between
       50,000 and 150,000 ....☐
    c. smaller town, with a population of less than
       50,000 ....☐
2. What is the average daily circulation of the newspaper?
    a. 1–5,000 ....☐
    b. 5,000–25,000 ....☐
    c. 25,000–100,000 ....☐
    d. 100,000–300,000 ....☐
    e. more than 300,000 ....☐
3. How many professional journalists are on your staff?
    a. 1–10 ....☐
    b. 11–25 ....☐
    c. 26–50 ....☐
    d. more than 50 ....☐

4. Which of the following applies to your organization?
      a. member of a newspaper chain ....☐
      b. independent publication ....☐

5. How many years have you worked as a professional journalist?
      a. 0–5 ....☐
      b. 6–10 ....☐
      c. 11–20 ....☐
      d. 21–30 ....☐
      e. more than 30 ....☐

6. Are there school newspapers or other media in high schools in your area?
      a. yes ....☐
      b. no ....☐
      c. uncertain ....☐

7. Do you have any contact with these media or people working with or in them?
      a. yes ....☐
      b. no ....☐

8. If "Yes," what kind of involvement do you have with them? (Please check as many as apply)
      a. student interns on your newspaper ....☐
      b. student articles published in your paper ......☐
      c. scholarships for students ....☐
      d. funds or equipment supplied for student use ....☐
      e. workshop sessions or lectures ....☐
      f. award programs ....☐
      g. periodic consultations with students or teachers ..☐

9. Have you attempted to arrange further contact between your organization and school journalists?
      a. yes ....☐
      b. no ....☐

10. If "Yes," have you encountered any of the following barriers to further involvement? (Please check as many as apply)
      a. lack of interest among students ....☐
      b. lack of interest among teachers or school administrators ....☐
      c. lack of talent among students ....☐
      d. lack of funds or time available to arrange a program ....☐
      e. none of the above ....☐

11. If "No," why do you not seek involvement with high school students? (Please check as many as apply)
      a. have no facilities for training high school students ....☐
      b. have no money available to use for high school students ....☐

    c. have no confidence in high school students' abilities in professional setting .... □
    d. none of the above .... □

12. Is there value in high school journalism? (Please check as many as apply)
    a. useful training for future careers in professional journalism .... □
    b. useful in introducing students to the idea of journalism as a career .... □
    c. significant as a forum for discussion within the school .... □
    d. insignificant in all these respects .... □

13. If you believe high school journalism currently is of little value, do you think there are reasonable changes which would make it valuable?
    a. yes .... □
    b. no .... □
    c. uncertain .... □
If "Yes," please elaborate _____
_____

14. Are students in most schools in your area permitted to exercise First Amendment rights in the production of school publications?
    a. yes .... □
    b. no .... □
    c. uncertain .... □

15. Have you discussed First Amendment rights for high school students with any teachers or students from high schools in your area?
    a. yes .... □
    b. no .... □

16. Do you consider that First Amendment rights should apply to high school students producing school publications? (Please check only one response)
    a. yes .... □
    b. no .... □
    c. under certain conditions .... □
    d. no opinion .... □

17. If other than "Yes," are students in most high schools in your area allowed enough editorial freedom in choosing the content of their publications?
    a. yes .... □
    b. no .... □
    c. uncertain .... □

18. Are you aware of the recent court decision in favor of high school students in censorship cases, e.g., *Tinker v. Des Moines,* etc.?
    a. yes .... □

b. no .... ☐

19. Do you think school teachers and administrators in your community are aware of such decisions?

a. yes .... ☐
b. no .... ☐
c. uncertain .... ☐

20. If "Yes," do you think they act in accordance with the First Amendment when decisions are necessary on contents of school publications?

a. yes .... ☐
b. no .... ☐
c. uncertain .... ☐

21. Do you believe that minority students in your area have equal access to journalism in high schools?

a. yes .... ☐
b. no .... ☐
c. uncertain .... ☐

22. Have you talked to any teachers or students in high schools in your area about minority access problems in high school journalism?

a. yes .... ☐
b. no .... ☐

23. Do you believe that high school students are aware of the importance of a free and vocal press in their *communities*?

a. yes .... ☐
b. no .... ☐
c. uncertain .... ☐

24. Do you believe that high school students are aware of the importance of a free and vocal press in their *schools*?

a. yes .... ☐
b. no .... ☐
c. uncertain .... ☐

Your comments will be appreciated about the questionnaire or high school journalism in general.

6. Content Analysis

July 27, 1973

Purpose

Content analysis of nearly 300 high school newspapers was undertaken by Commission staff to provide further information on the role of the student newspaper in the schools. In addition, the analysis sought to determine the effects of the following variables on the content of the papers:

a. geographical region
b. size of town
c. size of school
d. presence of advertisements

A fifth variable was the inclusion in the sample of award-winning newspapers from the Columbia High School Press Association (CSPA) journalism contest.

Methodology

Two hundred ninety-three high school newspapers from across the country were selected for the analysis. Selection of the sample was based upon (a) a nonsystematic effort to obtain a reasonable cross section of high schools and their papers, and (b) a state-by-state representation that reflects the population breakdown by region for the country.

The high school newspapers were selected from several sources: (1) 183 entries, including 53 award-winners, in the CSPA journalism contest, (2) newspapers collected by Ms. Dorothy McPhillips, Commission member and a former Journalism Education Association officer, from contacts she maintains with various high schools in the United States, (3) papers collected by Commission staff through field contacts.

In examining the role of high school newspapers, Commission staff focused on the emphasis these papers gave various subject areas. These categories were determined with the help of Dr. R. Hiebert, Dean of the School of Journalism at the University of Maryland at College Park, and Dr. Barbara Finkelstein of the School of Education, also at the University of Maryland. The categories were: (1) sports news, (2) social and school activities news, (3) student government coverage, (4) administration, academic, and faculty news, (5) creative items, (6) in-school protests and issues, (7) off-campus protest and issues, (8) all other off-campus news, and (9) miscellaneous.

A newspaper was analyzed according to the number of

items devoted to each of the nine categories. The items could be articles, editorials, letters to the editor, or photographs independent of other items.

Table 6, Appendix II, presents each category's percentage of the total number of items from all newspapers in the survey.

The distribution of these categories was cross-tabulated against each of five major factors: (1) region, (2) size of town, (3) size of school (available for 183 of the newspapers), (4) independent financial sources in the advertising, and (5) award winners of CSPA journalism contest. These comparisons are presented in Appendices III, IV, V, VI, and VII.

The tables reflect the weight each of the five factors has in conditioning the areas of concern emphasized by the surveyed high school newspapers.

The classification of items was completed by four graduate students from the School of Education at the University of Maryland at College Park, and resulting data was processed by the Computer Science Center at the College Park campus.

Results of the Analysis

As noted before, each region of the country was represented in the content analysis proportionately to its population vis-à-vis U.S. population statistics. Thus, seventy-eight papers were analyzed from Region I (comprised of the Northeastern states) while Region VII (Rocky Mountain states) were represented by only ten newspapers. Over one half of the papers came from towns having populations of under 50,000. Five-sixths of the newspapers in the analysis carried advertisements.

The content analysis revealed a tremendous uniformity in content among high school newspapers in every region of the country. Papers in Region IV (Midwest) and those in Region I (Northeast), for instance, were found to have approximately the same percentage of space assigned to any one particular category; the space occupied by a given category in any one region generally varied by no more than 3 or 4 percent from that in any other region. In addition, all papers were approximately the same length. In every region, sports and social events together comprised approximately 50 percent of the newspapers' items. In-

school and off-campus issues, protests, and local or national news made up approximately 20 percent of the total.
An average of 13 percent of items were "creative"; the
same percentage covered academic affairs and administra-
tive-faculty news. Three percent of the items were concerned with student government.

The size of the town in which the school papers were
produced proved to have an equally small effect upon the
general content. A slightly larger percentage of newspapers produced in large towns received medalist awards
from the Columbia Scholastic Press Association than did
newspapers from small towns. There was, however, no
appreciable difference between the percentages of space
given to the individual categories.

Newspapers carrying advertisements did not, for the
most part, differ in content from those without advertisements. One exception occurred in the categories concerned with protests and off-campus news: papers carrying
ads gave an additional 5 percent of their total coverage to
such issues than did those without ads. The former group
of papers were generally longer, consisting of an average
6.24 pages as opposed to an average of 5.0 pages in the
latter group.

As with the other variables, no appreciable difference
occurred in newspaper content as a function of the school
size. A slightly larger coverage of social events was noted
in the schools with populations of 500 students and under.

Newspapers with medalist awards from the CSPA were
found to be slightly longer than nonmedalists and had several
more items per paper. Medalist papers gave slightly less
coverage to creative works by students, but generally the
same coverage to other categories.

These results indicate several things. Most obviously, it
is evident that high school newspapers are primarily concerned with reporting sports and social events. Far less
coverage is given to in-school issues and protests and off-
campus news. The universality of this trend indicates a
common attitude as to what high school newspapers should
consider newsworthy, an attitude that apparently regards
controversial issues as relatively unimportant or inappropriate subjects for coverage.

A possibility exists that the avoidance of controversial
articles in high school newspapers stems partly from many
newspapers' financial dependence upon their schools, a

dependence that leaves them vulnerable to censorship from
school officials who can suspend funds at will. It was seen
in the content analysis that newspapers carrying advertisements, which are thus to some degree more independent,
donated somewhat more space to the coverage of protests,
student concerns, and off-campus news than did those
newspapers without ads. A study of newspapers with complete financial independence would indicate whether a
significant change is indeed affected by independence from
school financing.

Finally, based on this analysis, and confirmed by field
and research experience, there is evidence that the subject
matter of high school newspapers is not influenced by high
school journalism awards programs. The limited coverage
of student issues or concerns, other than sports and social
activities, dominates both the medalist and nonmedalist
papers.

Appendix I

1. *Coding Categories*

a) | Regions | #
of Papers | Component States |
|---|---|---|
| I | 78 | Maine, N.H., Vt., Mass., R.I., N.Y., N.J., Penn., Conn. |
| II | 40 | Md., Del., D.C., Va., W.Va., Ky., Tenn., N.C. |
| III | 22 | S.C., Ga., Fla., Ala., Miss., La., Ark. |
| IV | 51 | Ohio, Ind., Mich., Ill. |
| V | 37 | Wisc., Minn., N.D., S.D., Iowa |
| VI | 20 | Okla., Texas, Ariz., N.M. |
| VII | 10 | Colo., Wyo., Idaho, Nev., Mont., Utah |
| VIII | 35 | Calif., Oreg., Wash., Alaska, Hawaii |

b) *Size of Town*

Size of Population	Code Used
Up to 50,000 inhabitants	1
50,001–150,000 inhabitants	2
more than 150,000 inhabitants	3

c) *Size of School*

Size of Student Enrollment	Code Used
Unknown	0
1–1,000	1
501–1,000	2
1,001–1,500	3
1,501–2,000	4
2,001–2,500	5
More than 2,500	6

d) *Advertisements*   *Code*

Present	1
Absent	2

This means that mean values of this code for each section examined will fall between 1 and 2, coming closer to 1 than 2 where there is a predominance of papers using advertisements, and vice versa.

e) *Medalist/Nonmedalist papers*   (CSPA)

Category	Code
Medalist	1
Nonmedalist	0

This means that mean values of this code for each section examined will fall between 0 and 1, coming closer to 1 where there is a predominance of medalist papers in our sample, and closer to 0 where there is a predominance of nonmedalists.

Analysis Categories:

1. *Sports news:* All sports reports, news, stories about team members, coaches, etc.
2. *Social and activities news:* All club news, meetings reports, fund-raising items, school dances, stories about individual students including exchange students, travel stories, etc.
3. *Student government coverage:* All reports of student government meetings, elections, addresses of presidents, progress reports, etc.
4. *Administrative, academic, and faculty news:* Stories about administration changes, faculty changes, administration announcements; discussion of course topics or careers,

articles by faculty members, stories about or interviewing faculty members.

5. *Creative items:* Poetry, fantasies, cartoons, book/film/record reviews.

6. *In-school protests and issues:* All discussions of protest or problems of concern to students and occurring within the school.

7. *Off-campus protests and issues:* All items reporting or discussing protests, problems of concern to students, occurring outside school, e.g., social issues, minority problems, women's lib, civil rights in general, politics, the Vietnam war, etc.

8. *All other off-campus news:* Self-explanatory.

9. *Miscellaneous:* All items not clearly falling under any of the first eight categories.

Appendix II—Total Counts

Table 1.

Regions	No. of Papers
I	78
II	40
III	22
IV	51
V	37
VI	20
VII	10
VIII	35

Table 2.

Size of Town	No. of Papers
1–50,000	155
50,000–150,000	68
More than 150,000	70

Table 3.

Size of School		No. of Papers
– 0 –	Unknown	110
– 1 –	1–500	9
– 2 –	501–1,000	33
– 3 –	1,001–1,500	20
– 4 –	1,501–2,000	50
– 5 –	2,001–2,500	41
– 6 –	More than 2,500	29

Table 4.

Advertisements	244 papers
No advertisements	49 papers

Table 5.

Medalists	53
Nonmedalists	240

Table 6.
Overall Count of Items

	Category	No. of Items	Percent of Total
1.	Sports news	6,121	20.80
2.	Social & school activities news	8,482	28.90
3.	Student government coverage	895	3.03
4.	Administration, academic and faculty news	3,872	13.20
5.	Creative items	3,808	13.00
6.	In-school protests and issues	2,393	8.16
7.	Off-campus protest and issues	2,051	7.00
8.	All other off-campus news	1,199	4.08
9.	Miscellaneous	506	1.72
10.	Categories 1, 2 & 3 combined	15,498	52.80
11.	Categories 6, 7 & 8 combined	5,643	19.20
12.	Total	29,327	100.00

Appendix III

Region	I	II	III	IV	V	VI	VII	VIII
No. of Papers	78	40	22	51	37	20	10	35
Categories								
No. of pages (mean number)	5.72	5.85	6.91	6.14	6.22	7.35	4.00	5.91
Size of town (mean, 1–3)	1.54	1.62	1.86	1.73	1.57	2.35	1.90	1.80
Ads/no ads (mean, 1–2)	1.29	1.05	1.05	1.10	1.22	1.05	1.20	1.14
Medalist/nonmedalist (mean, 1–0)	0.32	0.30	0.32	0.51	0.22	0.25	0.10	0.66
Sports (mean percentage of total)	19.86	18.92	19.64	19.51	25.51	22.30	19.70	22.60
Social and activities (mean percentage of total)	25.94	30.28	33.59	33.32	26.92	30.45	29.90	25.14
Student gov't. (mean percentage of total)	3.79	2.80	2.95	2.00	1.78	3.20	3.50	4.43
Admin., academic, and faculty (mean percentage)	15.41	11.18	14.23	11.69	11.76	16.60	18.50	10.63
Creative (mean percentage of total)	12.01	14.25	9.45	13.20	16.11	11.55	8.80	14.14
In-school protests and issues (mean percentage)	8.95	8.83	7.91	7.88	6.54	6.25	8.80	8.89
Off-campus protests & issues (mean percentage)	8.04	7.75	6.86	5.39	6.49	4.65	6.50	8.29
All other off-campus issues (mean percentage)	4.12	4.88	3.68	5.47	2.35	3.75	1.60	4.43
Miscellaneous (mean percentage of total)	1.94	1.35	1.77	1.33	2.51	1.45	2.20	1.43
Total (mean no. of items)	30.72	30.58	32.73	28.73	24.03	30.15	25.60	29.14
Sports, social, student gov't. (mean percentage)	49.59	51.95	56.00	55.27	54.16	56.10	52.80	52.14
On- and off-campus protests and other off-campus news (mean percentage of total)	21.10	21.53	18.45	18.73	15.38	14.55	16.80	21.57

Appendix IV

Size of Town	less than 50,000	50,000–150,000	more than 150,000
Number of Papers	155	68	70
Categories			
Number of pages (mean number)	6.14	6.12	5.73
Ads/no ads (mean, 1–2)	1.19	1.10	1.14
Medalist/nonmedalist (mean, 1–0)	0.33	0.38	0.43
Sports (mean percentage of total)	20.52	22.13	20.36
Social and school activities (mean percentage of total)	29.65	27.53	28.77
Student government (mean percentage of total)	3.43	2.53	2.74
Admin., academic, and faculty (mean percentage of total)	13.18	12.88	13.76
Creative items (mean percentage of total)	13.49	11.43	13.29
In-school protests and issues (mean percentage of total)	8.16	9.06	7.31
Off-campus protest and issues (mean percentage of total)	6.43	7.94	7.36
All other off-campus news (mean percentage of total)	3.72	4.82	4.36
Miscellaneous items (mean percentage of total)	1.65	1.68	1.96
Total (mean no. of items)	29.70	28.10	29.39
Sports, social, student gov't. (mean percentage of total)	53.52	52.19	51.89
On- and off-campus protests and other off-campus news (mean percentage of total)	18.35	21.75	18.97

Appendix V

Advertisements   245:48

Categories	245 −1− Advertisements	48 −2− No Advertisements
Number of pages (mean number)	6.24	5.00
Size of town (mean, 1−3)	1.74	1.56
Medalist/nonmedalist (mean, 1−0)	0.37	0.33
Sports (mean percentage of total)	20.68	21.77
Social and school activities (mean percentage of total)	28.90	29.21
Student government (mean percentage of total)	3.19	2.38
Admin., academic, and faculty (mean percentage of total)	12.83	15.38
Creative items (mean percentage of total)	12.71	14.23
In-school protests and issues (mean percentage of total)	8.43	6.83
Off-campus protest and issues (mean percentage of total)	7.28	5.56
All other off-campus news (mean percentage of total)	4.36	2.96
Miscellaneous items (mean percentage of total)	1.73	1.71
Total (mean no. of items)	29.50	28.02
Sports, social, student gov't. (mean percentage of total)	52.71	53.40
On- and off-campus protests and other off-campus news (mean percentage of total)	20.05	15.38

Appendix VI

Size of School, Coded	0	1	2	3	4	5	6
Number of Schools	110	9	33	20	50	41	29
Categories							
Number of pages (mean number)		5.22	5.57	5.30	6.42	5.95	6.24
Size of town (mean, 1–3)		1.67	1.30	1.50	1.88	1.71	2.24
Ads/no ads (mean, 1–2)		1.33	1.15	1.15	1.06	1.15	1.14
Medalist/nonmedalist (mean, 1–0)		0.67	0.21	0.20	0.42	0.63	0.59
Sports (mean percentage of total)		15.89	20.79	18.60	19.72	22.07	23.35
Social and school activities (mean percentage of total)		35.56	30.97	31.15	31.44	28.46	30.69
Student government (mean percentage of total)		4.78	3.52	1.90	3.70	3.44	4.21
Admin, academic & faculty (mean percentage of total)		16.78	11.39	15.00	13.48	12.46	12.10
Creative items (mean percentage of total)		10.11	15.21	13.60	8.80	10.15	12.03
In-school protests and issues (mean percentage of total)		5.11	8.30	7.70	8.20	9.83	6.86
Off-campus protests & issues (mean percentage of total)		5.89	5.12	6.65	7.76	8.05	6.52
All other off-campus issues (mean percentage of total)		4.00	3.30	3.00	5.50	3.80	3.45
Miscellaneous items (mean percentage of total)		1.44	1.64	2.90	1.34	1.98	1.03
Total (mean no. of items)		26.44	32.03	30.05	31.90	29.29	30.41
Sports, social, student gov't. (mean percentage of total)		56.44	55.21	51.30	54.86	53.83	58.24
On- and off-campus protests and other off-campus news (mean percentage of total)		15.22	16.88	17.50	21.44	21.56	16.76

Appendix VII—Medalists

Categories	Medalist	Nonmedalist
Number of pages (mean number)	6.66	5.89
Size of town (mean, 1–3)	1.89	1.67
Ads/no ads (mean, 1–2)	1.17	1.16
Sports (mean percentage of total)	21.66	20.67
Social and school activities news (mean percentage of total)	30.42	28.64
Student government coverage (mean percentage of total)	3.57	2.95
Administration, academic and faculty news (mean percentage of total)	12.66	13.39
Creative items (mean percentage of total)	10.68	13.47
In-school protests and issues (mean percentage of total)	8.25	8.15
Off-campus protests and issues (mean percentage of total)	6.94	7.01
All other off-campus news (mean percentage of total)	4.11	4.13
Miscellaneous items (mean percentage of total)	1.85	1.69
Total (mean no. of items)	31.70	28.70
Sports, social, student gov't. coverage (mean percentage of total)	55.55	52.24
On- and off-campus protests and other off-campus news (mean percentage of total)	19.32	19.28

7. Selected Readings

This list is a selection of readings related to the Commission's work. It is not meant to be all-inclusive, but illustrative of materials the Commission and its staff found particularly helpful in planning and carrying forward this inquiry. Included are selected background readings, which in addition to books and articles from periodicals, include a list of current subject-related periodicals to which the reader may wish to subscribe.

This list is divided into five areas, four of which mirror directly the major sections of the Commission's Report: Censorship, Minority Access, Journalism Education, and Established Media. In addition, one area covers a list of nine books under the general heading "Education and Adolescence." While such a list could easily extend to hundreds of publications these particular ones are noted because of their unique value to the staff in its work.

Education and Adolescence

Coleman, James. *The Adolescent Society*. New York, Free Press, 1961.

Coles, Robert. *Children of Crisis*. Volume I, *A Study of Courage and Fear*, 1967; Volume II, *Migrants, Mountaineers, and Sharecroppers*, 1972; Volume III, *South Goes North*. Boston, Atlantic Monthly Press, 1972.

Dewey, John. *Democracy and Education*. New York, Macmillan Free Press, 1961.

Erikson, Erik. *Identity: Youth in Crisis*. New York, Norton, 1968.

Friedenberg, Edgar. *Coming of Age in America*. New York, Random House, 1965.

Goodman, Paul. *Growing Up Absurd*. New York, Random House, 1956.

Keniston, Kenneth. *Youth and Dissent*. New York, Harcourt Brace and Javonovich, 1971.

President's Science Advisory Committee. *Youth: Transition to Adulthood*. Washington, D.C., United States Department of Health, Education and Welfare, Office of Science and Technology, 1973.

Silberman, Charles. *Crisis in the Classroom*. New York, Harper and Row, 1970.

Press Law and the First Amendment

Books:

American Bar Association Special Committee on Youth Education for Citizenship. *Bibliography of Law-Related*

Curriculum Materials: Annotated, Chicago, ABA, 1974.

Birmingham, John. *Our Time is Now: Notes from the High School Underground.* New York, Praeger, 1970.

DeGrazia, Edward. *Censorship Landmarks.* New York, R. R. Bowker, 1969.

Emerson, Thomas I. *Toward a General Theory of the First Amendment.* New York, Vintage Press, 1963.

Learner, Lawrence. *The Paper Revolutionaries.* New York, Simon and Schuster, 1972.

Levine, Alan, with Eve Cary, Diane Divoky. *The Rights of Students.* New York, American Civil Liberties Union Handbook, Discus/Avon, 1973.

Nelson, Jack. *The Censors and the Schools.* Boston, Little, Brown and Company, 1963.

New York Civil Liberties Union Student Rights Project. *N.Y.C.L.U. Student Rights Project, Report on the First Two Years,* New York, N.Y.C.L.U., 1972. (For copies contact ERIC Document Reproduction Service, P.O. Drawer O, Bethesda, Maryland 20014).

Rubin, David. *The Rights of Teachers.* New York, An American Civil Liberties Union Handbook, Discus/Avon, 1972.

Articles:

Denton, David, E., "How Free Should School Press Be?—Existentialist Asks" *Communication: Journalism Education Today,* Volume 5, Summer 1972, pp. 2–3.

Kozol, Jonathan, "How Schools Train Children for Political Impotence," *Social Policy,* Volume 3, Number 2, July/August 1972.

Trager, Robert & Osterman, Robert, "Coying the Censorship Dragon" *Scholastic Editor,* December/January 1971, pp. 8–11.

Periodicals:

Freedom of Information Center Reports, FOI Center, Box 858, University of Missouri, Columbia, Missouri, 65201. ($.35 for back copies, $10/year)

Press Censorship Newsletter, The Reporters Committee for Freedom of the Press, Legal Defense and Research Fund, Room 1310, 1750 Pennsylvania Avenue N.W., Washington, D.C. 20006.

Minority Participation

(While a number of articles and periodicals are listed below, the Commission found few books dealing in this subject area.)

Books:

Kimbrough, Marvin. *Black Magazines: An Exploratory Study*. Austin, Texas, Center for Communications Research, 1973.

Murphy, Sharon Feyen. *Other Voices*. Dayton, Ohio, Pflaum, 1974.

U.S. Civil Rights Commission. *Towards Quality Education for Mexican Americans*. Volumes I-VI, Washington, D.C., U.S. Government Printing Office.

Watts, Dan. *Reprints from The Liberator*. Milwood, New York, Kraus Reprint Company.

Woseley, Ronald. *The Black Press, U.S.A.* Ames, Iowa, Iowa State University Press, 1971.

Articles:

"Cable Television Opportunities for Minorities," *Crisis*, N.A.A.C.P., New York 10019.

Wilkinson, Gerald, "Colonialism Through the Media—The Creation of CEE-TRUTH," *Medium Rare*, February 1974, AIPA News Bureau, Room 206, 1346 Connecticut Avenue N.W., Washington, D.C. 20036.

"Guide to Community Demands in License Challenges," Black Efforts for Soul in Television, 1015 North Carolina Avenue S.E., Washington, D.C. 20003.

"Help Wanted: More Minority Newsmen," Association of Professional Managing Editors, Personnel Committee. Write: Harold Lappin, *Saginaw News*, 203 South Washington Avenue, Saginaw, Michigan, 48605.

Periodicals:

Akwesasne Notes, Mohawk Nation via Rooseveltown, New York, 13683.

American Indian Media Director, 1974, American Indian Press Association, 1346 Connecticut Avenue N.W., Washington, D.C. 20036. ($25 per copy).

Ethnicity, Center for the Study of American Pluralism, University of Chicago, Chicago, Illinois 60637. ($12 per year).

Intercom, National Mexican American Anti-Defamation Committee, Inc., 1605 Connecticut Avenue N.W., Washington, D.C. 20009.

Journalism Council, Job/Scholarship Referral Bulletin for Minorities, published monthly for Journalism, Inc., by Minorities and Communication Division, Association for Education in Journalism, contact: Dr. Lionel Barrow, Jr., or Donna Pugh, University of Wisconsin-Milwaukee, Department of Mass Communication, Mitchell 214, Milwaukee, Wisconsin 53201.

Medium Rare, American Indian Press Association News Bureau, Room 206, 1346 Connecticut Avenue, N.W., Washington, D.C. 20036. ($10 per year).

Race Relations Reporter, Race Relations Information Center, Box 12156, Nashville, Tennessee 37212. ($10 per year).

Shove It, American Indian Press Association, 1346 Connecticut Avenue N.W., Room 206, Washington, D.C. 20036 ($1.50 per copy).

Wassaja, American Indian Historical Society, 1451 Masonic Avenue, San Francisco, California 94117.

Journalism Education

The five major reference categories as listed below are based upon a system developed by the Journalism Education Association following several years of special research and curriculum development workshops.

A Study of the Communication Process: worktext manuscript pending with Loyola University Press, Chicago, by Sharon Feyen Murphy.

TEACHER RESOURCE BOOKS:

Berlo, David K. *The Process of Communication.* New York, Holt, Rinehart & Winston, 1960.

Fabun, Don. *Communications: The Transfer of Meaning.* Beverly Hills, Glencoe Press, 1968.

Krupar, Karen. *Communication Games.* New York, The Free Press, 1973.

Schramm, Wilbur, Ithiel de Sola Pool, et al., eds. *Handbook of Communication.* Chicago, Rand McNally, 1973.

Mass Media Analysis:

Heintz, Ann, Reuter, Lawrence, and Conley, Elizabeth. *Mass Media.* Chicago, Loyola University Press, 1972. (Inductive student worktext)

TEACHER RESOURCE BOOKS:

Casty, Alan, ed., *Mass Media and Mass Man,* Holt, Rinehart & Winston, New York, 1968.

Emery, Edwin, Ault, Phillip and Agee, Warren, *Introduction to Mass Communication,* Dodd, Mead and Co., New York, 1970.

Wiseman, T. Jan and Molly J., *Creative Communications: Teaching Mass Media,* University of Minnesota, N.S.P.A., 1972.

Methods of Research and Investigation (observation, interviewing, secondary sources)

Heintz, Ann, Fitzgerald, Patricia and Fieweger, Margaret, *Independent Learning,* Ginn and Co., Lexington, Mass., 1974.

TEACHER RESOURCE BOOKS:

Barzun, Jacques and Graff, Henry F., *The Modern Researcher,* Harcourt, Brace & World, New York, 1970.

Reporting/Exposition: In an evaluation study supported by Quill & Scroll and published in October, 1972 by Laurence R. Campbell of Florida State University, the following student texts received the highest evaluation for publications productions and reporting:

Adams, J., and Stratton, K. *Presstime,* Englewood, N.J., Prentice-Hall Inc., 1969.

English, E., and Hach, C. *Scholastic Journalism,* 5th ed. Ames, Iowa, Iowa State University Press, 1972.

Moyes, N., and White, D. M. *Journalism in the Mass Media.* Boston, Ginn and Co., 1970.

TEACHER RESOURCE BOOKS:

Copple, Neale. *Depth Reporting.* Englewood Cliffs, N.J., Prentice-Hall, 1964.

Persuasion/Rhetoric

Heintz, Ann. *Persuasion*. Chicago, Loyola University Press, 1970. (Inductive student worktext)

TEACHER RESOURCE BOOKS:

Fogarty, Daniel J. *Roots for a New Rhetoric*. New York, Teachers College, Columbia University, 1959.

McGinnis, Joe. *The Selling of the President, 1972*. New York, Trident Press, 1973.

Weaver, Richard M. *Ethics of Rhetoric*. Chicago, Henry Regnery Co., 1953.

"What's Going On Here?" The EMC Corp. (180 E. 6th St., St. Paul, Minn. 55101) filmstrip, records, and activity materials.

Supplemental to these five curriculum needs are:

Electronic Media

Anderson, Chuck. *The Electronic Journalist: An Introduction to Video*. New York, Praeger, 1973.

United Press International. *Broadcast Stylebook*. New York, UPI (Write UPI, 220 East 42nd St., N.Y. 10017, for copies).

Videofreex. *The Spaghetti City Video Manual*. New York, Praeger, 1973.

Filmmaking

Coynik, David. *Movie Making*. Chicago, Loyola University Press, 1974.

Kuhns, William, and Giardint, Thomas F. *Behind the Camera*. Dayton, Ohio, Pflaum, 1970.

Smallman, Kirk. *Creative Filmmaking*. New York, Bantam, 1973.

Cable Television

Berks Cable Co. *A Story About People*. Reading, Pa., Berks Cable Co. (P.O. Box 107, Reading, Pa. 19603). Single copy free.

Community Cable TV and You. Special Feb., 1971, issue of *Challenge for Change Newsletter*, National Film Board of Canada (P.O. Box 6100 Montreal, Quebec, Canada). Single copy free.

Price, Monroe, and Wicklein, John. *Cable Television: A Guide for Citizen Action*. New York, Pilgrim Press,

1972. (Write the Office of Communication, 289 Park Ave. South, New York, New York 10010. $2.95).

Shafer, Jon. "Education and Cable TV, a Guide to Franchising and Utilization" ERIC publication (Box E, School of Education, Stanford University, Stanford, California 94035. $2.50).

Smith, Ralph Lee. *The Wired Nation.* New York, Harper & Row, 1972.

Source Catalog: Communications. "An Organizing Tool" Chicago, Swallow Press, Inc. (1139 Wabash Ave., Chicago, Ill. 60605. $1.00).

Periodical Citations

TEACHER ACCREDITATION IN JOURNALISM:

Windhauser, John, and Click, J. W., "Will the Real Journalism Teacher Please Stand Up," *Communication: Journalism Education Today, (C:JET)* Summer 1971, pp. 2–3.

JOURNALISM COMPETITIONS:

Pasqua, Tom, "Is There a Winning Formula? How Journalism Contest Judges Rate News," *C:JET*, Winter 1973, pp. 6–8.

JOURNALISM EDUCATION PRACTICES:

Danielson, Wayne A., "Can We Train Journalists Able to Face Tomorrow?" *C:JET*, Fall 1971, pp. 3–5. (Address by the President of AEJ to the AEJ Convention, August, 1971).

ELECTRONIC JOURNALISM:

C:JET, Winter issue 1974.

"Beginners Can Produce a Creditable Learning Experience," *C:JET*, Spring 1971, pp. 12–13.

Professional Journals

Cable Report, 192 N. Clark St., Chicago, Ill. 60601. $7/ year (Originally a supplement of the *Chicago Journalism Review*).

The C.S.P.A.A. Bulletin, 860 Van Vleet Oval, Suite 225, Norman, Oklahoma 73069. Free to GSPAA members.

Communication: Journalism Education Today, Box 884, Springfield, Mo. 65804. Official journal of the Journalism Education Association. (Single copy $3.00; included in $10 membership dues).

Journalism Quarterly, School of Journalism, University of Minnesota, Minneapolis, Minn. 55455. ($10/year).

Mass Media Booknotes, Dept. of Radio-TV-Film, Temple University, Philadelphia, Pa. 19122. Monthly ($3.50/year).

Media and Methods, 134 North Thirteenth St., Philadelphia, Pa. 19107. ($7/year).

Newspaper Fund Newsletter, Newspaper Fund, P.O. Box 300, Princeton, New Jersey 08540.

Scholastic Editor, National Scholastic Press Assn., 18 Journalism Bldg., University of Minnesota, Minneapolis, Minn. 55455. ($5.75/year).

Video Exchange Directory, Michael Goldberg, c/o Vancouver Art Gallery, 1145 W. Georgia St., Vancouver, B.C., Canada.

Established Media

(Following is a list of selected recent books and current periodicals concerning established media. No attempt is made to select from the numerous textbooks on the professional media.)

Books:

Bagdikigian, Ben. *The Effete Conspiracy: And Other Crimes of the Press.* New York, Harper and Row, 1972.

Crouse, Timothy. *The Boys on the Bus.* New York, Random House, 1974.

Friendly, Fred. *Due to Circumstances Beyond Our Control.* New York, Random House, 1967.

Gans, Herbert. *The Uses of Television and their Educational Implication: Preliminary Findings from a Survey of Adult and Adolescent New York Television Viewers.* New York, Center for Urban Education, 1968.

Hohenberg, John. *The Professional Journalist.* New York, Rinehart and Winston, 1969.

Johnson, Nicholas. *How to Talk Back to Your Television Set.* New York, Bantam, 1970.

Perry, James. *Us and Them: How the Press Covered the 1972 Election*. New York, Potter, 1973.

Peterson, Theodore, Jensen, Jay, and Rivels, William L. *The Mass Media in Modern Society*. New York, Holt, Rinehart and Winston, 1966.

Small, William. *Political Power and the Press*. New York, Norton, 1972.

Wolfe, Tom. *The New Journalism*. New York, Harper and Row, 1973.

Periodicals:

Chicago Journalism Review, 192 North Clark, Room 607, Chicago, Illinois 60601. ($7 per year).

Columbia Journalism Review, 700 Journalism Building, Columbia University, New York, 10027. ($12 per year).

Editor and Publisher, 850 Third Avenue, New York 10022. ($10 per year).

MORE Journalism Review, Box 576, Ansonia Station, New York 10023. ($7 per year).

8. Organizations

Following are some of the organizations with which the Commission was in contact and found helpful during its Inquiry. This is not meant to be an all-inclusive list, but one illustrative of organizations which may be helpful to students, teachers, and interested citizens depending upon the nature of a particular request and the areas of interest and expertise of the organization.

Legal Groups

Contact should be made with local legal services agencies, particularly affiliates of the American Civil Liberties Union (national headquarter is listed). Contact should also be made with local student and teachers rights groups.

Back up information and resources may be obtained from the following groups:

American Civil Liberties Union
22 East 40th Street
New York, New York 10019

Freedom of Information Center
School of Journalism
Box 858
University of Missouri
Columbia, Missouri 65201

Harvard Center for Law & Education
38 Kirkland Street
Cambridge, Massachusetts 02138

National Juvenile Law Center
3642 Lindell Boulevard
St. Louis, Missouri 63108

Reporter's Committee for Freedom of the Press
c/o Fred T. Sirhan
New York Times News Bureau
1920 L Street, N.W.
Washington, D.C. 20036

Youth Law Center
759 Turk Street
San Francisco, California 94102

Minority Participation

Local Human Relations groups, the N.A.A.C.P., and civil rights groups should be contacted for general information and services. Back up information and resources may be obtained from the following groups:

American Indian Press Association
1346 Connecticut Avenue, N.W.
Washington, D.C. 20036

Bilingual Bicultural Coalition on the Mass Media
2158 Commerce Street
San Antonio, Texas 78207

Black Efforts for Soul in T.V.
1015 North Carolina Avenue, S.E.
Washington, D.C. 20003

Cable Communications Resource Center
1900 L Street, N.W.
Washington, D.C. 20036

Coalition for the Enforcement of
  Equality in Television and Radio
  Utilization of Time and Hours
  (CEE-TRUTH—This is a coalition
  of Indians and Chicanos in New Mexico)
201 Hermosa, N.E.
Albuquerque, New Mexico 87107

Ideas, Inc.
  (resource organization working to
  replicate *Foxfire*)
1785 Massachusetts Avenue, N.W.
Washington, D.C. 20036

Indian Law Center
School of Law
University of New Mexico
Albuquerque, New Mexico 87106

Journalism Council, Inc.
Department of Journalism
1021 Main Building
New York University
New York, New York 10003

N.A.A.C.P. Legal Defense &
  Educational Fund, Inc.
10 Columbus Circle
New York, New York 10019

Native American Rights Fund
1506 Broadway
Boulder, Colorado 80302

Journalism Education

Local chapters of national journalism organizations and
regional scholastic press associations should be contacted
for general information and services. Back up information
and resources may be obtained from the following:

Association for Education in Journalism
c/o Dr. Harld Wilson
School of Journalism

Murphy Hall
University of Minnesota
Minneapolis, Minnesota 55455

Blair Summer School for Journalism
Blairstown, New Jersey 07825

Columbia Scholastic Press Association
Box 11 Central Mail Room
Columbia University
New York, New York 10027

Journalism Education Association
c/o Sr. Rita Jeanne
FSPA
St. Rose Convent
912 Market Street
La Crosse, Wisconsin 54601

National Education Association
1201 16th Street, N.W.
Washington, D.C. 20036

National Scholastic Press Association
University of Minnesota
18 Journalism Building
Minneapolis, Minnesota 55455

The Newspaper Fund
Box 300
Princeton, New Jersey 08540

Northwestern University
School of Journalism
c/o Jack Williams
202 Fiske Hall
National High School Institute
Evanston, Illinois 60201

Quill and Scroll Society
University of Iowa
Iowa City, Iowa 52240

Student Press in America Archives
John C. Behrens, Curator
Burrston Road
Utica, New York 13502

National Indian Media Training Center
All-Indian Pueblo Council
  Communications Project

P.O. Box 6053
1000 Indian School Road
Albuquerque, New Mexico 87017

Texas Institute for Educational Development
311 North Zarzamora
San Antonio, Texas 78207

Electronic and Cable TV

Association for Educational Communication
  and Technology
1201 16th Street, N.W.
Washington, D.C. 20036

Cable Television Information Center
The Urban Institute
2100 M Street, N.W.
Washington, D.C. 20036

Citizens Communication Center
1914 Sunderland Place, N.W.
Washington, D.C. 20036

Federal Communications Commission
1919 M Street, N.W.
Washington, D.C. 20554

Joint Council on Educational Tele-
  Communications
1126 16th Street, N.W.
Washington, D.C. 20036

National Association for Media Action
Allen Fredrickson
Community Access TV
Santa Cruz, California

Videofreex
Media Bus
Maple Tree Farm
Lanesville, New York 12450

Professional Journalism Organizations

American Newspaper Publishers
Association Foundation
Box 17407
Dulles International Airport
Washington, D.C. 20041

American Society of Newspaper Editors
1350 Sullivan Trail
Box 551
Eaton, Pennsylvania 18042

National Newspaper Publishers Association
P.O. Box 1546
Washington, D.C. 20013

Society of Professional Journalists
Sigma Delta Chi
35 East Wacker Drive
Chicago, Illinois 60601
    (Please contact local chapters)

The Fourth Estate Alternative
Box 11176
Palo Alto, California 94306

Women in Communications, Inc.
830-A Shoal Creek Boulevard
Austin, Texas 78758

Organizations Supporting Youth Action and Journalism

Contact local youth groups for information and resources in your area. Back up support and resource information may be obtained from the following regional and national organizations:

American Friends Service Committee
1520 Spruce Street
Philadelphia, Pennsylvania 19102

Children's Defense Fund
1763 R Street, N.W.
Washington, D.C. 20009

Governor's Youth Action Program
contact: John Schaller
427 Cleveland Avenue
Columbus, Ohio 43215

National Commission on Resources for Youth
36 West 44th Street
New York, New York 10036

National Endowment for the Humanities
Youth Grants In Humanities
806 15th Street, N.W.
Washington, D.C. 20004

National Youth Alternatives
St. Margaret's Church
1830 Connecticut Avenue, N.W.
Washington, D.C. 20009

School Desegregation Project
Southern Regional Council
52 Fairlie Street, N.W.
Atlanta, Georgia 30303

The Youth Project
1000 Wisconsin Avenue, N.W.
Washington, D.C. 20007

The Youth Project
294 Page Street
San Francisco, California 94102

The Youth Project
87 Walton Street
Suite 504
Atlanta, Georgia 30303

Appendix C

1. The Lion

Lyons Township High School
LaGrange & Western Springs, Illinois
Vol. 63, No. 11, March 9, 1973

Dialogue

The Issue—can *Lion* endorsements be justified?

Lion decisions, with rare exception, are made by student editors. Its adviser operates within the school's articulated policy of press freedom. "Students are free to choose the issue and to discuss it broadly and forthrightly with honesty and integrity," Supt. Dr. Donald Reber wrote recently.

While not agreeing with everything published, Adviser Mr. John Wheeler does not censor material. However adviser and editors could not reach a consensus on the issue of endorsing General Assembly candidates, and his judgment prevailed. Alternative editorial approaches were then suggested. At the editors' request, he has submitted a statement. We invite you to share the exchange of viewpoints.

We at the *Lion* believe that it is our responsibility to inform the student body of important events taking place at LT. Another of our prime responsibilities is to provide leadership to the student body.

With this in mind, we had planned to cover the important points of each candidate's platform in a news story and then endorse candidates we felt were qualified.

Our prime concern was to find out if the candidates had established goals and a workable mechanism for implementation of these goals.

This would be revealed in a 15–20 minute interview where each candidate could be closely questioned.

Those who, in our opinion, had set goals and a workable mechanism for implementation would have been endorsed. To those who did not meet these qualifications, suggestions would have been offered.

The reaction to our plans was immediate. The candidates met and decided that they were not sure they wanted the *Lion* to endorse candidates, and consequently they decided that they would not come in to be interviewed.

Their main contention was that endorsing one candidate over another would give an unfair advantage to the endorsed candidate. We never intended to be fair in this respect. We believe that because we have analyzed and criticized General Assembly a good deal, we are responsible to the students to present to them a slate we feel could make General Assembly a vital part of LT.

We wanted to provide more thought on the part of the candidates and the student body. We believe that endorsements would have forced candidates to consider their platform more carefully.

If a candidate were not endorsed, he would have had to prove to the students that he was indeed the right person for the job. The endorsed candidate would have had to maintain his position. Thus a dialogue between the candidates and the students would have resulted.

Then the limited campaigning allotment for each candidate would have had to be directed at issues that concerned the students and not a meaningless propaganda. The students would have had to be given definite statements by the candidates.

Some contend that the *Lion* has too much power and that a candidate endorsed would be a candidate elected. We believe that the student body is intelligent enough to weigh our recommendations with what they hear and see. Most students have little contact with General Assembly. Campaigning in the past has taken on the characteristic of a nice game to play.

We believe that student government can and should be more than that. To accomplish this, meaningful dialogue between the students and candidates is necessary. We believe that endorsement would have helped to bring this about.

Endorsement Not Beneficial

by Mr. John Wheeler

Because I could not support a *Lion* editorial board decision to endorse specific candidates for General Assembly election, I regrettably exercised a seldom used authority granted by the school which is the paper's publisher, and overruled its resolution. While appreciating the board's high motives, I came to believe that endorsement would not benefit student government or the newspaper. First, editorial advocacy could give a decided edge (or disadvantage if there were voter backlash) to some nominees. Since the paper is published infrequently (unlike a metropolitan or college daily), there would be no opportunity for those not endorsed to respond. Spirited dialogue through letters by supporters and opponents is eliminated. To argue that candidates would have chances to respond at the all-school assemblies or through materials purchased through their $5 allotted campaign fund is irrelevant—the limited time and material are not intended to retort positions taken by a newspaper which circulates nearly 5,000 copies.

Then there are the candidates themselves. Unlike the professionals or even some who run for college government offices, most have little acquaintance with the shrewd intricacies of politicking. Moreover, student government, as part of the educational arrangement, should encourage participation. The reaction of most candidates to hearing that the *Lion* was contemplating endorsement is significant, especially in light of the number of candidates. Most initially refused to be interviewed about their positions; some wondered whether they wished to run for office. None said he wanted the *Lion* to make Olympian judgments.

Also because the campaign period is short, candidates do not develop definite campaign strategies. Although those who chose to be were interviewed for about 20 minutes by a panel of *Lion* editors and could freely voice their views, I do not believe the interviews were of sufficient length to provide a basis for political support or rejection. It would be arrogant of the paper to instruct others how to vote based on such evidence.

It is the *Lion*'s rightful position in its editorials to urge readers directly or through representatives to undertake actions. But there is, I believe, an important, though subtle, difference between endorsing an action that the paper believes worthwhile and openly backing nominees. After all, people, not newspapers, decide the merits of a cause and act accordingly.

The American election process requires individual voters to pass judgment on those who aspire to public office. Fundamentally, it is a newspaper's responsibility to report fairly and accurately candidates' positions, which the *Lion* has honestly tried to do. It is each voter's responsibility to consider candidates and issues and decide if he will vote, and for whom. The *Lion* should exercise its influence by striving to reveal candidates' positions, not telling voters whom they should choose for their officers.

Ram-Page

Ranson Junior High School
Charlotte, North Carolina
Vol. 9, No. 5, March 2, 1973

Student Walkout

by Kim Holbrook
9th Grade Student

Wednesday, February 7, the 9th Grade class had a walkout to protest being sent out of an assembly by Mr. Deal. The assembly was planned for the 9th graders to hear North Mecklenburg's band, The Blue Notes.

Mr. Deal claimed he asked the students to get quiet 3 times, but the 9th graders paid no attention, so he sent them back to class. He also claimed the 7th Grade got quiet after being asked to do so. Many students, including 7th graders, disagreed with this. Several different 7th graders said, "We were just as loud as the 9th graders."

Mr. Deal then went to two different classes and accused 2 different girls of "Standing up and yelling." This upset the 9th graders greatly, especially one of the classes Mr. Deal had come into.

A small group of students from this class decided to come up to their room during lunch to discuss the problem. This small group got bigger and bigger until the whole room was packed with angry students. After a few minutes, Mr. Ray came into the room and asked them to get back to the plaza. Everyone objected, so Mr. Ray just listened until he got an idea of what was going on.

The bell rang for 7th period. Mr. Deal asked 2 students to go to his office so they could talk over the problem. By this time ⅔ of the 9th Grade had assembled at the back of the school and refused to go to class. Mr. Deal came out and asked for a group of 4 students to come to the office to act as spokesmen for the crowd.

Apparently, the 9th graders didn't like the idea, since more than 4 went. The group was then ordered to get back to class. The students turned away from the office and went back out to join the walkout, refusing to go to class.

Mr. Deal came out and announced to the group that they were all officially suspended and were to leave the school grounds immediately.

Mr. Ray came out to the group and tried to make a deal with them. He would tell Mr. Deal they were willing to go back to class if he would "un-suspend" them. Most of the group agreed with him, so he got permission for the group to return to class.

At the teachers' meeting that afternoon, many of the teachers voiced their opinion on how they felt about the incident. A few teachers let Mr. Deal know what the students' complaints were. It was brought up that many of the students thought Mr. Deal made all the rules and ran everything, and the students could not have a say in anything.

Thursday, the day after the walkout, the student council met. Mr. Deal was asked many questions. The 9th Grade was promised that the Blue Notes would return to RJH for another concert if possible. They also got a pep rally. From now on, the 9th Grade will attend all pep rallies with 7th and 8th graders rotating.

Mr. Deal has asked that from now on whenever the student body has a complaint, they should ask a student council member to see him or a panel of teachers about it.

The Sword & Shield

Keenan High School
Columbia, South Carolina
Vol. 2, Issue 3, Nov. 6, 1972

How can Keenan students prepare to face a life of living in a multi-racial America? And how can people with different racial outlooks raise their children free of prejudices? Is it possible for us, the next generation of parents, to avoid future conflict between ourselves and our children if their ideas on race differ from ours?

Many parents have no intentions of helping their children develop without racial prejudices. This type of parent may perform a disservice to their children and their country and they must assume full responsibility for the consequences.

The first place that a child learns racial prejudice is in his home. Ten years ago white society's attitudes toward blacks were expressed indirectly in books, broadcasts and plays that portrayed blacks as "happy-go-lucky" and "shiftless" or as depraved and dangerous criminals.

Today many white Americans accept these images as mere stereotypes but many still suffer from the old delusions.

Blacks often see whites as being middle-class citizens and people that blacks must "conquer" in order to gain a little bit of power. This is constantly being proved with "Black On" marches and boycotts against white merchants who fail to hire adequate numbers of black salesclerks.

Parents, sometimes unaware of their racial bias, spread it on to their children. Young children may become confused when the parents talk one way and act another. For example, there is the white mother who says she isn't prejudiced but resents blacks moving into her apartment building or neighborhood.

If one is unaware or will not admit his prejudices, he is more likely to become inconsistent and defensive in his actions toward racial matters. It is better for a person to acknowledge his prejudices rather than hiding them. . . .

Children adapt quickly to the negative attitudes their playmates and parents display. Even though nothing disparaging may be said, children sense that something is wrong about minority groups or races if their parents shun one another at school events or public affairs.

It is important that parents who acknowledge an irrational prejudice allow their children to form more rational attitudes. . . . Children appreciate honesty and willingness to permit them to hold different opinions.

Parents who force their ideas and thinkings on their youngsters deprive them of the opportunity to think for themselves and encourage rebellion.

Editor and Publisher

April 13, 1974

"ASNE Survey Shows Minimal Gain in Black Reporters"

Minority employment on news staffs has crept up at a barely measurable rate of an estimated one-fourth of one percent nationally since 1973, according to the American Society of Newspaper Editors' Committee on Minority Employment Report.

The study entitled "Don't Steal My Black Reporter," will be distributed to ASNE members at their annual meeting in Atlanta, April 16–19.

The Committee, in its third year of a "fact-finding patrol," has come to the conclusion that "a strong majority of U.S. editors favor increased opportunities for members of the minority groups." However, according to the report, a lack of progress has made some editors hypersensitive to the point that they ignore queries from fellow editors. Others simply express frustration.

Poll Response Drops

This year's committee report covers responses from 148 editors spread over the country, or 62% of those who received questionnaires. This is 33% under the 1972 canvass of a 95.6% return.

The 1974 report considers the issues of minority quality and availability, recruiting, development, quota systems, minority turnover, the economy's forecast on minority employment and the regional patterns in hiring practices.

The ASNE Committee on Minority Employment is composed of Norman E. Isaacs, Columbia University, chairman; James Batten, *Charlotte* (N.C.) *Observer*; Charles O. Kilpatrick, *San Antonio* (Tex.) *News* and *Express*; C. K. McClatchy, *Sacramento* (Calif.) *Bee,* and George R. Packard, *Philadelphia Bulletin.*

The Committee's 1972 report estimated total professional newsroom employment of minority individuals to be three-quarters of one percent. The 1973 report said that the "Second-Reconstruction had fallen victim to weariness and general disaffection, but that the total appeared to have gained slightly."

The current 1974 report precludes that there is no clear estimate but that the findings indicate that the gross national rate may have moved upwards to one percent.

Quality and Availability

There are two aspects that affect minority hiring distinctly: "quality" and "availability," according to the Committee's report. The report states, "Many editors focused on the tension between their determination to maintain their newspapers' editorial standards and their eagerness to hire blacks, many of whom have sharply weaker credentials than average white applicants."

A southern editor was quoted in the Committee's findings to substantiate the "quality" factor: "A problem is trying to bring along poorly prepared candidates who may have promise. The cultural and educational background of blacks still is a large handicap. I am largely optimistic. . . ."

Another southern editor summed it up more bluntly in the Committee's report: "We want more blacks—but we want those who can do the job."

On the question of "quality," the ASNE Committee

firmly states in the report that "American newspaper editors must accept their share of the responsibility for what has gone on and goes on, within the nation's classrooms."

In fact, in the Committee's two prior reports, recommendations were made for editors to pay more attention to the educational standards of local schools, and particularly, to conduct regular, determined examinations of the high school counseling systems to make sure untrained, ill-informed advisors are not "poor-mouthing" journalism as a desirable career.

The 1974 report concludes: "There is little evidence to indicate that ASNE members have heeded the advice."

Editors Favor Recruitment

In a positive light, the Committee reports that a strong majority of editors favor increased minority employment and many of the editors responded with more descriptions of active recruitment efforts than previously.

Some of the comments included in the recruitment section of the report included editors' efforts to notify minority sources in the local area about available openings; communicating more thoroughly with all colleges and universities in a specific area; visiting higher education institutions to explain the newspaper's interest in hiring minorities; ensuring minorities' chance to prove themselves through intern programs; sponsoring of students in special minority programs at universities.

These efforts are encouraging, however, the Committee reports many of the respondents stated clearly that while interested, no special recruiting efforts were being exerted.

Turnover Complaint

One of the biggest complaints raised by editors in the polling, according to the recent report, centers on high turnover or "raiding." One editor quoted in the study said, "Turnover is ridiculous. The demand for blacks is high, and those who have been on the staff tend to leave quickly for better jobs."

On the subject of a quota system, the ASNE Committee reports that "only among editors in the western tier of states came expressions in support of a 'quota' pattern." One editor in the report said he wanted "at least a 20%

ethnic minority." Two expressed the hope of reflecting the "proportionate percentage of minority groups and women."

However, numerous editors were strongly opposed to quotas. Again and again, editors attributed in the study felt that ability, experience, competition, were more relevant than hiring under a quota system.

This quality and experience proving ground is not necessarily the right answer. The ASNE 1974 report presents an argument by James Aronson in the *Antioch Review,* which rebuts the "quality" pronouncements:

"One thing editors could do," he wrote, "is abandon the 'qualification' standard which is rarely raised when a bright, talented, untutored white youngster comes along and they are challenged to take a chance. While professional standards obviously have changed, and college degrees seem almost mandatory for a newspaper job today, there was a time when no-degree Italians, Jews and Irish developed into some of the best-known by-lines in the newspaper industry. But they were white. There are no rules of thumb to prevent similar experiments with black youngsters—particularly when on-the-job training programs have come into fashion—except the unwritten rules or prejudice in the minds of editors and their assistants."

The Committee affirms Aronson's reflections on editor's attitudes. However, its research indicates that "blanket condemnation is unfair to a great many editors, who have been thinking hard about the problem."

The report states: "Training programs for minority staffers do exist on some larger papers and one Southern editor advanced the thesis that it is NOT an editorial problem but a corporate one."

The Southern editor wrote that a company must put more pressure on newsrooms to hire minorities and create more training positions which compensate for initially weak staffers by "over-complement allowances and a full-time recruiting program."

Economy Forecast: Freezes

Another important issue brought up by editors in the polling concerned the state of the economy and what it forecasts about minority employment. Points brought up included the freezes on overall hiring in the newsrooms.

The Committee findings show that pressures to employ

minority staffers has dropped somewhat. Committee member McClatchy noted in the report that the pressure to do something and the "willingness to make the effort" seem to be concentrated in the metropolitan areas. He termed this "understandable since there is less concentration of minority population in the smaller cities and towns."

Self-pressure

"Self-pressure" was evidenced in the pollings. A western editor was quoted in the report as feeling too self-conscious and hypocritical to spout "non-discrimination platitudes," when he didn't have a minority editorial employee other than one female Mexican-American.

The report summarized that several Midwestern and Upper-Midwestern editors noted a similar tendency: "A decrease in minority pressure, but a marked increase in what one termed militancy by women for more women in news jobs."

What does this all add up to? The Committee states that they feel frustration but they still cling to hope. "There is a distinct regional pattern. What improvement in numbers there has been seems to have come in the East, South and a few Far West states. There has been no change in New England and the situation in the Southwest is glum and static. The Midwest has moved ahead, but only fractionally, and spottily."

Committee Conclusions

The Committee concludes in its report, that after three years of repeated checking it has served its purpose for the time being. One of the reasons the Committee gives for recommending suspension presently is the 1974 drop in retained questionnaires.

In summary, the Committee says that "the great pressure of the late 1960's and early 1970's has receded." They state that "further progress will come slowly, as the awareness of newspapers' genuine demand for black talent trickles into the black communities and gradually produces a more adequate supply of capable applicants. In the short run, there is little question that demand for black newsmen and newswomen will vastly outstrip the supply."

Index

Action Programs, recom-
     mended by Com-
     mission, 145–49
Ahee, Carl, 20–23
Alling, Duncan, 169
American Civil Liberties
     Union, 35, 148, 162
American Newspapers Pub-
     lishers Association,
     109, 127, 129
American Society of News-
     paper Editors
     (ASNE), 55–57, 137,
     147, 151–52, 153–54
Anaheim Union High School
     District, 25–26
Antioch Review, 254
Antonelli v. Hammond, 162
Arevalo, Abraham, 38, 60
Aronson, James, 254
Awakening, 41

Ballance, Gilbert, 100–1, 122
Baltimore County (Md.)
     High Schools, 35
Barron's National Business,
     127
Batten, James, 252
Beamer, Judge George, 6–7
Berkeley (Calif.) High
     School, 73, 92
Black Spectrum, 70, 124
Black Voice, 64
Blackwell v. Issaquena, 163
Blair Summer School for
     Journalism, 107, 112,
     169

Blank, Karent, 169, 170
Blatchford, Nick, 169
Borenstein v. Jones, 163
Boston Globe, 132
Brahma Tales, 44
Bronx (N. Y.) High School of
     Science, 68
Brown, David, 75, 99–100
Browne (Washington, D. C.)
     Junior High School, 64
Bureau of Indian Affairs, 76
*Burke v. Board of Education
     of Township of
     Livingston,* 163
Burnside v. Byars, 163

Canoga Park (Calif.) High
     School, 96
Carnegie Study of the Educa-
     tion of Educators, 36n
Carroll (Texas) High School,
     17
Cartselos, Ted, 68
Cary Eve, 162
Cassidy, Cynthia, 86
Castro, Armando, 16–19
Catalyst, 62
Censorship
     administrative, 24–28
     advisors, 29–37
     Commission recommenda-
          tions on, 141–42
     kinds of materials censored,
          40–47
     Legal Guide for High
          School Journalists,
          153–63

Censorship *(continued)*
  model guidelines for student
    publications, 164–66
  Parent Teacher Associa-
    tions, 36
  resource organizations, 237
  selected readings on, 228–
    29
  specific Commission
    findings on, 47–49
  student, 37–40
Commission Consultation
  Meetings, 169–70
Centennial (Ore.) High
  School, 131
Chancellor of the City of
  New York, 39
Charlotte Observer, 124, 252
Chicago Board of Education,
  9, 10
Chisme, El (The Gossip), 60
Clepper, Lori, 45
Cohen, Jeanne, 38
Columbia Graduate School of
  Journalism, 56
Columbia Scholastic Press
  Association (CSPA),
  108, 109, 216, 117
Commission Hearing Sites,
  169
*Communications: Journalism
  Education Today*, 32,
  95
Conley, Micaela, 63–64, 69
Content Analysis, high school
  newspapers, 44, 215–
  27
Cope, Lew, 130
Corpus Christi Caller, 17
Crisis in the Classroom, 36–
  37, 36n–37n
Crusader, 25
Cruttenden, Edward, 105–6
Cunningham, James, 42
Curtis Publishing Co. v. Butts,
  162

Daily Jacket, 66, 73–74, 92
Dellemere, Craig, 70, 104

*Dickey v. Alabama State
  Board of Education*,
  162
Di Grazia, Tom, 5, 6
Divoky, Diane, 162
Doubloon, 27
Dow Jones & Co., Inc. 127
Dow Jones News Service, 127
Dunbar (Washington, D. C.)
  High School, 42
DuShane Fund, 23

East Chicago Media Center,
  102
Editor & Publisher, 57n, 207,
  251
Editor & Publisher Yearbook,
  208
*Eisner v. Stamford Board of
  Education*, 47, 47n,
  163
El Chicano, 16, 18
Electronic media, 97–103, 112
Empire State School Press
  Association, 39
Endry, Joseph, 27–28
Erasmus (N. Y.) High
  School, 53, 68
Established Media
  attitudes toward high school
    press, 117–23
  Commission recommenda-
    tion on, 144–45
  contacts with high school
    press, 123–26
  programs initiated by,
    126–32
  resource organizations,
    240–41
  selected readings on, 235–
    36
  specific Commission
    findings on, 137–38
  statements from profes-
    sional journalists:
    Patterson, Eugene, 133;
    Wicker, Tom, 134–36;
    Winship, Thomas, 132–
    33

Federal Communications Commission, 103

Financial Weekly, 127

Finkelstein, Barbara, 216

First Amendment
  and official school publication, 154–59
    "Disruption" clause of legal standards, 185–86
    legal limitations, 182–85
    libel, 184–85
  and unofficial papers, 159–61
    prior review, 160–61
    sale on school grounds, 161

Fisher, Patti, 73–74, 92

Fodor, Marilyn, 30

Fourth Street I, 58

"Four-Way Test" of Rotary International, 20–24

Foxfire, 86–87, 89, 169

Free Youth, 13–14

Freedom of the Press in College and High School, 162

Fuhrman, Janice, 11–16, 18

Fujishima v. the Board of Education, 9, 10, 163

García, Abel, 68

Garinger (N. C.) High School, 100, 122–23

Garrett County (Md.) High Schools, 35

Garrick, Jr., James W., 69, 82–83, 89

Ginsburg v. United States, 162

Gonzáles, Angel, 61

Gonzáles, Fred, 58

Gotham Herald, The, 68

Grambs, Jean, 92–93, 169, 170

Grasinger, Sandra, 29

Greer, Bill, 129

Griffin, John, 37–38

Growald, Paul, 45–46

Guerra, Carlos, 59, 71, 91

Gutiérrez, Fernando, 70–71, 124–25

Haaran (N. Y.) High School, 99

Hannahs v. Endry, 27n, 163

Harris Poll (Louis Harris), 36

"Harry", 36

Harford County (Md.) High Schools, 36

Haynes, Charles E., 17–18, 19

Heintz, Sister Ann Christine, 95, 98–99, 170

Hickson, Linnell, 30–31

Hiebert, Ray, 216

Hirsh, Sharlene, 104

Holbrook, Kim, 46, 248–49

Hopkins, Demetrius, 8–10

Hornets Buzz, 11

Houston, Ulysses, 64–65

Hoyekiya, 76

Hunt, Chet, 93

Hunt, Jr., Deason L. 44–45

Hurley, Rod, 38, 39

Illinois Arts Council, 101

Isaacs, Norman, 56–57, 252

Jacket, The (Daily Jacket), 66, 73, 92

Jacobs v. Board of School Commissioners of Indianapolis, 162, 163

J. E. A., 32

James, Fletcher, 64

Jones, Carolyn, 105

Jones, Chuck, 86

Journalism Education Association (J. E. A.), 23, 55, 94–96, 189, 201, 216

Journalism and Journalism Education advisor and teacher roles, 89–94
  Commission recommendations on, 143–44
  as preparation for career, 105–6

Journalism and Journalism
(continued)
  resource organizations,
    238–40
  role in high school, 81–89
  scholastic journalism
    organizations, 108–11
  selected readings in, 231–35
  specific Commission find-
    ings on, 111–13
  teacher training for, 89–91
  unofficial media, 104–5

Keenan (S. C.) High School,
  81–82, 87, 89, 250
Kemp, Susan, 29
Keyishian v. Board of
  Regents, 162
Kilpatrick, Charles O., 252
King, Steve, 169
Koppell v. Levine, 162

Lane Technical (Ill.) High
  School, 7, 10
Lee v. Board of Regents, 162
Legal Defense Fund, 148
Levene, Alan H. 162, 170
Libel, 39–40, 156, 158, 160,
  164, 165
Liberty Link, 3
Lion, 31–32, 33n, 83–84,
  245–48
Lipsky, Alan, 38–39, 69–70
Little Big Horn (Ill.) High
  School, 77
Lomita de Libertad, La, 60
López, Ruth, 62
Los Alamitos (Calif.), 25
Los Angeles Board of Educa-
  tion, The, 96
Los Angeles Journalism
  Teachers Association,
  96
Los Angeles Times, 96
Loudell, Allan, 84
Lucas, Roy, 23
Ludlow, Lynn, 121
Lynch, Phyllis, 71

Magazin, 124
Maniloff, Howard, 67, 88–89
Martin, Trudy, 30, 42
Martinez, Suzanne, 169
Matter of Brociner, 163
Matter of Williams, 162, 163
Maynard, Robert, 169
McAllen (Texas) High
  School, 16, 17
McArthur (Texas) High
  School, 35, 44
McClatchy, C. K. 252
McGovern, George, 81
McPhillips, Dorothy, 25–26,
  93, 170, 216
Mercantini, Sam, 43, 106–7
"Metro Newsbeat," 129
Mexican-American Youth
  Organization, 16
Milford County (Md.) High
  Schools, 36
Miller v. California, 162
Mills (Calif.) High School,
  42
Minneapolis Star, 129
Minneapolis Tribune, 130
Minor, Lorraine, 61–62
Minority Participation
  Commission recommenda-
    tions on, 142–43
  coverage of minority news,
    69–71
  electronic media, 74–75
  financial problems, 71–72
  high school press work-
    shops, 72
  non-minority attitudes,
    69–71
  and percentage of minori-
    ties in schools, 61–66
  in professional journalism,
    53–57
  recruiting of, 72–74
  resource organizations,
    237–38
  scheduling, affect on, 71
  selected readings in, 230–31

Minority Participation
    (continued)
  specific Commission
    findings on, 77–78
  staff selection, 67–69
  tracking, 72
  unofficial papers, 58–61
Mishawaka (Ind.) High
    School, 34
Missouri Scholastic Press
    Association, 170
Monitor Patriot Co. v. Roy,
    162
Montgomery County (Md.)
    High Schools, 35
Morris, Homer M., 16, 17
Mounds View (Minn.) High
    School, 45
Mulcahy, David, 44

National Council of Teachers
    of English, 189, 201
National Education Associa-
    tion, 23, 29
National Fund for Humani-
    ties, 86
National High School Insti-
    tute (Northwestern
    University), 107
National Observer, The, 127
National Scholastic Press
    Association, 109
National Youth Journalism
    Project, 145–46
Navies, Richard, 66
New York City High School
    Press Council, 26
New York Times, The, 70,
    104, 124, 132
*New York Times Co. v.
    Sullivan,* 162
"Newspaper in the Class-
    room," 129
Newspaper Fund, The, 112,
    126–28, 131–32
*Nicholson v. Board of Educa-
    tion, Torrance Unified
    School District, et al.,*
    21n, 22n, 23n

Nicholson, Don Patrick,
    19–24, 25, 95
Nienke, Melody, 86
Nixon, Richard M., 81
Northwestern Summer School
    of Journalism, 72, 112
Novato (Calif.) High School,
    11, 13, 18
Nyquist, Ewald, New York
    State Commissioner of
    Education, 158

Obscenity, 39, 40–41, 156–58,
    160, 164, 165
Office of Economic Oppor-
    tunity, 91
Office of Educational Devel-
    opment, Department
    of Human Resources
    122, 144
Oglala (S. D.) High School,
    76
Oglala Light, 76
Ohio ACLU, 27n
Ollinger, Lilly, 101–2
Olympic (N. C.), 124
O'Malley, Charles, 108–9
Onderdonk, Stanley, 11–14
Oppressed, The, 8–10
Ottaway Group, 127

Packard, George R., 252
Parent Teacher Associations,
    36
*Paris Adult Art Theater v.
    Slaton,* 162
Patterson, Eugene C., 132, 133
Philadelphia Bulletin, 252
Piñon, Fernando, 91, 106
Plummer, Abe, 75
Plylar, David, 35
Poxon v. Board of Education,
    163
Prologue (Ill.) High School,
    101

Quarterman v. Byrd, 163
Quill and Scroll, 29, 44, 54

Quill and Scroll, 109–11

Rabin, David, 7–11
Radio Television News Directors Association, 122
Ram-Page, 44, 46n, 85, 248–49
Ramage, Trilla, 169
Ranson (N. C.) Junior High School, 44, 46, 85, 87, 248
Reber, Donald D., 84, 245
Reporters Committee for Freedom of the Press, 130–32
Reporters Committee Press Censorship Newsletter, 131
Resource Organizations, 236–42
  in electronic media, 240–41
  in First Amendment issues, 136–37
  in journalism education, 238–40
  in minority participation, 237–38
  in professional journalism, 240–41
  in youth action, 241–42
Reyna, Wendy, 75
Reyes, Dominguez, 55–56
Reynoldsburg (Ohio) High School, 27
Robert F. Kennedy Memorial, 131
Rights of Students, The, 162
Roemer III, John, 35
Rolling Hills (Calif.) High School, 29
Rosenbloom v. Metromedia, Inc., 162
Ross, Ami, 38
Rowe v. Campbell Union High School District, 163
Rubin, Richard, 125

Sacramento Bee, 252
St. Mary Center for Learning, 61, 97
St. Petersburg Times, 132
San Antonio News and Express, 252
San Francisco Call-Bulletin, 54
San Francisco Chronicle, 14
San Francisco News, 54
Sanders v. Martin, 163
School Publications, model guidelines for, 164–66
  official, 164–66
  unofficial, 165–66
Schultz, Marilyn, 131
Science Survey, 68
Schwartz, Joseph, 22
Scoville v. Board of Education of Joliet Township, 162
Scribner, Harvey, Chancellor of the New York City public schools, 156
Segal, Danny, 38, 39, 53, 68, 71
Selected Readings, 227–36
  education and adolescence, 228
  established media, 235–36
  journalism education, 231–35
  minority participation, 230–31
  press law and the First Amendment, 228–29
Seventh U. S. Circuit Court of Appeals, 9, 161
Shanley v. Northeast Independent School District, 163
Shore (Washington, D. C.) Junior High School, 125
Sigma Delta Chi, 130, 132
Silberman, Charles, 36–37, 170
Sills, James, 46, 85–86

Singing Sands, 75

South Bend Community School Corp., 6

South Bend Tribune, 33–34, 123–24

Still, Douglas, 169

Student Supplement, 34

Sullivan v. Houston Independent School District, 163

Sullivan, Kathleen, 31

Sulok, Nancy, 33–34

Supreme Court, 37, 153–54, 158

Surveys
American Society of Newspaper Editors, 55–57, 251–54
Commission
faculty, 33, 91, 189–201
managing editors, 40, 57, 105
student, 33, 65–66
teacher, 201–7
Harris, 36, 126
National Education Association, 29
Quill and Scroll, 44
Roper, 126
Texas High School Newspapers, 44–45

Sword and Shield, The, 82, 89, 250–51

Talking Leaves, 77

Texas Institute for Educational Development, 59, 60, 61

Thomas, Adolphus, 53–55

Thunderbolt, 30

Tillman, Deborah, 42–43

Time, Inc. v. Hill, 162

Tinker v. Des Moines Independent School District, 3n, 154, 159–61, 162, 163

Title III, Innovative Program of the Elementary and

Title III *(continued)*
Secondary Education Act of 1965, 129

Torrance Board of Education, 23

Torrance (Calif.) High School, 20

Torrance News Torch, 20–21

Torrance (Calif.) school district, 19

Traeger, Robert, 162

Trevino, Mario, 53, 61

Trujillo v. Love, 162

Tsá Aszi, 75, 87

University of Missouri, 107

University of Wisconsin Extension at Madison, 107, 112

"Upward Bound," 149

Urban Journalism Workshop, Washington, D. C., 104, 112, 128

Vandor, Ron, 26–27

Van Hecke, Fay, 74, 124

Videopolis, 101

Viewer, The, 45

Vought v. Van Buren Public Schools, 162

Walker, Tillie, 170

Wall Street Journal, The, 127

Wasko, John, 102

Watergate, 23

WCGC, 123

Wesolek v. The Board of Trustees, South Bend Community School Corporation, 163

Wesolek, Jenn, 3–7, 15, 30, 40

Wheel, The, 16, 18

Wheeler, John, 31–33, 245, 247–48

Wicker, Tom, 132, 134–36

Wieboldt Foundation, 101

Wiener, Mike, 96

Wiggington, B. Eliot, 86–87, 89, 169
Williams, Jack, 72, 122
Winship, Thomas, 132–33
WLTL–FM, 84
WNDU, 102
Woodring, Virginia, 95

Woodrow Wilson (Calif.) High School, 53, 55
WTCI, 122

Youth Coalition, The, 3

Zucker v. Panitz, 162

JACK NELSON

Jack Nelson was born in Talladega, Alabama, and raised in Alabama, Mississippi, and Georgia. He studied economics at Georgia State College and was a Nieman Fellow at Harvard University for one year. A reporter for twenty-four years, he has won several national and state news awards. In 1960, as a reporter for *The Atlanta Constitution,* he received the Pulitzer Prize for local news coverage. As Atlanta bureau chief of the *Los Angeles Times* from 1965–70, Mr. Nelson covered every major civil rights story in the South. In 1970 he joined the *Los Angeles Times* Washington bureau as an investigative reporter.

Mr. Nelson is also a founder and executive committee member of the Reporters Committee for Freedom of the Press, and co-author of three books, including *The Censors and the Schools* and *The Orangeburg Massacre.*